CAMBRIDGE LIBRAR

Books of enduring scho

Literary Studies

This series provides a high-quality selection of early printings of literary works, textual editions, anthologies and literary criticism which are of lasting scholarly interest. Ranging from Old English to Shakespeare to early twentieth-century work from around the world, these books offer a valuable resource for scholars in reception history, textual editing, and literary studies.

George Eliot's Life

Best known for his brief marriage to George Eliot, John Walter Cross (1840–1924) compiled this three-volume 'autobiography' of 1885 from his late wife's journals and letters. Eliot was never married to her long-term partner G.H. Lewes, and she courted further scandal when she married Cross, twenty years her junior, in the spring of 1880. While these volumes offer a valuable insight into Eliot's private reflections, what is perhaps most telling is the material left out or rewritten in Cross's efforts to lend his wife's unconventional life some respectability, which he does at the expense of what one reviewer described as Eliot's 'salt and spice'. *George Eliot's Life* will be of particular interest to scholars of nineteenth-century biography and literature. Volume 2 covers the years 1858–66, including Eliot's initial success in fiction and her travels in Italy, Holland, and along the Rhine.

Cambridge University Press has long been a pioneer in the reissuing of out-of-print titles from its own backlist, producing digital reprints of books that are still sought after by scholars and students but could not be reprinted economically using traditional technology. The Cambridge Library Collection extends this activity to a wider range of books which are still of importance to researchers and professionals, either for the source material they contain, or as landmarks in the history of their academic discipline.

Drawing from the world-renowned collections in the Cambridge University Library, and guided by the advice of experts in each subject area, Cambridge University Press is using state-of-the-art scanning machines in its own Printing House to capture the content of each book selected for inclusion. The files are processed to give a consistently clear, crisp image, and the books finished to the high quality standard for which the Press is recognised around the world. The latest print-on-demand technology ensures that the books will remain available indefinitely, and that orders for single or multiple copies can quickly be supplied.

The Cambridge Library Collection will bring back to life books of enduring scholarly value (including out-of-copyright works originally issued by other publishers) across a wide range of disciplines in the humanities and social sciences and in science and technology.

George Eliot's Life

As Related in her Letters and Journals

VOLUME 2: FAMOUS

EDITED BY JOHN WALTER CROSS

CAMBRIDGE
UNIVERSITY PRESS

CAMBRIDGE UNIVERSITY PRESS

Cambridge, New York, Melbourne, Madrid, Cape Town, Singapore,
São Paolo, Delhi, Dubai, Tokyo

Published in the United States of America by Cambridge University Press, New York

www.cambridge.org
Information on this title: www.cambridge.org/9781108020077

This edition first published 1885
This digitally printed version 2010

ISBN 978-1-108-02007-7 Paperback

GEORGE ELIOT'S LIFE

VOL. II.—FAMOUS

"OUR FINEST HOPE IS FINEST MEMORY"

MISS EVANS, ÆT 30.

Engraved by G J Stodart from a Painting by M D'Albert-Durade

GEORGE ELIOT'S LIFE

AS

RELATED IN HER LETTERS
AND JOURNALS

ARRANGED AND EDITED BY HER HUSBAND

J. W. CROSS

IN THREE VOLUMES

VOL. II.

WILLIAM BLACKWOOD AND SONS
EDINBURGH AND LONDON
MDCCCLXXXV

CONTENTS OF THE SECOND VOLUME.

CHAPTER VIII.

JANUARY 1858 TO DECEMBER 1858.

PAGE

Success of 'Scenes of Clerical Life'—'Adam Bede,' . 1

CHAPTER IX

JANUARY 1859 TO MARCH 1860.

'The Mill on the Floss,' 79

CHAPTER X.

MARCH TO JUNE 1860.

First Journey to Italy, ... 164

CHAPTER XI.

JULY 1860 TO DECEMBER 1861.

'Silas Marner'—'Romola' begun, . . . 255

CHAPTER XII.

JANUARY 1862 TO DECEMBER 1865.

'Romola'—'Felix Holt,' 329

CHAPTER XIII.

JANUARY 1866 TO DECEMBER 1866.

Tour in Holland and on the Rhine, . . . 419

ILLUSTRATIONS TO THE SECOND VOLUME.

PORTRAIT OF GEORGE ELIOT. Engraved by G. J. Stodart, ... *Frontispiece.*

FACSIMILE OF GEORGE ELIOT'S HANDWRITING, *At end.*

GEORGE ELIOT'S LIFE.

CHAPTER VIII.

Jan. 2.—George has returned this evening from a week's visit to Vernon Hill. On coming up-stairs he said—"I have some very pretty news for you,—something in my pocket." I was at a loss to conjecture, and thought confusedly of possible opinions from admiring readers, when he drew the 'Times' from his pocket—to-day's number, containing a review of the 'Scenes of Clerical Life.' He had happened to ask a gentleman in the railway carriage coming up to London to allow him to look at the 'Times,' and felt quite agitated and tremulous when his eyes alighted on the review. Finding he had time to go into town before the train started, he bought a copy there. It is a highly favourable notice, and, as far as it goes, appreciatory.

Journal, 1858.

Journal, 1858.

When G. went into town he called at Nutt's, and Mrs Nutt said to him, "I think you don't know our curate. *He* says the author of 'Clerical Scenes' is a High Churchman; for though Mr Tryan is said to be Low Church, his feelings and *actions* are those of a High Churchman." (The curate himself being of course High Church.) There were some pleasant scraps of admiration also gathered for me at Vernon Hill. Doyle happening to mention the treatment of children in the stories, Helps said—"Oh, he is a great writer!"

I wonder how I shall feel about these little details ten years hence, if I am alive. At present I value them as grounds for hoping that my writing may succeed, and so give value to my life: as indications that I can touch the hearts of my fellow-men, and so sprinkle some precious grain as the result of the long years in which I have been inert and suffering. But at present fear and trembling still predominate over hope.

Jan. 5.—To-day the 'Clerical Scenes' came in their two-volume dress, looking very handsome.

Jan. 8.—News of the subscription—580, with a probable addition of 25 for Longmans. Mudie has taken 350. When we used to talk of the probable subscription, G. always said, "I daresay it will be

250!" (The final number subscribed for was 650.) Journal, 1858.

I ordered copies to be sent to the following persons—Froude, Dickens, Thackeray, Tennyson, Ruskin, Faraday, the author of 'Companions of my Solitude,' Albert Smith, Mrs Carlyle.

On the 20th of January I received the following letter from Dickens.

"TAVISTOCK HOUSE, LONDON,
Monday, 17*th Jan.* 1858.

Letter from Charles Dickens to George Eliot, 18th Jan. 1858.

"MY DEAR SIR,—I have been so strongly affected by the two first tales in the book you have had the kindness to send me, through Messrs Blackwood, that I hope you will excuse my writing to you to express my admiration of their extraordinary merit. The exquisite truth and delicacy, both of the humour and the pathos of these stories, I have never seen the like of; and they have impressed me in a manner that I should find it very difficult to describe to you, if I had the impertinence to try.

"In addressing these few words of thankfulness to the creator of the Sad Fortunes of the Rev. Amos Barton, and the sad love-story of Mr Gilfil, I am (I presume) bound to adopt the

Letter from Charles Dickens to George Eliot, 18th Jan. 1858.

name that it pleases that excellent writer to assume. I can suggest no better one: but I should have been strongly disposed, if I had been left to my own devices, to address the said writer as a woman. I have observed what seemed to me such womanly touches in those moving fictions, that the assurance on the title-page is insufficient to satisfy me even now. If they originated with no woman, I believe that no man ever before had the art of making himself mentally so like a woman since the world began.

"You will not suppose that I have any vulgar wish to fathom your secret. I mention the point as one of great interest to me—not of mere curiosity. If it should ever suit your convenience and inclination to show me the face of the man, or woman, who has written so charmingly, it will be a very memorable occasion to me. If otherwise, I shall always hold that impalpable personage in loving attachment and respect, and shall yield myself up to all future utterances from the same source, with a perfect confidence in their making me wiser and better.—Your obliged and faithful servant and admirer, CHARLES DICKENS.

"GEORGE ELIOT, Esq."

Jan. 21.—To-day came the following letter from Froude.

Journal, 1858.

"NORTHDOWN HOUSE, BIDEFORD,
17*th Jan.* 1858.

Letter from J. A. Froude to George Eliot, 17th Jan. 1858.

"DEAR SIR,—I do not know when I have experienced a more pleasant surprise than when, on opening a book parcel two mornings ago, I found it to contain 'Scenes of Clerical Life,' 'From the author.' I do not often see 'Blackwood;' but in accidental glances I had made acquaintance with 'Janet's Repentance,' and had found there something extremely different from general magazine stories. When I read the advertisement of the republication, I intended fully, at my leisure, to look at the companions of the story which had so much struck me, and now I find myself sought out by the person whose workmanship I had admired, for the special present of it.

"You would not, I imagine, care much for flattering speeches; and to go into detail about the book would carry me farther than at present there is occasion to go. I can only thank you most sincerely for the delight which it has given me; and both I myself, and my wife, trust that the acquaintance which we seem to have made

Letter from J. A. Froude to George Eliot, 17th Jan. 1858.

with you through your writings may improve into something more tangible. I do not know whether I am addressing a young man or an old—a clergyman or a layman. Perhaps, if you answer this note, you may give us some information about yourself. But at any rate, should business or pleasure bring you into this part of the world, pray believe that you will find a warm welcome if you will accept our hospitality.—Once more, with my best thanks, believe me, faithfully yours, J. A. FROUDE."

Letter to Miss Sara Hennell, 17th Jan. 1858.

I have long ceased to feel any sympathy with mere antagonism and destruction; and all crudity of expression marks, I think, a deficiency in subtlety of thought as well as in breadth of moral and poetic feeling. Mr William Smith, the author of 'Thorndale,' is an old acquaintance of Mr Lewes's. I should say an old *friend*, only I don't like the too ready use of that word. Mr Lewes admires and esteems him very highly. He is a very accomplished man—a bachelor, with a small independent income; used to write very effective articles on miscellaneous subjects in 'Blackwood.' I shall like to know what you think of 'Thorndale.' I don't know whether you look out for Ruskin's books whenever they appear. His little book on the 'Political Economy of Art' contains some magnificent passages, mixed up with stupendous specimens of arrogant absurdity on some economical points. But I venerate him as one of the great teachers of the day. The grand doctrines of truth and sincerity in art, and the nobleness and solemnity of our human life, which he teaches with the inspiration of a Hebrew prophet, must be stirring up young minds in a promising way. The two last volumes of 'Modern Painters' contain, I think, some of the finest writing of the age. He is strongly akin to the sublimest part of Wordsworth—whom, by-the-by, we are reading with fresh admiration for his beauties and tolerance for his faults. Our present plans are: to remain here till about the end of March, then to go to Munich, which I long to see. We shall live there several months, seeing the wonderful galleries in leisure moments. Our living here is so much more expensive than living abroad, that we save more than the expenses of our journeying; and as our work can be as well done there as here for some months, we lay in much more capital, in the shape of knowledge and experience, by going abroad.

Letter to Miss Sara Hennell, 17th Jan. 1858.

Jan. 18.—I have begun the 'Eumenides,' having finished the 'Choephoræ.' We are reading

Journal, 1858.

Journal, 1858.

Wordsworth in the evening—at least G. is reading him to me. I am still reading aloud Miss Martineau's History.

Letter to John Blackwood, 21st Jan. 1858.

I am sure you will be interested in Dickens's letter, which I enclose, begging you to return it as soon as you can, and not to allow any one besides yourself and Major Blackwood to share in the knowledge of its contents. There can be no harm, of course, in every one's knowing that Dickens admires the 'Scenes,' but I should not like any more specific allusion made to the words of a private letter. There can hardly be any climax of approbation for me after this; and I am so deeply moved by the finely-felt and finely-expressed sympathy of the letter, that the iron mask of my *incognito* seems quite painful in forbidding me to tell Dickens how thoroughly his generous impulse has been appreciated. If you should have an opportunity of conveying this feeling of mine to him in any way, you would oblige me by doing so. By-the-by, you probably remember sending me, some months ago, a letter from the Rev. Archer Gurney—a very warm, simple-spoken letter—praising me for qualities which I most of all care to be praised for. I should like to send him a copy of the 'Scenes,' since I could make no acknowledgment of his letter in any other way. I don't know his address, but perhaps Mr Langford would be good enough to look it out in the Clergy List.

Jan. 23.—There appeared a well-written and enthusiastic article on 'Clerical Scenes' in the 'Statesman.' We hear there was a poor article in the 'Globe'—of feebly written praise—the previous week, but beyond this, we have not yet heard of any notices from the press. Journal, 1858.

Jan. 26.—Came a very pleasant letter from Mrs Carlyle, thanking the author of 'Clerical Scenes' for the present of his book, praising it very highly, and saying that her husband had promised to read it when released from his mountain of history.

"5 CHEYNE ROW, CHELSEA,
21*st Jan.* 1858.

"DEAR SIR,—I have to thank you for a surprise, a pleasure, and a—consolation (!) all in one book! And I do thank you most sincerely. I cannot divine what inspired the good thought to send *me* your book, since (if the name on the title-page be your real name) it could not have been personal regard; there has never been a George Eliot among my friends or acquaintance. But neither, I am sure, could *you* Letter from Mrs Carlyle to George Eliot, 21st Jan. 1858.

Letter from Mrs Carlyle to George Eliot, 21st Jan. 1858.

divine the circumstances under which I should read the book, and the particular benefit it should confer on me! I read it—at least the first volume—during one of the most (physically) wretched nights of my life; sitting up in bed, unable to get a wink of sleep for fever and sore throat, and it helped me through that dreary night as well—better than—the most sympathetic helpful friend watching by my bedside could have done!

"You will believe that the book needed to be something more than a "new novel" for me; that I *could* at my years, and after so much reading, read it in positive torment, and be beguiled by it of the torment! that it needed to be the one sort of book, however named, that still takes hold of me, and that grows rarer every year—a *human* book—written out of the heart of a live man, not merely out of the brain of an author — full of tenderness and pathos, without a scrap of sentimentality, of sense without dogmatism, of earnestness without twaddle—a book that makes one *feel friends* at once and for always with the man or woman who wrote it!

"In guessing at why you gave me this good

gift, I have thought amongst other things, 'Oh, perhaps it was a delicate way of presenting the novel to my husband, he being over head and ears in *history*.' If that was it, I compliment you on your *tact!* for my husband is much likelier to read the 'Scenes' on *my* responsibility than on a venture of his own—though, as a general rule, never opening a novel, he has engaged to read this one whenever he has some leisure from his present task.

Letter from Mrs Carlyle to George Eliot, 21st Jan. 1858.

"I hope to know some day if the person I am addressing bears any resemblance in external things to the idea I have conceived of him in my mind—a man of middle age, with a wife, from whom he has got those beautiful *feminine* touches in his book—a good many children, and a dog that he has as much fondness for as I have for my little Nero! For the rest—not just a clergyman, but brother or first cousin to a clergyman! How ridiculous all this *may* read beside the reality. Anyhow—I honestly confess I am very curious about you, and look forward with what Mr Carlyle would call 'a good, healthy, genuine desire' to shaking hands with you some day.—In the meanwhile, I remain, your obliged JANE W. CARLYLE."

Journal, 1858.

Jan. 30.—Received a letter from Faraday, thanking me very gracefully for the present of the 'Scenes.' Blackwood mentions, in enclosing this letter, that Simpkin & Marshall have sent for twelve additional copies—the first sign of a move since the subscription. The other night we looked into the life of Charlotte Brontë, to see how long it was before 'Jane Eyre' came into demand at the libraries, and we found it was not until six weeks after publication. It is just three weeks now since I heard news of the subscription for my book.

Letter from M. Faraday to George Eliot, 28th Jan. 1858.

"ROYAL INSTITUTION, 28*th Jan.* 1858.

"SIR,—I cannot resist the pleasure of thanking you for what I esteem a great kindness: the present of your thoughts embodied in the two volumes you have sent me. They have been, and will be again, a very pleasant relief from mental occupation among my own pursuits. Such rest I find at times not merely agreeable, but essential.—Again thanking you, I beg to remain, your very obliged servant,

M. FARADAY.

"GEORGE ELIOT, Esq., &c., &c."

Journal, 1858.

Feb. 3.—Gave up Miss Martineau's History last night, after reading some hundred pages in the second volume. She has a sentimental, rhetorical style in this history which is fatiguing and not instructive. But her history of the Reform movement is very interesting. Journal, 1858.

Feb. 4.—Yesterday brought the discouraging news, that though the book is much talked of, it moves very slowly. Finished the 'Eumenides.' Bessie Parkes has written asking me to contribute to the 'Englishwoman's Journal,' a new monthly, which, she says, "We are beginning with £1000, and great social interest."

Feb. 16.—To-day G. went into the City and saw Langford, for the sake of getting the latest news about our two books—his 'Sea-side Studies' having been well launched about a fortnight or ten days ago, with a subscription of 800. He brought home good news. The 'Clerical Scenes' are moving off at a moderate but steady pace. Langford remarked, that while the press had been uniformly favourable, not one *critical* notice had appeared. G. went to Parker's in the evening, and gathered a little gossip on the subject. Savage, author of the 'Falcon Family,' and now editor of the 'Examiner,' said he was reading the 'Scenes'—had read some of them already in 'Blackwood,' but was now reading the volume. "G. Eliot was a writer of great

Journal, 1858.

merit." A barrister named Smythe said he had seen "the Bishop" reading them the other day. As a set-off against this, Mrs Schlesinger "couldn't bear the book." She is a regular novel reader; but hers is the first unfavourable opinion we have had.

Feb. 26.—We went into town for the sake of seeing Mr and Mrs Call, and having our photographs taken by Mayall.

Feb. 28.—Mr John Blackwood called on us, having come to London for a few days only. He talked a good deal about the 'Clerical Scenes' and George Eliot, and at last asked, "Well, am I to see George Eliot this time?" G. said, "Do you wish to see him?" "As he likes—I wish it to be quite spontaneous." I left the room, and G. following me a moment, I told him he might reveal me. Blackwood was kind, came back when he found he was too late for the train, and said he would come to Richmond again. He came on the following Friday and chatted very pleasantly—told us that Thackeray spoke highly of the 'Scenes,' and said *they were not written by a woman.* Mrs Blackwood is *sure* they are not written by a woman. Mrs Oliphant, the novelist, too, is confident on the same side. I gave Blackwood the MS. of my new novel, to the end of the second scene in the wood. He opened it, read the first page, and smiling, said, "This will do." We walked with him to Kew, and had a good deal of talk. Found, among other things, that he had lived two years in Italy when he was a youth, and that he admires Miss Austen. Journal, 1858.

Since I wrote these last notes, several encouraging fragments of news about the 'Scenes' have come to my ears—especially that Mrs Owen Jones and her husband—two very different people—are equally enthusiastic about the book. But both have detected the woman.

Letter to Miss Sara Hennell, 2d March 1858.

Perhaps we may go to Dresden, perhaps not: we leave room for the *imprévu,* which Louis Blanc found so sadly wanting in Mr Morgan's millennial village. You are among the exceptional people who say pleasant things to their friends, and don't feel a too exclusive satisfaction in their misfortunes. We like to hear of your interest in Mr Lewes's books — at least, *I* am very voracious of such details. I keep the pretty letters that are written to him; and we have had some really important ones from the scientific big-wigs about the 'Sea-side Studies.' The reception of the book in that quarter has been quite beyond our expectations. Eight hundred copies were sold at once. There is a great deal of close hard work in the book, and every one

Letter to Miss Sara Hennell, 2d March 1858.

who knows what scientific work is necessarily perceives this. Happily many have been generous enough to express their recognition in a hearty way.

I enter so deeply into everything you say about your mother. To me that old, old popular truism, "We can never have but one mother," has worlds of meaning in it, and I think with more sympathy of the satisfaction you feel in at last being allowed to wait on her than I should of anything else you could tell me. I wish we saw more of that sweet human piety that feels tenderly and reverently towards the aged. [*Apropos* of some incapable woman's writing she adds.] There is something more piteous almost than soapless poverty in this application of feminine incapacity to literature. We spent a very pleasant couple of hours with Mr and Mrs Call last Friday. It was worth a journey on a cold dusty day to see two faces beaming kindness and happiness.

Letter to Miss Sara Hennell, 26th March 1858.

I enclose a letter which will interest you. It is affecting to see how difficult a matter it often is for the men who would most profit by a book to purchase it, or even get a reading of it, while stupid Jopling of Reading or elsewhere thinks nothing of giving a guinea for a work which he will simply put on his shelves.

When do you bring out your new poem? I presume you are already in the sixth canto. It is true you never told me you intended to write a poem, nor have I heard any one say so who was likely to know. Nevertheless I have quite as active an imagination as you, and I don't see why I shouldn't suppose you are writing a poem as well as you suppose that I am writing a novel. Seriously, I wish you would not set rumours afloat about me. They are injurious. Several people, who seem to derive their notions from Ivy Cottage,[1] have spoken to me of a supposed novel I was going to bring out. Such things are damaging to me.

Letter to Chas. Bray, March 1858.

Thanks for your disclaimer. It shows me that you take a right view of the subject. There is no undertaking more fruitful of absurd mistakes than that of "guessing" at authorship; and as I have never communicated to any one so much as an *intention* of a literary kind, there can be none but imaginary data for such guesses. If I withhold anything from my friends which it would gratify them to know, you will believe, I hope, that I have good reasons for doing so, and I am sure those friends will understand me when I ask them to

Letter to Chas. Bray, 31st March 1858.

[1] The Brays' new house.

Letter to Chas. Bray, 31st March 1858.

further my object—which is not a whim but a question of solid interest—by complete silence. I can't afford to indulge either in vanity or sentimentality about my work. I have only a trembling anxiety to do what is in itself worth doing, and by that honest means to win very necessary profit of a temporal kind. "There is nothing hidden that shall not be revealed" in due time. But till that time comes—till I tell you myself, "This is the work of my hand and brain"—don't believe anything on the subject. There is no one who is in the least likely to know what I can, could, should, or would write.

Journal, 1858.

April 1, 1858.—Received a letter from Blackwood containing warm praise of 'Adam Bede,' but wanting to know the rest of the story in outline before deciding whether it should go in the Magazine. I wrote in reply refusing to tell him the story.

Journal, April 1858.

On Wednesday evening, April 7th, we set off on our journey to Munich, and now we are comfortably settled in our lodgings, where we hope to remain three months at least. I sit down in my first leisure moments to write a few recollections of our journey, or rather of our twenty-four hours' stay at Nürnberg; for the rest of our journey was

Journal, April 1858.

mere endurance of railway and steamboat in cold and sombre weather, often rainy. I ought to except our way from Frankfort to Nürnberg, which lay for some distance—until we came to Bamberg—through a beautifully varied country. Our view both of Würzburg and Bamberg, as we hastily snatched it from our railway carriage, was very striking — great old buildings, crowning heights that rise up boldly from the plain in which stand the main part of the towns. From Bamberg to Nürnberg the way lay through a wide rich plain sprinkled with towns. We had left all the hills behind us. At Bamberg we were joined in our carriage by a pleasant-looking, elderly couple who spoke to each other and looked so affectionately, that we said directly, "Shall we be so when we are old?" It was very pretty to see them hold each others' gloved hands for a minute like lovers. As soon as we had settled ourselves in our inn at Nürnberg—the Baierische Hof—we went out to get a general view of the town. Happily it was not raining, though there was no sun to light up the roof and windows.

How often I had thought I should like to see Nürnberg, and had pictured to myself narrow streets with dark quaint gables! The reality was not at

Journal, April 1858.

all like my picture, but it was ten times better. No sombre colouring, except the old churches: all was bright and varied, each *façade* having a different colour — delicate green, or buff, or pink, or lilac—every now and then set off by the neighbourhood of a rich reddish brown. And the roofs always gave warmth of colour with their bright red or rich purple tiles. Every house differed from its neighbour, and had a physiognomy of its own, though a beautiful family likeness ran through them all, as if the burghers of that old city were of one heart and one soul, loving the same delightful outlines, and cherishing the same daily habits of simple ease and enjoyment in their balcony-windows when the day's work was done.

The balcony window is the secondary charm of the Nürnberg houses; it would be the principal charm of any houses that had not the Nürnberg roofs and gables. It is usually in the centre of the building, on the first floor, and is ornamented with carved stone or wood, which supports it after the fashion of a bracket. In several of these windows we saw pretty family groups—young fair heads of girls or of little children, with now and then an older head surmounting them. One can fancy that these windows are the pet places for family joys—that papa

Journal, April 1858.

seats himself there when he comes home from the warehouse, and the little ones cluster round him in no time. But the glory of the Nürnberg houses is the roofs, which are no blank surface of mere tiling, but are alive with lights and shadows, cast by varied and beautiful lines of windows and pinnacles and arched openings. The plainest roof in Nürnberg has its little windows lifting themselves up like eyelids, and almost everywhere one sees the pretty hexagonal tiles. But the better houses have a central, open sort of pavilion in the roof, with a pinnacle, surmounted by a weathercock. This pavilion has usually a beautifully carved, arched opening in front, set off by the dark background which is left by the absence of glass. One fancies the old Nürnbergers must have gone up to these pavilions to smoke in the summer and autumn days. There is usually a brood of small windows round this central ornament, often elegantly arched and carved. A wonderful sight it makes to see a series of such roofs surmounting the tall, delicate-coloured houses. They are always high-pitched, of course, and the colour of the tiles was usually of a bright red. I think one of the most charming vistas we saw was the Adler-Gasse on the St Lorenz side of the town. Sometimes, instead of the high-pitched roof, with

Journal, April 1858.

its pavilion and windows, there is a richly ornamented gable fronting the street; and still more frequently we get the gables at right angles with the street at a break in the line of houses.

Coming back from the Burg, we met a detachment of soldiers, with their band playing, followed by a stream of listening people; and then we reached the market-place, just at the point where stands "The Beautiful Fountain"—an exquisite bit of florid Gothic, which has been restored in perfect conformity with the original. Right before us stood the Frauen-Kirche, with its fine and unusual *façade*, the chief beauty being a central chapel used as the choir, and added by Adam Krafft. It is something of the shape of a mitre, and forms a beautiful gradation of ascent towards the summit of the *façade*. We heard the organ, and were tempted to enter—for this is the one Catholic church in Nürnberg. The delicious sound of the organ and voices drew us farther and farther in among the standing people, and we stayed there I don't know how long, till the music ceased. How the music warmed one's heart! I loved the good people about me, even to the soldier who stood with his back to us, giving us a full view of his close-cropped head, with its pale-yellowish hair standing up in

Journal, April 1858.

bristles on the crown, as if his hat had acted like a forcing-pot. Then there was a little baby in a close-fitting cap on its little round head, looking round with bright black eyes as it sucked its bit of bread. Such a funny little complete face—rich brown complexion and miniature Roman nose. And then its mother lifted it up that it might see the rose-decked altar, where the priests were standing. How music, that stirs all one's devout emotions, blends everything into harmony—makes one feel part of one whole which one loves all alike, losing the sense of a separate self. Nothing could be more wretched as art than the painted Saint Veronica opposite me, holding out the sad face on her miraculous handkerchief. Yet it touched me deeply; and the thought of the Man of Sorrows seemed a very close thing—not a faint hearsay.

We saw Albert Dürer's statue by Rauch, and Albert Dürer's house—a striking bit of old building, rich dark-brown, with a truncated gable and two wooden galleries running along the gable end. My best wishes and thanks to the artists who keep it in repair, and use it for their meetings. The vistas from the bridges across the muddy Pegnitz, which runs through the town, are all quaint and picturesque; and it was here that we saw some

Journal, April 1858.

of the *shabbiest*-looking houses—almost the only houses that carried any suggestion of poverty, and even here it was doubtful. The town has an air of cleanliness and wellbeing, and one longs to call one of those balconied apartments one's own home, with their flower-pots, clean glass, clean curtains, and transparencies turning their white backs to the street. It is pleasant to think there is such a place in the world where many people pass peaceful lives.

On arriving at Munich, after much rambling, we found an advertisement of "Zwei elegant möblirte Zimmer," No. 15 Luitpold Strasse; and to our immense satisfaction found something that looked like cleanliness and comfort. The bargain was soon made—twenty florins per month. So here we came last Tuesday, the 13th April. We have been taking sips of the Glyptothek and the two Pinacotheks in the morning, not having settled to work yet. Last night we went to the opera—"Fra Diavolo"—at the Hof-Theater. The theatre ugly, the singing bad. Still, the orchestra was good, and the charming music made itself felt in spite of German throats. On Sunday, the 11th, we went to the Pinacothek, straight into the glorious Rubens Saal. Delighted afresh in the picture of "Samson and Delilah," both for the painting and character of the figures. Delilah, a magnificent blonde, seated in a chair, with a transparent white garment slightly covering her body, and a rich red piece of drapery round her legs, leans forward, with one hand resting on her thigh, the other, holding the cunning shears, resting on the chair—a posture which shows to perfection the full, round, living arms. She turns her head aside to look with sly triumph at Samson, —a tawny giant, his legs caught in the red drapery, shorn of his long locks, furious with the consciousness that the Philistines are upon him, and that this time he cannot shake them off. Above the group of malicious faces and grappling arms, a hand holds a flaming torch. Behind Delilah, and grasping her arm, leans forward an old woman, with hard features full of exultation.

Journal, April 1858.

This picture, comparatively small in size, hangs beside the "Last Judgment," and in the corresponding space, on the other side of the same picture, hangs the sublime "Crucifixion." Jesus alone, hanging dead on the Cross, darkness over the whole earth. One can desire nothing in this picture: the grand, sweet calm, of the dead face, calm and satisfied amidst all the traces of anguish, the real livid flesh, the thorough mastery with

Journal, April 1858.

which the whole form is rendered, and the isolation of the supreme sufferer, make a picture that haunts one like a remembrance of a friend's deathbed.

April 12 (*Monday*).—After reading Anna Mary Howitt's book on Munich and Overbeck on Greek art, we turned out into the delicious sunshine to walk in the Theresien Wiese, and have our first look at the colossal "Bavaria," the greatest work of Schwanthaler. Delightful it was to get away from the houses into this breezy meadow, where we heard the larks singing above us. The sun was still too high in the west for us to look with comfort at the statue, except right in front of it, where it eclipsed the sun; and this front view is the only satisfactory one. The outline made by the head and arm on a side view is almost painfully ugly. But in front, looking up to the beautiful, calm face, the impression it produces is sublime. I have never seen anything, even in ancient sculpture, of a more awful beauty than this dark colossal head, looking out from a background of pure, pale-blue sky. We mounted the platform to have a view of her back, and then walking forward, looked to our right hand and saw the snow-covered Alps! Sight more to me than

Journal, April 1858.

all the art in Munich, though I love the *art* nevertheless. The great, wide-stretching earth and the all-embracing sky—the birthright of us all—are what I care most to look at. And I feel intensely the new beauty of the sky here. The blue is so exquisitely clear, and the wide streets give one such a broad canopy of sky. I felt more inspirited by our walk to the Theresien Platz than by any pleasure we have had in Munich.

April 16.—On Wednesday we walked to the Theresien Wiese to look at the "Bavaria" by sunset, but a shower came on and drove us to take refuge in a pretty house built near the Ruhmeshalle, whereby we were gainers, for we saw a charming family group: a mother with her three children—the eldest a boy with his book, the second a three-year-old maiden, the third a sweet baby-girl of a year and a half; two dogs, one a mixture of the setter and pointer, the other a turnspit; and a relation or servant ironing. The baby cried at the sight of G. in beard and spectacles, but kept her eyes turning towards him from her mother's lap, every now and then seeming to have overcome her fears, and then bursting out crying anew. At last she got down and lifted the tablecloth to peep at his legs, as if to see the monster's nether parts.

Letter to Miss Sara Hennell, 17th April 1858.

We have been just to take a sip at the two Pinacotheks and at the Glyptothek. At present the Rubens Saal is what I most long to return to. Rubens gives me more pleasure than any other painter, whether that is right or wrong. To be sure, I have not seen so many pictures, and pictures of so high a rank, by any other great master. I feel sure that when I have seen as much of Raphael I shall like him better; but at present Rubens, more than any one else, makes me feel that painting is a great art, and that he was a great artist. His are such real, breathing men and women, moved by passions, not mincing and grimacing, and posing in mere aping of passion! What a grand, glowing, forceful thing life looks in his pictures—the men such grand-bearded, grappling beings, fit to do the work of the world; the women such real mothers. We stayed at Nürnberg only twenty-four hours, and I felt sad to leave it so soon. A pity the place became Protestant, so that there is only one Catholic church, where one can go in and out as one would. We turned into the famous St Sebald's for a minute, where a Protestant clergyman was reading in a cold, formal way under the grand Gothic arches. Then we went to the Catholic church, the Frauen-Kirche, where the organ and voices were giving forth a glorious mass; and we stood with a feeling of brotherhood among the standing congregation till the last note of the organ had died out.

Letter to Miss Sara Hennell, 17th April 1858.

April 23.—Not being well enough to write, we determined to spend our morning at the Glyptothek and Pinacothek. A glorious morning—all sunshine and blue sky. We went to the Glyptothek first, and delighted ourselves anew with the "Sleeping Faun," the "Satyr and Bacchus," and the "Laughing Faun" ("Fauno colla Macchia"). Looked at the two young satyrs reposing with the pipe in their hands — one of them charming in the boyish, good-humoured beauty of the face, but both wanting finish in the limbs, which look almost as if they could be produced by a turning-machine. But the conception of this often-repeated figure is charming: it would make a garden seem more peaceful in the sunshine. Looked at the old Silenus too, which is excellent. I delight in these figures, full of droll animation, flinging some nature, in its broad freedom, in the eyes of small-mouthed mincing narrowness.

Journal, 1858.

We went into the modern Saal also, glancing on

Journal, 1858.

our way at the Cornelius frescoes, which seem to me stiff and hideous. An Adonis, by Thorwaldsen, is very beautiful.

Then to the Pinacothek, where we looked at Albert Dürer's portrait again, and many other pictures, among which I admired a group by Jordaens: "A satyr eating, while a peasant shows him that he can blow hot and cold at the same time;" the old grandmother nursing the child, the father with the key in his hand, with which he has been amusing baby, looking curiously at the satyr, the handsome wife, still more eager in her curiosity, the quiet cow, the little boy, the dog and cat—all are charmingly conceived.

April 24.—As we were reading this afternoon, Herr Oldenbourg came in, invited us to go to his house on Tuesday, and chatted pleasantly for an hour. He talked of Kaulbach, whom he has known very intimately, being the publisher of the 'Reineke Fuchs.' The picture of the "Hunnen Schlacht" was the first of Kaulbach's on a great scale. It created a sensation, and the critics began to call it a "Weltgeschichtliches Bild." Since then Kaulbach has been seduced into the complex, wearisome, symbolical style, which makes the frescoes at Berlin enormous puzzles.

When we had just returned from our drive in the Englische Garten, Bodenstedt pleasantly surprised us by presenting himself. He is a charming man, and promises to be a delightful acquaintance for us in this strange town. He chatted pleasantly with us for half an hour, telling us that he is writing a work, in five volumes, on the 'Contemporaries of Shakspeare,' and indicating the nature of his treatment of the Shakspearian drama—which is historical and analytical. Presently he proposed that we should adjourn to his house and have tea with him; and so we turned out all together in the bright moonlight, and enjoyed his pleasant chat until ten o'clock. His wife was not at home, but we were admitted to see the three sleeping children—one a baby about a year and a half old—a lovely waxen thing. He gave the same account of Kaulbach as we had heard from Oldenbourg: spoke of Genelli as superior in genius, though he has not the fortune to be recognised: recited some of Hermann Lingg's poetry, and spoke enthusiastically of its merits. There was not a word of detraction about any one—nothing to jar on one's impression of him as a refined noble-hearted man. Journal, 1858.

April 27.—This has been a red-letter day. In the morning Professor Wagner took us over his

Journal, 1858.

"Petrifacten Sammlung," giving us interesting explanations; and before we left him we were joined by Professor Martius, an animated clever man, who talked admirably, and invited us to his house. Then we went to Kaulbach's studio, talked with him, and saw with especial interest the picture he is preparing as a present to the New Museum. In the evening, after walking in the Theresien Wiese, we went to Herr Oldenbourg's, and met Liebig the chemist, Geibel and Heyse the poets, and Carrière, the author of a work on the Reformation. Liebig is charming, with well-cut features, a low quiet voice, and gentle manners. It was touching to see his hands, the nails black from the roots, the skin all grimed.

Heyse is like a painter's poet, ideally beautiful; rather brilliant in his talk, and altogether pleasing. Geibel is a man of rather coarse texture, with a voice like a kettledrum, and a steady determination to deliver his opinions on every subject that turned up. But there was a good deal of ability in his remarks.

April 30.—After calling on Frau Oldenbourg, and then at Professor Bodenstedt's, where we played with his charming children for ten minutes, we went to the theatre to hear Prince Radziwill's music to the "Faust." I admired especially the earlier part, the Easter-morning song of the spirits, the Beggar's song, and other things, until after the scene in Auerbach's cellar, which is set with much humour and fancy. But the scene between Faust and Marguerite is bad—"Meine Ruh ist hin" quite pitiable, and the "König im Thule" not good. Gretchen's second song, in which she implores help of the Schmerzensreiche, touched me a good deal.

Journal, 1858.

May 1.—In the afternoon Bodenstedt called, and we agreed to spend the evening at his house—a delightful evening. Professor Löher, author of 'Die Deutschen in America,' and another much younger *Gelehrter*, whose name I did not seize, were there.

May 2.—Still rainy and cold. We went to the Pinacothek, and looked at the old pictures in the first and second Saal. There are some very bad and some fine ones by Albert Dürer: of the latter, a full-length figure of the Apostle Paul, with the head of Mark beside him, in a listening attitude, is the one that most remains with me. There is a very striking "Adoration of the Magi," by Johannes van Eyck, with much merit in the colouring, perspective, and figures. Also, "Christ carrying His Cross," by Albert Dürer, is striking. "A woman

Journal, 1858.

raised from the dead by the imposition of the Cross," is a very elaborate composition, by Böhms, in which the faces are of first-rate excellence.

In the evening we went to the opera and saw the "Nord Stern."

May 10. — Since Wednesday I have had a wretched cold and cough, and been otherwise ill, but I have had several pleasures nevertheless. On Friday, Bodenstedt called with Baron Schack to take us to Genelli's, the artist of whose powers Bodenstedt had spoken to us with enthusiastic admiration. The result to us was nothing but disappointment: the sketches he showed us seemed to us quite destitute of any striking merit. On Sunday we dined with Liebig, and spent the evening at Bodenstedt's, where we met Professor Bluntschli, the jurist, a very intelligent and agreeable man, and Melchior Meyr, a maker of novels and tragedies, otherwise an ineffectual personage.

Letter to Miss Sara Hennell, 10th May 1858.

Our life here is very agreeable—full of pleasant novelty, although we take things quietly and observe our working hours just as if we were at Richmond. People are so kind to us that we feel already quite at home, sip *baierisch Bier* with great tolerance, and talk bad German with more and more *aplomb*. The place, you know, swarms with professors of all sorts—all *gründlich*, of course, and one or two of them great. There is no one we are more charmed with than Liebig. Mr Lewes had no letter to him—we merely met him at an evening party; yet he has been particularly kind to us, and seems to have taken a benevolent liking to me. We dined with him and his family yesterday, and saw how men of European celebrity may put up with greasy cooking in private life. He lives in very good German style, however; has a handsome suite of apartments, and makes a greater figure than most of the professors. His manners are charming—easy, graceful, benignant, and all the more conspicuous because he is so quiet and low-spoken among the loud talkers here. He looks best in his laboratory, with his velvet cap on, holding little phials in his hand, and talking of Kreatine and Kreatinine in the same easy way that well-bred ladies talk scandal. He is one of the professors who has been called here by the present king—Max—who seems to be a really sensible man among kings: gets up at five o'clock in the morning to study, and every Saturday evening has a gathering of the first men in science and literature, that he may benefit by their opinions on important subjects. At this *Tafel-rund* every

Letter to Miss Sara Hennell, 10th May 1858.

Letter to Miss Sara Hennell, 10th May 1858.

man is required to say honestly what he thinks; every one may contradict every one else; and if the king suspects any one of a polite insincerity, the too polished man is invited no more. Liebig, the three poets—Geibel, Heyse, and Bodenstedt—and Professor Löher, a writer of considerable mark, are always at the *Tafel-rund* as an understood part of their functions; the rest are invited according to the king's direction. Bodenstedt is one of our best friends here—enormously instructed, after the fashion of Germans, but not at all stupid with it.

We were at the Siebolds' last night to meet a party of celebrities, and, what was better, to see the prettiest little picture of married life—the great comparative anatomist (Siebold) seated at the piano in his spectacles playing the difficult accompaniments to Schubert's songs, while his little round-faced wife sang them with much taste and feeling. They are not young. Siebold is grey, and probably more than fifty—his wife perhaps nearly forty; and it is all the prettier to see their admiration of each other. She said to Mr Lewes, when he was speaking of her husband, "Ja, er ist ein netter Mann, nicht wahr?"[1]

We take the art in very small draughts at

[1] "He is really a charming man, is he not?"

present — the German hours being difficult to adjust to our occupations. We are obliged to dine at *one!* and of course when we are well enough must work till then. Two hours afterwards all the great public exhibitions are closed, except the churches. I *cannot* admire much of the modern German art. It is for the most part elaborate lifelessness. Kaulbach's great compositions are huge charades; and I have seen nothing of his equal to his own "Reineke Fuchs." It is an unspeakable relief, after staring at one of his pictures—the "Destruction of Jerusalem," for example, which is a regular child's puzzle of symbolism—to sweep it all out of one's mind,—which is very easily done, for nothing grasps you in it,—and call up in your imagination a little Gerard Dow that you have seen hanging in a corner of one of the cabinets. We have been to his *atelier*, and he has given us a proof of his "Irrenhaus,"[1] a strange sketch, which he made years ago—very terrible and powerful. He is certainly a man of great faculty, but is, I imagine, carried out of his true path by the ambition to produce "Weltgeschichtliche Bilder," which the German critics may go into raptures about. His "Battle of the Huns," which is the most

Letter to Miss Sara Hennell, 10th May 1858.

[1] Picture of interior of a Lunatic Asylum.

Letter to Miss Sara Hennell, 10th May 1858.

impressive of all his great pictures, was the first of the series. He painted it simply under the inspiration of the grand myth about the spirits of the dead warriors rising and carrying on the battle in the air. Straightway the German critics began to smoke furiously that vile tobacco which they call *æsthetik,* declared it a "Weltgeschichtliches Bild," and ever since Kaulbach has been concocting these pictures in which, instead of taking a single moment of reality and trusting to the infinite symbolism that belongs to all nature, he attempts to give you at one view a succession of events—each represented by some group which may mean "Whichever you please, my little dear."

I must tell you something else which interested me greatly, as the first example of the kind that has come under my observation. Among the awful mysterious names, hitherto known only as marginal references whom we have learned to clothe with ordinary flesh and blood, is Professor Martius, (Spix and Martius), now an old man, and rich after the manner of being rich in Germany. He has a very sweet wife—one of those women who remain pretty and graceful in old age—and a family of three daughters and one son, all more than grown up. I learned that she is Catholic, that her daughters are Catholic, and her husband and son Protestant—the children having been so brought up according to the German law in cases of mixed marriage. I can't tell you how interesting it was to me to hear her tell of her experience in bringing up her son conscientiously as a Protestant, and then to hear her and her daughters speak of the exemplary priests who had shown them such tender fatherly care when they were in trouble. They are the most harmonious, affectionate family we have seen; and one delights in such a triumph of human goodness over the formal logic of theorists.

Letter to Miss Sara Hennell, 10th May 1858.

May 13.—Geibel came and brought me the two volumes of his poems, and stayed chatting for an hour. We spent the evening quietly at home.

Journal, 1858.

May 14.—After writing, we went for an hour to the Pinacothek, and looked at some of the Flemish pictures. In the afternoon we called at Liebig's, and he went a long walk with us—the long chain of snowy mountains in the hazy distance. After supper I read Geibel's 'Junius Lieder.'

May 15. — Read the 18th chapter of 'Adam Bede' to G. He was much pleased with it. Then we walked in the Englische Garten, and heard the band, and saw the Germans drinking their beer. The park was lovely.

Journal, 1858.

May 16.—We were to have gone to Grosshesselohe with the Siebolds, and went to *Frühstück* with them at 12, as a preliminary. Bodenstedt was there to accompany us. But heavy rain came on, and we spent the time till 5 o'clock in talking, hearing music, and listening to Bodenstedt's 'Epic on the Destruction of Novgorod.' About seven, Liebig came to us and asked us to spend the evening at his house. We went, and found Voelderndorff, Bischoff and his wife, and Carrière and Frau.

May 20.—As I had a feeble head this morning, we gave up the time to seeing pictures, and went to the *Neue Pinacothek.* A "Lady with Fruit, followed by three Children," pleased us more than ever. It is by Wichmann. The two interiors of Westminster Abbey by Ainmueller admirable. Unable to admire Rothmann's Greek Landscapes, which have a room to themselves. Ditto Kaulbach's "Zerstörung von Jerusalem."

We went for the first time to see the collection of porcelain paintings, and had really a rich treat. Many of them are admirable copies of great pictures. The sweet "Madonna and Child," in Raphael's early manner: a "Holy Family," also in the early manner, with a Madonna the exact type of the St Catherine; and a "Holy Family" in the later manner, something like the "Madonna della Sedia," are all admirably copied. So are two of Andrea del Sarto's—full of tenderness and calm piety. Journal, 1858.

May 23.—Through the cold wind and white dust we went to the Jesuits' church to hear the music. It is a fine church in the Renaissance style, the vista terminating with the great altar, very fine, with all the crowd of human beings covering the floor. Numbers of men!

In the evening we went to Bodenstedt's, and saw his wife for the first time—a delicate creature, who sang us some charming Bavarian *Volkslieder.* On Monday we spent the evening at Löhers'—Baumgarten, *ein junger Historiker,* Oldenbourg, and the Bodenstedts meeting us.

Delicious *Mai-trank,* made by putting the fresh *Waldmeister*—a cruciferous plant with a small white flower, something like Lady's Bedstraw—into mild wine, together with sugar, and occasionally other things.

May 26.—This evening I have read aloud 'Adam Bede,' chap. xx. We have begun Ludwig's 'Zwischen Himmel und Erde.'

May 27.—We called on the Siebolds to-day,

Journal, 1858.

then walked in the Theresien Wiese, and saw the mountains gloriously. Spent the evening at Prof. Martius's, where Frau Erdl played Beethoven's Andante and the Moonlight Sonata admirably.

May 28.—We heard from Blackwood this morning. Good news in general, but the sale of our books not progressing at present.

Letter to John Blackwood, 28th May 1858.

It is invariably the case that when people discover certain points of coincidence in a fiction with facts that happen to have come to their knowledge, they believe themselves able to furnish a key to the whole. That is amusing enough to the author, who knows from what widely sundered portions of experience — from what a combination of subtle, shadowy suggestions, with certain actual objects and events, his story has been formed. It would be a very difficult thing for me to furnish a key to my stories myself. But where there is no exact memory of the past, any story with a few remembered points of character or of incident may pass for a history.

We pay for our sight of the snowy mountains here by the most capricious of climates. English weather is steadfast compared with Munich weather. You go to dinner here in summer and come away from it in winter. You are languid among trees and feathery grass at one end of the town, and are shivering in a hurricane of dust at the other. This inconvenience of climate, with the impossibility of dining (well) at any other hour than one o'clock, is not friendly to the stomach—that great seat of the imagination. And I shall never advise an author to come to Munich except *ad interim.* The great Saal, full of Rubens's pictures, is worth studying; and two or three precious bits of sculpture, and the sky on a fine day, always puts one in a good temper—it is so deliciously clear and blue, making even the ugliest buildings look beautiful by the light it casts on them.

Letter to John Blackwood, 28th May 1858.

May 30.—We heard "William Tell"—a great enjoyment to me.

Journal, 1858.

June 1.—To Grosshesselohe with a party. Siebold and his wife, Prof. Löher, Fräulein von List, Fräulein Thiersch, Frau von Schaden and her pretty daughter. It was very pretty to see Siebold's delight in nature. The strange whim of Schwanthaler's — the Burg von Schwaneck — was our destination.

June 10.—For the last week my work has been rather scanty, owing to bodily ailments. I am at the end of chap. xxi., and am this morning

Journal, 1858.

going to begin chap. xxii. In the interim our chief pleasure has been a trip to Starnberg by ourselves.

June 13.—This morning at last free from headache, and able to write. I am entering on my history of the birthday, with some fear and trembling. This evening we walked, between eight and half-past nine, in the Wiese, looking toward Nymphenburg. The light delicious—the west glowing; the faint crescent moon and Venus pale above it; the larks filling the air with their songs, which seemed only a little way above the ground.

Letter to Miss Sara Hennell, 14th June 1858.

Words are very clumsy things. I like less and less to handle my friends' sacred feelings with them. For even those who call themselves intimate know very little about each other—hardly ever know just *how* a sorrow is felt, and hurt each other by their very attempts at sympathy or consolation. We can bear no hand on our bruises. And so I feel I have no right to say that I know *how* the loss of your mother—"the only person who ever leaned on you"—affects you. I only know that it must make a deeply-felt crisis in your life, and I know that the better from having felt a great deal about my own mother and father, and from having the keenest remembrance of all that experience. But for this very reason I know that I can't measure what the event is to you; and if I were near you I should only kiss you and say nothing. People talk of the feelings dying out as one gets older; but at present my experience is just the contrary. All the serious relations of life become so much more real to me—pleasure seems so slight a thing, and sorrow and duty and endurance so great. I find the least bit of real human life touch me in a way it never did when I was younger.

Letter to Miss Sara Hennell, 14th June 1858.

June 17.—This evening G. left me to set out on his journey to Hofwyl to see his boys.

Journal, 1858.

June 18.—Went with the Siebolds to Nymphenburg; called at Professor Knapp's, and saw Liebig's sister, Frau Knapp—a charming, gentle-mannered woman, with splendid dark eyes.

June 22.—Tired of loneliness, I went to the Frau von Siebold, chatted with her over tea, and then heard some music.

June 23.—My kind little friend (Frau von Siebold) brought me a lovely bouquet of roses this morning, and invited me to go with them in the evening to the theatre to see the new comedy, the "Drei Candidaten," which I did—a miserably poor affair.

June 24.—G. came in the evening, at 10 o'clock

Journal, 1858.

—after I had suffered a great deal in thinking of the possibilities that might prevent him from coming.

June 25.—This morning I have read to G. all I have written during his absence, and he approves it more than I expected.

July 7.—This morning we left Munich, setting out in the rain to Rosenheim by railway. The previous day we dined and sat a few hours with the dear charming Siebolds, and parted from them with regret—glad to leave Munich, but not to leave the friends who had been so kind to us. For a week before, I had been ill—almost a luxury, because of the love that tended me. But the general languor and sense of depression, produced by Munich air and way of life, was no luxury, and I was glad to say a last good-bye to the quaint pepper-boxes of the Frauen-Kirche.

Munich to Dresden, 1858.

At the Rosenheim station we got into the longest of omnibuses, which took us to the *Gasthof*, where we were to dine and lunch, and then mount into the *Stell-wagen*, which would carry us to Prien, on the borders of the Chiem See. Rosenheim is a considerable and rather quaint-looking town, interrupted by orchards, and characterised in a passing glance by the piazzas that are seen everywhere fronting the shops. It has a grand view of the mountains, still a long way off. The afternoon was cloudy, with intermittent rain, and did not set off the landscape. Nevertheless I had much enjoyment in this four or five hours' journey to Prien. The little villages, with picturesque, wide gables, projecting roofs, and wooden galleries—with abundant orchards — with felled trunks of trees and stacks of fir-wood, telling of the near neighbourhood of the forest—were what I liked best in this ride.

We had no sooner entered the steamboat to cross the Chiem See than it began to rain heavily, and I kept below, only peeping now and then at the mountains and the green islands, with their monasteries. From the opposite bank of the See we had a grand view of the mountains, all dark purple under the clouded sky. Before us was a point where the nearer mountains opened and allowed us a view of their more distant brethren, receding in a fainter and fainter blue—a marsh in the foreground, where the wild-ducks were flying. Our drive from this end of the lake to Traunstein was lovely—through fertile, cultivated land, everywhere married to bits of forest. The green meadow or the golden corn sloped upwards towards pine woods, or the bushy

Munich to Dresden, 1858.

greenness seemed to run with wild freedom far out into long promontories among the ripening crops. Here and there the country had the aspect of a grand park from the beautiful intermingling of wood and field, without any line of fence.

Then came the red sunset, and it was dark when we entered Traunstein, where we had to pass the night. Among our companions in the day's journey had been a long-faced, cloaked, slow and solemn man, whom George called the author of 'Eugene Aram,' and I Don Quixote, he was so given to serious remonstrance with the vices he met on the road. We had been constantly deceived in the length of our stages—on the principle, possibly, of keeping up our spirits. The next morning there was the same tenderness shown about the starting of the *Stellwagen:* at first it was to start at seven, then at half-past, then when another *Wagen* came with its cargo of passengers. This was too much for Don Quixote; and when the stout, red-faced *Wirth* had given him still another answer about the time of starting, he began, in slow and monotonous indignation, "Warum lügen sie so? Sie werden machen dass kein Mensch diesen Weg kommen wird,"[1] &c. Whereupon the

[1] "Why do you tell such lies? The result of it will be that no one will travel this way."

Wirth looked red-faced, stout, and unwashed as before, without any perceptible expression of face supervening.

The next morning the weather looked doubtful, and so we gave up going to the König See for that day, determining to ramble on the Mönchsberg and enjoy the beauties of Salzburg instead. The morning brightened as the sun ascended, and we had a delicious ramble on the Mönchsberg—looking down on the lovely, peaceful plain below the grand old Untersberg, where the sleeping Kaiser awaits his resurrection in that "good time coming;" watching the white mist floating along the sides of the dark mountains, and wandering under the shadow of the plantation, where the ground was green with luxuriant hawkweed, as at Nymphenburg, near Munich. The outline of the castle and its rock is remarkably fine, and reminded us of Gorey in Jersey. But we had a still finer view of it when we drove out to Aigen. On our way thither we had sight of the Watzmann, the highest mountain in Bavarian Tyrol —emerging from behind the great shoulder of the Untersberg. It was the only mountain within sight that had snow on its summit. Once at Aigen, and descended from our carriage, we had a delicious walk, up and up, along a road of continual steps, by

Munich to Dresden, 1858.

the course of the mountain-stream, which fell in a series of cascades over great heaps of boulders; then back again, by a roundabout way, to our vehicle and home, enjoying the sight of old Watzmann again, and the grand mass of Salzburg Castle on its sloping rock.

We encountered a *table-d'hôte* acquaintance who had been to Berchtesgaden and the König See, driven through the salt-mine, and had had altogether a perfect expedition on this day, when we had not had the courage to set off. Never mind! we had enjoyed our day.

We thought it wisest the next morning to renounce the König See, and pursue our way to Ischl by the *Stell-wagen.* We were fortunate enough to secure two places in the *coupé,* and I enjoyed greatly the quiet outlook, from my comfortable corner, on the changing landscape—green valley and hill and mountain; here and there a picturesque Tyrolese village, and once or twice a fine lake.

The greatest charm of charming Ischl is the crystal Traun, surely the purest of streams. Away again early the next morning in the *coupé* of the *Stell-wagen,* through a country more and more beautiful, high woody mountains sloping

Munich to Dresden, 1858.

steeply down to narrow fertile green valleys, the road winding amongst them so as to show a perpetual variety of graceful outlines where the sloping mountains met in the distance before us. As we approached the Gmunden See, the masses became grander and more rocky, and the valley opened wider. It was Sunday, and when we left the *Stell-wagen*, we found quite a crowd in Sunday clothes standing round the place of embarkation for the steamboat that was to take us along the lake. Gmunden is another pretty place at the head of the lake, but apart from this one advantage, inferior to Ischl. We got on to the slowest of railways here, getting down at the station near the falls of the Traun, where we dined at the pleasant inn, and fed our eyes on the clear river again hurrying over the rocks. Behind the great fall there is a sort of inner chamber, where the water rushes perpetually over a stone altar. At the station, as we waited for the train, it began to rain, and the good-natured-looking woman asked us to take shelter in her little station-house,—a single room not more than eight feet square, where she lived with her husband and two little girls all the year round. The good couple looked more contented than half the well-lodged people in the

Munich to Dresden, 1858.

world. He used to be a *drozchky* driver; and after that life of uncertain gains, which had many days quite penniless and therefore dinnerless, he found his present position quite a pleasant lot.

On to Linz, when the train came, gradually losing sight of the Tyrolean mountains and entering the great plain of the Danube. Our voyage the next day in the steamboat was unfortunate: we had incessant rain till we had passed all the finest parts of the banks. But when we had landed, the sun shone out brilliantly, and so our entrance into Vienna, through the long suburb, with perpetual shops and odd names (Prschka, for example, which a German in our omnibus thought not at all remarkable for consonants!) was quite cheerful. We made our way through the city and across the bridge to the Weissen Ross, which was full: so we went to the Drei Rosen, which received us. The sunshine was transient: it began to rain again when we went out to look at St Stephen's, but the delight of seeing that glorious building could not be marred by a little rain. The tower of this church is worth going to Vienna to see.

The aspect of the city is that of an inferior Paris; the shops have an elegance that one sees nowhere else in Germany; the streets are clean, the houses tall and stately. The next morning we had a view of the town from the Belvedere Terrace—St Stephen's sending its exquisite tower aloft from among an almost level forest of houses and inconspicuous churches. It is a magnificent collection of pictures at the Belvedere; but we were so unfortunate as only to be able to see them once, the gallery being shut up on the Wednesday; and so, many pictures have faded from my memory, even of those which I had time to distinguish. Titian's "Danaë" was one that delighted us: besides this, I remember Giorgione's "Lucrezia Borgia" with the cruel, cruel eyes; the remarkable head of Christ; a proud Italian face in a red garment, I think by Correggio; and two heads by Denner, the most wonderful of all his wonderful heads that I have seen. There is an "Ecce Homo" by Titian, which is thought highly of, and is splendid in composition and colour, but the Christ is abject, the Pontius Pilate vulgar; amazing that they could have been painted by the same man who conceived and executed the "Christo della Moneta"! There are huge Veroneses, too, splendid and interesting.

The Liechtenstein collection we saw twice, and that remains with me much more distinctly—the room full of Rubens's history of Decius, more mag-

Munich to Dresden, 1858.

nificent even than he usually is in colour; then his glorious "Assumption of the Virgin," and opposite to it the portraits of his two boys; the portrait of his lovely wife going to the bath, with brown drapery round her; and the fine portraits by Vandyke, especially the pale delicate face of Wallenstein with blue eyes and pale auburn locks.

Another great pleasure we had at Vienna—next after the sight of St Stephen's and the pictures—was a visit to Hyrtl, the anatomist, who showed us some of his wonderful preparations, showing the vascular and nervous systems in the lungs, liver, kidneys, and intestinal canal of various animals. He told us the deeply interesting story of the loss of his fortune in the Vienna revolution of '48. He was compelled by the revolutionists to attend on the wounded for three days' running. When at last he came to his house to change his clothes he found nothing but four bare walls! His fortune in Government bonds was burnt along with the house, as well as all his precious collection of anatomical preparations, &c. He told us that since that great shock his nerves have been so susceptible that he sheds tears at the most trifling events, and has a depression of spirits which often keeps him silent for days. He only received a very slight sum from Government in compensation for his loss.

One evening we strolled in the Volksgarten and saw the "Theseus killing the Centaur" by Canova, which stands in a temple built for its reception. But the garden to be best remembered by us was that at Schönbrunn, a labyrinth of stately avenues with their terminal fountains. We amused ourselves for some time with the menagerie here, the lions especially, who lay in dignified sleepiness till the approach of feeding-time made them open eager eyes and pace impatiently about their dens.

We set off from Vienna in the evening with a family of Wallachians as our companions, one of whom, an elderly man, could speak no German, and began to address G. in Wallachian, as if that were the common language of all the earth. We managed to sleep enough for a night's rest, in spite of intense heat and our cramped positions, and arrived in very good condition at Prague in the fine morning.

Out we went after breakfast, that we might see as much as possible of the grand old city in one day; and our morning was occupied chiefly in walking about and getting views of striking exteriors. The most interesting things we saw were the Jewish

Munich to Dresden, 1858.

burial-ground (the Alter Friedhof) and the old synagogue. The Friedhof is unique—with a wild growth of grass and shrubs and trees, and a multitude of quaint tombs in all sorts of positions, looking like the fragments of a great building, or as if they had been shaken by an earthquake. We saw a lovely dark-eyed Jewish child here, which we were glad to kiss in all its dirt. Then came the sombre old synagogue, with its smoked groins, and lamp for ever burning. An intelligent Jew was our *cicerone*, and read us some Hebrew out of the precious old book of the law.

After dinner we took a carriage and went across the wonderful bridge of St Jean Nepomuck, with its avenue of statues, towards the Radschin—an ugly straight-lined building, but grand in effect from its magnificent site, on the summit of an eminence crowded with old massive buildings. The view from this eminence is one of the most impressive in the world—perhaps as much from one's associations with Prague as from its visible grandeur and antiquity. The cathedral close to the Radschin is a melancholy object on the outside—left with unfinished sides like scars. The interior is rich, but sadly confused in its ornamentation, like so many of the grand old churches—hideous altars of bastard style disgracing exquisite Gothic columns —cruelest of all in St Stephen's at Vienna!

Munich to Dresden, 1858.

We got our view from a *Damen Stift*[1] (for ladies of family), founded by Maria Theresa, whose blond beauty looked down on us from a striking portrait. Close in front of us, sloping downwards, was a pleasant orchard; then came the river, with its long, long bridge and grand gateway; then the sober-coloured city, with its surrounding plain and distant hills. In the evening we went to the theatre—a shabby, ugly building—and heard Spohr's "Jessonda."

The next morning early by railway to Dresden—a charming journey—for it took us right through the Saxon Switzerland, with its castellated rocks and firs. At four o'clock we were dining comfortably at the Hotel de Pologne, and the next morning (Sunday) we secured our lodgings—a whole apartment of six rooms, all to ourselves, for 18s. per week! By nine o'clock we were established in our new home, where we were to enjoy six weeks' quiet work, undisturbed by visits and visitors. And so we did. We were as happy as princes—are not—George writing at the far corner of the great *salon*, I at my *Schrank* in my own private room, with closed doors. Here I wrote the latter half of the

[1] Charitable Institution for Ladies.

Munich to Dresden, 1858.

second volume of 'Adam Bede' in the long mornings that our early hours—rising at six o'clock—secured us. Three mornings in the week we went to the Picture Gallery from twelve till one. The first day we went was a Sunday, when there is always a crowd in the Madonna Cabinet. I sat down on the sofa opposite the picture for an instant; but a sort of awe, as if I were suddenly in the living presence of some glorious being, made my heart swell too much for me to remain comfortably, and we hurried out of the room. On subsequent mornings we always came, in the last minutes of our stay, to look at this sublimest picture; and while the others, except the "Christo della Moneta" and Holbein's Madonna, lost much of their first interest, this became harder and harder to leave. Holbein's Madonna is very exquisite—a divinely gentle, golden-haired blonde, with eyes cast down, in an attitude of unconscious, easy grace—the loveliest of all the Madonnas in the Dresden Gallery, except the Sistine. By the side of it is a wonderful portrait by Holbein, which I especially enjoyed looking at. It represents nothing more lofty than a plain, weighty man of business, a goldsmith; but the eminently fine painting brings out all the weighty, calm, good sense that lies in a first-rate character of that order.

We looked at the Zinsgroschen (Titian's), too, every day, and after that at the great painter's Venus, fit for its purity and sacred loveliness to hang in a temple with Madonnas. Palma's Venus, which hangs near, was an excellent foil, because it is pretty and pure in itself; but beside the Titian it is common and unmeaning. Munich to Dresden, 1858.

Another interesting case of comparison was that between the original Zinsgroschen and a copy by an Italian painter, which hangs on the opposite wall of the cabinet. This is considered a fine copy, and would be a fine picture if one had never seen the original; but all the finest effects are gone in the copy.

The four large Correggios hanging together,—the *Nacht;* the Madonna with St Sebastian, of the smiling graceful character, with the little cherub riding astride a cloud; the Madonna—with St Hubert; and a third Madonna—very grave and sweet, painted when he was nineteen,—remain with me very vividly. They are full of life, though the life is not of a high order; and I should have surmised, without any previous knowledge, that the painter was among the first masters of *technique.* The Magdalen is sweet in conception, but seems to have less than the usual merit of Correggio's pictures

Munich to Dresden, 1858.

as to painting. A picture we delighted in extremely was one of Murillo's—"St Rodriguez, fatally wounded, receiving the Crown of Martyrdom." The attitude and expression are sublime, and strikingly distinguished from all other pictures of Saints I have ever seen. He stands erect in his scarlet and white robes, with face upturned, the arms held simply downward, but the hands held open in a receptive attitude. The silly cupid-like angel holding the martyr's crown in the corner spoils all.

I did not half satisfy my appetite for the rich collection of Flemish and Dutch pictures here—for Teniers, Ryckart, Gerard Dow, Terburg, Mieris, and the rest. Rembrandt looks great here in his portraits, but I like none of the other pictures by him; the Ganymede is an offence. Guido is superlatively odious in his Christs, in agonised or ecstatic attitudes,—much about the level of the accomplished London beggar. Dear, grand old Rubens does not show to great advantage, except in the charming half-length "Diana returning from Hunting," the "Love Garden," and the sketch of his "Judgment of Paris."

The most popular Murillo, and apparently one of the most popular Madonnas in the gallery, is the simple, sad mother with her child, without the least divinity in it, suggesting a dead or sick father, and imperfect nourishment in a garret. In that light it is touching. A fellow traveller in the railway to Leipzig told us he had seen this picture in 1848 with nine bullet-holes in it! The firing from the hotel of the Stadt Rom bore directly on the Picture Gallery.

Munich to Dresden, 1858.

Veronese is imposing in one of the large rooms—the "Adoration of the Magi," the "Marriage at Cana," the "Finding of Moses," &c., making grand masses of colour on the lower part of the walls; but to me he is ignoble as a painter of human beings.

It was a charming life—our six weeks at Dresden. There were the open-air concerts at the Grosser Garten and the Brühl'sche Terrace; the Sommer Theater, where we saw our favourite comic actor Merbitz; the walks into the open country, with the grand stretch of sky all round; the Zouaves, with their wondrous make-ups as women; Räder, the humorous comedian at the Sink'sche Bad Theater; our quiet afternoons in our pleasant *salon*—all helping to make an agreeable fringe to the quiet working time.

Letter to Miss Sara Hennell, 28th July 1858.

Since I wrote to you last I have lived through a great deal of exquisite pleasure. First an attack of illness during our last week at Munich, which I reckon among my pleasures because I was nursed

Letter to Miss Sara Hennell, 28th July 1858.

so tenderly. Then a fortnight's unspeakable journey to Salzburg, Ischl, Linz, Vienna, Prague, and finally Dresden, which is our last resting-place before returning to Richmond, where we hope to be at the beginning of September. Dresden is a proper climax; for all other art seems only a preparation for feeling the superiority of the Madonna di San Sisto the more. We go three days a-week to the gallery, and every day—after looking at other pictures—we go to take a parting draught of delight at Titian's Zinsgroschen and the *Einzige* Madonna. In other respects I am particularly enjoying our residence here—we are so quiet, having determined to know no one and give ourselves up to work. We both feel a happy change in our health from leaving Munich, though I am reconciled to our long stay there by the fact that Mr Lewes gained so much from his intercourse with the men of science there, especially Bischoff, Siebold, and Harless. I remembered your passion for autographs, and asked Liebig for his on your account. I was not sure that you would care enough about the handwriting of other luminaries; for there is such a thing as being European and yet obscure — a fixed star visible only from observatories.

You will be interested to hear that I saw Strauss

at Munich. He came for a week's visit before we left. I had a quarter of an hour's chat with him alone, and was very agreeably impressed by him. He looked much more serene, and his face had a far sweeter expression, than when I saw him in that dumb way at Cologne. He speaks with very choice words, like a man strictly truthful in the use of language. Will you undertake to tell Mrs Call from me that he begged me to give his kindest remembrances to her and to her father,[1] of whom he spoke with much interest and regard as his earliest English friend? I dare not begin to write about other things or people that I have seen in these crowded weeks. They must wait till I have you by my side again, which I hope will happen some day.

Letter to Miss Sara Hennell, 28th July 1858.

From Dresden, one showery day at the end of August, we set off to Leipzig, the first stage on our way home. Here we spent two nights; had a glimpse of the old town with its fine market; dined at Brockhaus's; saw the picture-gallery, carrying away a lasting delight in Calame's great landscapes and De Dreux's dogs, which are far better worth seeing than De la Roche's "Napoleon at Fontainebleau"—considered the glory of the gallery; went

Journal, 1858.

[1] Dr Brabant.

Journal, 1858.

with Victor Carus to his museum and saw an Amphioxus; and finally spent the evening at an open-air concert in Carus's company. Early in the morning we set off by railway, and travelled night and day till we reached home on the 2d September.

Letter to Miss Sara Hennell, 5th Sept. 1858.

Will you not write to the author of 'Thorndale' and express your sympathy? He is a very diffident man, who would be susceptible to that sort of fellowship; and one should give a gleam of happiness where it is possible. I shall write you nothing worth reading for the next three months, so here is an opportunity for you to satisfy a large appetite for generous deeds. You can write to me a great many times without getting anything worth having in return.

Letter to Miss Sara Hennell, 6th Oct. 1858.

Thanks for the verses on Buckle. I'm afraid I feel a malicious delight in them, for he is a writer who inspires me with a personal dislike: not to put too fine a point on it, he impresses me as an irreligious, conceited man.

Long ago I had offered to write about Newman, but gave it up again.

The second volume of 'Adam Bede' had been sent to Blackwood on 7th September, the third had followed two months later, and there are the following entries in the Journal in November:—

Nov. 1.—I have begun Carlyle's 'Life of Frederic the Great,' and have also been thinking much of my own life to come. This is a moment of suspense, for I am awaiting Blackwood's opinion and proposals concerning 'Adam Bede.' Journal, 1858.

Nov. 4.—Received a letter from Blackwood containing warm praise of my third volume, and offering £800 for the copyright of 'Adam Bede' for four years. I wrote to accept.

Nov. 10.—Wilkie Collins and Mr Pigott came to dine with us after a walk by the river. I was pleased with Wilkie Collins,—there is a sturdy uprightness about him that makes all opinion and all occupation respectable.

Nov. 16.—Wrote the last word of 'Adam Bede' and sent it to Mr Langford. *Jubilate.*

History of 'Adam Bede.'

The germ of 'Adam Bede' was an anecdote told me by my Methodist Aunt Samuel (the wife of my father's younger brother),—an anecdote from her own experience. We were sitting together one afternoon during her visit to me at Griff, probably in 1839 or 1840, when it occurred to her to tell me how she had visited a condemned criminal,—a very ignorant girl, who had murdered her child and re-

History of 'Adam Bede.'

fused to confess; how she had stayed with her praying through the night, and how the poor creature at last broke out into tears, and confessed her crime. My aunt afterwards went with her in the cart to the place of execution; and she described to me the great respect with which this ministry of hers was regarded by the official people about the gaol. The story, told by my aunt with great feeling, affected me deeply, and I never lost the impression of that afternoon and our talk together; but I believe I never mentioned it, through all the intervening years, till something prompted me to tell it to George in December 1856, when I had begun to write the 'Scenes of Clerical Life.' He remarked that the scene in the prison would make a fine element in a story; and I afterwards began to think of blending this and some other recollections of my aunt in one story, with some points in my father's early life and character. The problem of construction that remained was to make the unhappy girl one of the chief *dramatis personæ,* and connect her with the hero. At first I thought of making the story one of the series of "Scenes," but afterwards, when several motives had induced me to close these with "Janet's Repentance," I determined on making what we always called in our conversation "My Aunt's Story" the subject of a long novel, which I accordingly began to write on the 22d October 1857. History of 'Adam Bede.'

The character of Dinah grew out of my recollections of my aunt, but Dinah is not at all like my aunt, who was a very small, black-eyed woman, and (as I was told, for I never heard her preach) very vehement in her style of preaching. She had left off preaching when I knew her, being probably sixty years old, and in delicate health; and she had become, as my father told me, much more gentle and subdued than she had been in the days of her active ministry and bodily strength, when she could not rest without exhorting and remonstrating in season and out of season. I was very fond of her, and enjoyed the few weeks of her stay with me greatly. She was loving and kind to me, and I could talk to her about my inward life, which was closely shut up from those usually round me. I saw her only twice again, for much shorter periods,—once at her own home at Wirksworth in Derbyshire, and once at my father's last residence, Foleshill.

The character of Adam and one or two incidents connected with him were suggested by my father's early life; but Adam is not my father any more than Dinah is my aunt. Indeed, there is not a

History of 'Adam Bede.'

single portrait in 'Adam Bede;' only the suggestions of experience wrought up into new combinations. When I began to write it, the only elements I had determined on, besides the character of Dinah, were the character of Adam, his relation to Arthur Donnithorne, and their mutual relations to Hetty—*i.e.*, to the girl who commits child-murder,—the scene in the prison being, of course, the climax towards which I worked. Everything else grew out of the characters and their mutual relations. Dinah's ultimate relation to Adam was suggested by George, when I had read to him the first part of the first volume: he was so delighted with the presentation of Dinah, and so convinced that the readers' interest would centre in her, that he wanted her to be the principal figure at the last. I accepted the idea at once, and from the end of the third chapter worked with it constantly in view.

The first volume was written at Richmond, and given to Blackwood in March. He expressed great admiration of its freshness and vividness, but seemed to hesitate about putting it in the Magazine, which was the form of publication he, as well as myself, had previously contemplated. He still *wished* to have it for the Magazine, but desired to know the course of the story. At *present* he saw

History of 'Adam Bede.'

nothing to prevent its reception in 'Maga,' but he would like to see more. I am uncertain whether his doubts rested solely on Hetty's relation to Arthur, or whether they were also directed towards the treatment of Methodism by the Church. I refused to tell my story beforehand, on the ground that I would not have it judged apart from my *treatment*, which alone determines the moral quality of art; and ultimately I proposed that the notion of publication in 'Maga' should be given up, and that the novel should be published in three volumes at Christmas, if possible. He assented.

I began the second volume in the second week of my stay at Munich, about the middle of April. While we were at Munich, George expressed his fear that Adam's part was too passive throughout the drama, and that it was important for him to be brought into more direct collision with Arthur. This doubt haunted me, and out of it grew the scene in the wood between Arthur and Adam; the fight came to me as a *necessity* one night at the Munich opera, when I was listening to "William Tell." Work was slow and interrupted at Munich, and when we left I had only written to the beginning of the dance on the Birthday Feast; but at Dresden I wrote uninterruptedly and with great

History of 'Adam Bede.'

enjoyment in the long, quiet mornings, and there I nearly finished the second volume—all, I think, but the last chapter, which I wrote here in the old room at Richmond in the first week of September, and then sent the MS. off to Blackwood. The opening of the third volume—Hetty's journey—was, I think, written more rapidly than the rest of the book, and was left without the slightest alteration of the first draught. Throughout the book I have altered little; and the only cases I think in which George suggested more than a verbal alteration, when I read the MS. aloud to him, were the first scene at the Farm, and the scene in the wood between Arthur and Adam, both of which he recommended me to "space out" a little, which I did.

When, on October 29, I had written to the end of the love-scene at the Farm, between Adam and Dinah, I sent the MS. to Blackwood, since the remainder of the third volume could not affect the judgment passed on what had gone before. He wrote back in warm admiration, and offered me, on the part of the firm, £800 for four years' copyright. I accepted the offer. The last words of the third volume were written and despatched on their way to Edinburgh, November the 16th, and now on the last day of the same month I have written this slight history of my book. I love it very much, and am deeply thankful to have written it, whatever the public may say to it—a result which is still in darkness, for I have at present had only four sheets of the proof. The book would have been published at Christmas, or rather early in December, but that Bulwer's 'What will he do with it?' was to be published by Blackwood at that time, and it was thought that this novel might interfere with mine. History of 'Adam Bede.'

> The manuscript of 'Adam Bede' bears the following inscription:—"To my dear husband, George Henry Lewes, I give the MS. of a work which would never have been written but for the happiness which his love has conferred on my life."

I shall be much obliged if you will accept for me Tauchnitz's offer of £30 for the English reprint of 'Clerical Scenes.' And will you also be so good as to desire that Tauchnitz may register the book in Germany, as I understand that is the only security against its being translated without our knowledge; and I shudder at the idea of my books being turned into hideous German by an incompetent translator. Letter to John Blackwood, 25th Nov 1858.

I return the proofs by to-day's post. The dialect

Letter to John Blackwood, 25th Nov. 1858.

must be toned down all through in correcting the proofs, for I found it impossible to keep it subdued enough in writing. I am aware that the spelling which represents a dialect perfectly well to those who know it by the ear, is likely to be unintelligible to others. I hope the sheets will come rapidly and regularly now, for I dislike lingering, hesitating processes.

Your praise of my ending was very warming and cheering to me in the foggy weather. I'm sure if I have written well, your pleasant letters have had something to do with it. Can anything be done in America for 'Adam Bede'? I suppose not—as my name is not known there.

Journal, 1858.

Nov. 25.—We had a visit from Mr Bray, who told us much that interested us about Mr Richard Congreve, and also his own affairs.

Letter to Mrs Bray, 26th Nov. 1858.

I am very grateful to you for sending me a few authentic words from your own self. They are unspeakably precious to me. I mean that quite literally, for there is no putting into words any feeling that has been of long growth within us. It is easy to say how we love *new* friends, and what we think of them, but words can never trace out all the fibres that knit us to the old. I have been thinking of you incessantly in the waking hours, and feel a growing hunger to know more precise details about you. I am of a too sordid and anxious disposition, prone to dwell almost exclusively on fears instead of hopes, and to lay in a larger stock of resignation than of any other form of confidence. But I try to extract some comfort this morning from my consciousness of this disposition, by thinking that nothing is ever so bad as my imagination paints it. And then I know there are incommunicable feelings within us capable of creating our best happiness at the very time others can see nothing but our troubles. And so I go on arguing with myself, and trying to live inside *you* and looking at things in all the lights I can fancy you seeing them in, for the sake of getting cheerful about you in spite of Coventry.

Letter to Mrs Bray, 26th Nov. 1858.

The well-flavoured molluscs came this morning. It was very kind of you: and if you remember how fond I am of oysters, your good-nature will have the more pleasure in furnishing my *gourmandise* with the treat. I have a childish delight in any little act of genuine friendliness towards us—and yet not childish, for how little we thought of people's goodness towards us when we were children. It takes a good deal of experience to tell one the rarity of a thoroughly disinterested kindness.

Letter to Chas. Bray, Christmas Day, 1858.

Letter to John Blackwood, 28th Dec. 1858.

I see with you entirely about the preface: indeed I had myself anticipated the very effects you predict. The deprecatory tone is not one I can ever take willingly, but I am conscious of a shrinking sort of pride which is likely to warp my judgment in many personal questions, and on that ground I distrusted my own opinion.

Mr Lewes went to Vernon Hill yesterday for a few days' change of air, but before he went, he said, "Ask Mr Blackwood what he thinks of putting a mere advertisement at the beginning of the book to this effect: As the story of 'Adam Bede' will lose much of its effect if the development is foreseen, the author requests those critics who may honour him with a notice to abstain from telling the story." I write my note of interrogation accordingly "?"

Pray do not begin to read the second volume until it is all in print. There is necessarily a lull of interest in it to prepare for the crescendo. I am delighted that you like my Mrs Poyser. I'm very sorry to part with her and some of my other characters—there seems to be so much more to be done with them. Mr Lewes says she gets better and better as the book goes on; and I was certainly conscious of writing her dialogue with heightening gusto. Even in our imaginary worlds there is the sorrow of parting. Letter to John Blackwood, 28th Dec. 1858

I hope the Christmas weather is as bright in your beautiful Edinburgh as it is here, and that you are enjoying all other Christmas pleasures too without disturbance.

I have not yet made up my mind what my next story is to be, but I must not lie fallow any longer when the new year is come.

Dec. 25 (*Christmas-Day*).—George and I spent this wet day very happily alone together. We are reading Scott's life in the evenings with much enjoyment. I am reading through Horace in this pause. Journal, 1858.

Dec. 31.—The last day of the dear old year, which has been full of expected and unexpected happiness. 'Adam Bede' has been written, and the second volume is in type. The first number of George's 'Physiology of Common Life'—a work in which he has had much happy occupation—is published to-day; and both his position as a scientific writer and his inward satisfaction in that part of his studies have been much heightened during the past year. Our double life is more and more blessed—more and more complete.

I think this chapter cannot more fitly conclude than with the following extract from Mr G. H. Lewes's Journal, with which Mr Charles Lewes has been good enough to furnish me:—

"*Jan.* 28, 1859.—Walked along the Thames towards Kew to meet Herbert Spencer, who was to spend the day with us, and we chatted with him on matters personal and philosophical. I owe him a debt of gratitude. My acquaintance with him was the brightest ray in a very dreary, *wasted* period of my life. I had given up all ambition whatever, lived from hand to mouth, and thought the evil of each day sufficient. The stimulus of his intellect, especially during our long walks, roused my energy once more and revived my dormant love of science. His intense theorising tendency was contagious, and it was only the stimulus of a *theory* which could then have induced me to work. I owe Spencer another and a deeper debt. It was through him that I learned to know Marian—to know her was to love her,—and since then my life has been a new birth. To her I owe all my prosperity and all my happiness. God bless her!"

SUMMARY.

JANUARY 1858 TO DECEMBER 1858.

'Times' reviews 'Scenes of Clerical Life'—Helps's opinion—Subscription to the 'Scenes'—Letter from Dickens, 18th Jan. 1858—Letter from Froude, 17th Jan.—Letter to Miss Hennell—Mr Wm. Smith, author of 'Thorndale'—Ruskin—Reading the 'Eumenides' and Wordsworth—Letter to John Blackwood on Dickens's Letter—Letter from Mrs Carlyle—Letter from Faraday—'Clerical Scenes' moving—John Blackwood calls, and George Eliot reveals herself—Takes MS. of first part of 'Adam Bede'—Letters to Charles Bray on reports of authorship—Visit to Germany—Description of Nürnberg — The Frauen - Kirche — Effect of the music—Albert Dürer's house—Munich—Lodgings—Pinacothek — Rubens — Crucifixion — Theresien Wiese—Schwanthaler's "Bavaria"—The Alps—Letter to Miss Hennell—Contrast between Catholic and Protestant worship—Glyptothek—Pictures—Statues—Cornelius frescoes—Herr Oldenbourg—Kaulbach — Bodenstedt — Professor Wagner — Martius—Liebig — Geibel — Heyse — Carrière — Prince Radziwill's "Faust"—Professsr Löher—Baron Schack—Genelli—Professor Bluntschli—Letter to Miss Hennell—Description of Munich life — Kaulbach's pictures — The Siebolds — The Neue Pinacothek—Pictures and porcelain painting—Mme. Bodenstedt—Letter to Blackwood—Combinations of artist in writing—Hears "William Tell"—Expedition to Grosshesselohe — Progress with 'Adam Bede'—Letter to Miss Hennell on death of her mother—Mr Lewes goes to Hofwyl

—Frau Knapp — Mr Lewes returns — Leave Munich for Traunstein—Salzburg—Ischl—Linz—By Danube to Vienna —St Stephen's—Belvedere pictures—Liechtenstein collection —Hyrtl the anatomist—Prague—Jewish burial-ground and the old synagogue—To Dresden—Latter half of second volume of 'Adam Bede' written—First impression of Sistine Madonna—"The Tribute-money"—Holbein's Madonna—The Correggios—Dutch school—Murillo—Letter to Miss Hennell —Description of life at Dresden—Health improved—Mention of Strauss at Munich—Dresden to Leipzig—Home to Richmond—Letter to Miss Hennell—Opinion of Buckle—Blackwood offers £800 for 'Adam Bede'—Wilkie Collins and Mr Pigott—History of 'Adam Bede'—Letter to Charles Bray—Disinterested kindness—Letter to Blackwood suggesting preface to 'Adam Bede' — Reading Scott's Life and Horace—Review of year—Extract from G. H. Lewes's Journal.

CHAPTER IX.

Jan. 12.—We went into town to-day and looked in the 'Annual Register' for cases of *inundation.* Letter from Blackwood to-day, speaking of renewed delight in 'Adam Bede,' and proposing 1st Feb. as the day of publication. Read the article in yesterday's 'Times' on George's 'Sea-side Studies'—highly gratifying. We are still reading Scott's life with great interest; and G. is reading to me Michelet's book 'De l'Amour.' Journal, 1859.

Jan. 15.—I corrected the last sheets of 'Adam Bede,' and we afterwards walked to Wimbledon to see our new house, which we have taken for seven years. I hired the servant—another bit of business done: and then we had a delightful walk across Wimbledon Common and through Richmond Park homeward. The air was clear and cold—the sky magnificent.

Jan. 31.—Received a cheque for £400 from

Journal, 1859.

Blackwood, being the first instalment of the payment for four years' copyright of 'Adam Bede.' To-morrow the book is to be subscribed, and Blackwood writes very pleasantly—confident of its "great success." Afterwards we went into town, paid money into the bank, and ordered part of our china and glass towards housekeeping.

Letter to John Blackwood, 31st Jan. 1859.

Enclosed is the formal acknowledgment, bearing my signature, and with it let me beg you to accept my thanks — *not* formal but heartfelt — for the generous way in which you have all along helped me with words and with deeds.

The impression 'Adam Bede' has made on you and Major Blackwood—of whom I have always been pleased to think as concurring with your views—is my best encouragement, and counterbalances, in some degree, the depressing influences to which I am peculiarly sensitive. I perceive that I have not the characteristics of the "popular author," and yet I am much in need of the warmly expressed sympathy which only popularity can win.

A good subscription would be cheering, but I can understand that it is not decisive of success or non-success. Thank you for promising to let me know about it as soon as possible.

Feb. 6.—Yesterday we went to take possession of Holly Lodge, Wandsworth, which is to be our dwelling, we expect, for years to come. It was a deliciously fresh bright day—I will accept the omen. A letter came from Blackwood telling me the result of the subscription to 'Adam Bede,' which was published on the 1st.: 730 copies, Mudie having taken 500 on the publisher's terms —*i.e.*, ten per cent on the sale price. At first he had stood out for a larger reduction, and would only take 50, but at last he came round. In this letter Blackwood told me the first *ab extra* opinion of the book, which happened to be precisely what I most desired. A cabinet-maker (brother to Blackwood's managing clerk) had read the sheets, and declared that the writer must have been brought up to the business, or at least had listened to the workmen in their workshop. Journal, 1859.

Feb. 12.—Received a cheering letter from Blackwood, saying that he finds 'Adam Bede' making just the impression he had anticipated among his own friends and connections, and enclosing a parcel from Dr John Brown "To the author of 'Adam Bede.'" The parcel contained 'Rab and his Friends,' with an inscription.

Letter to John Blackwood, 13th Feb. 1859.

Will you tell Dr John Brown, that when I read an account of 'Rab and his Friends' in a newspaper, I wished I had the story to read at full length; and I thought to myself the writer of 'Rab' would perhaps like 'Adam Bede.'

When you have told him this, he will understand the peculiar pleasure I had on opening the little parcel with 'Rab' inside, and a kind word from Rab's friend. I have read the story twice—once aloud, and once to myself, very slowly, that I might dwell on the pictures of Rab and Ailie, and carry them about with me more distinctly. I will not say any commonplace words of admiration about what has touched me so deeply: there is no adjective of that sort left undefiled by the newspapers. The writer of 'Rab' *knows* that I must love the grim old mastiff with the short tail and the long dewlaps—that I must have felt present at the scenes of Ailie's last trial.

Thanks for your cheering letter. I will be hopeful—if I can.

Letter to Miss Sara Hennell, 19th Feb. 1859.

You have the art of writing just the sort of letters I care for—sincere letters, like your own talk. We are tolerably settled now, except that we have only a temporary servant; and I shall not be quite at ease until I have a trustworthy woman who will manage without incessant dogging. Our home is very comfortable, with far more of vulgar indulgences in it than I ever expected to have again; but you must not imagine it a snug place, just peeping above the holly bushes. Imagine it rather as a tall cake, with a low garnish of holly and laurel. As it is, we are very well off, with glorious breezy walks, and wide horizons, well ventilated rooms, and abundant water. If I allowed myself to have any longings beyond what is given, they would be for a nook quite in the country, far away from palaces—Crystal or otherwise—with an orchard behind me full of old trees, and rough grass and hedgerow paths among the endless fields where you meet nobody. We talk of such things sometimes, along with old age and dim faculties, and a small independence to save us from writing drivel for dishonest money. In the meantime the business of life shuts us up within the environs of London and within sight of human advancements, which I should be so very glad to believe in without seeing.

Letter to Miss Sara Hennell, 19th Feb. 1859.

Pretty Arabella Goddard we heard play at Berlin —play the very things you heard as a *bonne bouche* at the last—none the less delightful from being so

Letter to Miss Sara Hennell, 19th Feb. 1859.

unlike the piano playing of Liszt and Clara Schumann, whom we had heard at Weimar,—both great, and one the greatest.

Thank you for sending me that authentic word about Miss Nightingale. I wonder if she would rather rest from her blessed labours, or live to go on working? Sometimes, when I read of the death of some great sensitive human being, I have a triumph in the sense that they are at rest; and yet, along with that, such deep sadness at the thought that the rare nature is gone for ever into darkness, and we can never know that our love and reverence can reach him, that I seem to have gone through a personal sorrow when I shut the book and go to bed. I felt in that way the other night when I finished the life of Scott aloud to Mr Lewes. He had never read the book before, and has been deeply stirred by the picture of Scott's character—his energy and steady work, his grand fortitude under calamity, and the spirit of strict honour to which he sacrificed his declining life. He loves Scott as well as I do.

We have met a pleasant-faced, bright-glancing man, whom we set down to be worthy of the name, Richard Congreve. I am curious to see if our *Ahnung* will be verified.

One word of gratitude to *you* first before I write any other letters. Heaven and earth bless you for trying to help me. I have been blasphemous enough sometimes to think that I had never been good and attractive enough to win any little share of the honest, disinterested friendship there is in the world: one or two examples of late had given that impression, and I am prone to rest in the least agreeable conviction the premisses will allow. I need hardly tell you what I want, you know it so well: a servant who will cause me the least possible expenditure of time on household matters. I wish I were not an anxious, fidgety wretch, and could sit down content with dirt and disorder. But anything in the shape of an *anxiety* soon grows into a monstrous vulture with me, and makes itself more present to me than my rich sources of happiness — such as too few mortals are blessed with. You know me. Since I wrote this, I have just had a letter from my sister Chrissey—ill in bed, consumptive—regretting that she ever ceased to write to me. It has ploughed up my heart.

Letter to Mrs Bray, 24th Feb. 1859.

Mrs Carlyle's ardent letter will interest and amuse you. I reckon it among my best triumphs that she found herself " in charity with the whole human race " when she laid the book down. I

Letter to John Blackwood, 24th Feb. 1859.

Letter to John Blackwood, 24th Feb. 1859.

want the philosopher himself to read it, because the *pre*-philosophic period—the childhood and poetry of his life—lay among the furrowed fields and pious peasantry. If he *could* be urged to read a novel! I should like, if possible, to give him the same sort of pleasure he has given me in the early chapters of 'Sartor,' where he describes little Diogenes eating his porridge on the wall in sight of the sunset, and gaining deep wisdom from the contemplation of the pigs and other "higher animals" of *Entepfuhl.*

Your critic was *not* unjustly severe on the 'Mirage Philosophy'—and I confess the 'Life of Frederic' was a painful book to me in many respects; and yet I shrink, perhaps superstitiously, from any written or spoken word which is as strong as my inward criticism.

I needed your letter very much—for when one lives apart from the world, with no opportunity of observing the effect of books except through the newspapers, one is in danger of sinking into the foolish belief that the day is past for the recognition of genuine truthful writing, in spite of recent experience that the newspapers are no criterion at all. One such opinion as Mr Caird's outweighs a great deal of damnatory praise from ignorant journalists.

It is a wretched weakness of my nature to be so strongly affected by these things; and yet how is it possible to put one's best heart and soul into a book and be hardened to the result—be indifferent to the proof whether or not one has really a vocation to speak to one's fellow-men in that way? Of course one's vanity is at work; but the main anxiety is something entirely distinct from vanity.

Letter to John Blackwood, 24th Feb. 1859.

You see I mean you to understand that my feelings are very respectable, and such as it will be virtuous in you to gratify with the same zeal as you have always shown. The packet of newspaper notices is not come yet. I will take care to return it when it *has* come.

The best news from London hitherto is that Mr Dallas is an enthusiastic admirer of Adam. I ought to except Mr Langford's reported opinion, which is that of a person who has a voice of his own, and is not a mere echo.

Otherwise, Edinburgh has sent me much more encouraging breezes than any that have come from the sweet south. I wonder if all your other authors are as greedy and exacting as I am. If so, I hope they appreciate your attention as much. Will you oblige me by writing a line to Mrs Carlyle for me. I don't like to leave her second letter (she wrote a

Letter to John Blackwood, 24th Feb. 1859.

very kind one about the 'Clerical Scenes') without any sort of notice. Will you tell her that the sort of effect she declares herself to have felt from 'Adam Bede' is just what I desire to produce—gentle thoughts and happy remembrances; and I thank her heartily for telling me, so warmly and generously, what she has felt. That is not a pretty message: revise it for me, pray, for I am weary and ailing, and thinking of a sister who is slowly dying.

Letter to John Blackwood, 25th Feb. 1859.

The folio of notices duly came, and are returned by to-day's post. The friend at my elbow ran through them for me, and read aloud some specimens to me, some of them ludicrous enough. The 'Edinburgh Courant' has the ring of sincere enjoyment in its tone; and the writer there makes himself so amiable to me, that I am sorry he has fallen into the mistake of supposing that Mrs Poyser's original sayings are remembered proverbs! I have no stock of proverbs in my memory; and there is not one thing put into Mrs Poyser's mouth that is not fresh from my own mint. Please to correct that mistake if any one makes it in your hearing.

I have not ventured to look into the folio myself; but I learn that there are certain threatening marks, in ink, by the side of such stock sentences as "best novel of the season," or "best novel we have read for a long time," from such authorities as the 'Sun,' or 'Morning Star,' or other orb of the newspaper firmament—as if these sentences were to be selected for reprint in the form of advertisement. I shudder at the suggestion. Am I taking a liberty in entreating you to keep a sharp watch over the advertisements, that no hackneyed puffing phrase of this kind may be tacked to my book? One sees them garnishing every other advertisement of trash: surely no being "above the rank of an idiot" can have his inclination coerced by them; and it would gall me, as much as any trifle could, to see my book recommended by an authority who doesn't know how to write decent English. I believe that your taste and judgment will concur with mine in the conviction that no quotations of this vulgar kind can do credit to a book; and that unless something looking like the real opinion of a tolerably educated writer, in a respectable journal, can be given, it would be better to abstain from "opinions of the press" altogether. I shall be grateful to you if you will save me from the results of any agency but your own—or at least of any agency that is not under your rigid criticism in this matter.

Letter to John Blackwood, 25th Feb. 1859.

Pardon me if I am overstepping the author's limits in this expression of my feelings. I confide in your ready comprehension of the irritable class you have to deal with.

Journal, 1859.

Feb. 26.—Laudatory reviews of 'Adam Bede' in the 'Athenæum,' 'Saturday,' and 'Literary Gazette.' The 'Saturday' criticism is characteristic: Dinah is not mentioned!

The other day I received the following letter, which I copy, because I have sent the original away:—

"To the Author of 'Adam Bede.'

"CHESTER ROAD, SUNDERLAND.

Letter from E. Hall to Geo. Eliot.

"DEAR SIR,—I got the other day a hasty read of your 'Scenes of Clerical Life,' and since that a glance at your 'Adam Bede,' and was delighted more than I can express; but being a poor man, and having enough to do to make 'ends meet,' I am unable to get a read of your inimitable books.

"Forgive, dear sir, my boldness in asking you to give us a cheap edition. You would confer on us a great boon. I can get plenty of trash for a few pence, but I am sick of it. I felt so different when I shut your books, even though it was but a kind of 'hop, skip, and jump' read.

"I feel so strongly in this matter, that I am determined to risk being thought rude and officious, and write to you. Letter from E. Hall to Geo. Eliot.

"Many of my working brethren feel as I do, and I express their wish as well as my own. Again asking your forgiveness for intruding myself upon you—I remain, with profoundest respect, yours, &c., E. HALL."

I have written to Chrissey, and shall hear from her again. I think her writing was the result of long, quiet thought—the slow return of a naturally just and affectionate mind to the position from which it had been thrust by external influence. She says: "My object in writing to you is to tell you how very sorry I have been that I ceased to write, and neglected one who, under all circumstances, was kind to me and mine. *Pray believe* me when I say it will be the greatest comfort I can receive to know that you are *well* and *happy*. Will you write once more?" &c. I wrote immediately, and I desire to avoid any word of reference to anything with which she associates the idea of alienation. The past is abolished from my mind. I only want her to feel that I love her and care for her. The servant trouble seems Letter to Miss Sara Hennell, 26th Feb. 1859.

Letter to Miss Sara Hennell, 26th Feb. 1859.

less mountainous to me than it did the other day. I was suffering physically from unusual worrit and muscular exertion in arranging the house, and so was in a ridiculously desponding state. I have written no end of letters in answer to servants' advertisements, and we have put our own advertisement in the 'Times'—all which amount of force, if we were not philosophers and therefore believers in the conservation of force, we should declare to be lost. It is so pleasant to know these high doctrines—they help one so much. Mr and Mrs Richard Congreve have called on us. We shall return the call as soon as we can.

Journal, 1859.

March 8.—Letter from Blackwood this morning saying that "'Bedesman' has turned the corner and is coming in a winner." Mudie has sent for 200 additional copies (making 700), and Mr Langford says the West End libraries keep sending for more.

March 14.—My dear sister wrote to me about three weeks ago, saying she regretted that she had ever ceased writing to me, and that she has been in a consumption for the last eighteen months. To-day I have a letter from my niece Emily, telling me her mother had been taken worse, and cannot live many days.

March 14. — Major Blackwood writes to say "Mudie has just made up his number of 'Adam Bede' to 1000. Simpkins have sold their subscribed number, and have had 12 to-day. Everyone is talking of the book." Journal, 1859.

March 15. — Chrissey died this morning at a quarter to 5.

March 16.—Blackwood writes to say I am "a popular author, as well as a great author." They printed 2090 of 'Adam Bede,' and have disposed of more than 1800, so that they are thinking about a second edition. A very feeling letter from Froude this morning. I happened this morning to be reading the 30th Ode, B. III. of Horace—"Non omnis moriar."

The news you have sent me is worth paying a great deal of pain for, past and future. It comes rather strangely to me, who live in such unconsciousnesss of what is going on in the world. I am like a deaf person, to whom some one has just shouted that the company round him have been paying him compliments for the last half hour. Let the best come, you will still be the person outside my own home who *first* gladdened me about 'Adam Bede;' and my success will always please me the better because you will share the pleasure. Letter to John Blackwood, 17th March 1859.

Letter to John Blackwood, 17th March 1859.

Don't think I mean to worry you with many such requests—but will you copy for me the enclosed short note to Froude? I know you will, so I say "thank you."

Letter to J. A. Froude from George Eliot.

DEAR SIR,—My excellent friend and publisher, Mr Blackwood, lends me his pen to thank you for your letter, and for his sake I shall be brief.

Your letter has done me real good—the same sort of good as one has sometimes felt from a silent pressure of the hand and a grave look in the midst of smiling congratulations.

I have nothing else I care to tell you that you will not have found out through my books, except this one thing: that, so far as I am aware, you are only the *second* person who has shared my own satisfaction in Janet. I think she is the least popular of my characters. You will judge from that, that it was worth your while to tell me what you felt about her.

I wish I could help you with words of equal value; but, after all, am I not helping you by saying that it was well and generously done of you to write to me?—Ever faithfully yours,

GEORGE ELIOT.

It was worth your while to write me those feeling words, for they are the sort of things that I keep in my memory and feel the influence of a long, long while. Chrissey's death has taken from the possibility of many things towards which I looked with some hope and yearning in the future. I had a very special feeling towards her—stronger than any third person would think likely.

Letter to Miss Sara Hennell, 21st March 1859.

March 24.—Mr Herbert Spencer brought us word that 'Adam Bede' had been quoted by Mr Charles Buxton in the House of Commons: "As the farmer's wife says in 'Adam Bede,' 'It wants to be hatched over again and hatched different.'"

Journal, 1859.

March 26.—George went into town to-day and brought me home a budget of good news that compensated for the pain I had felt in the coldness of an old friend. Mr Langford says that Mudie "thinks he must have another hundred or two of 'Adam'—has read the book himself, and is delighted with it." Charles Reade says it is "the finest thing since Shakspeare"—placed his finger on Lisbeth's account of her coming home with her husband from their marriage—praises enthusiastically the style—the way in which the author handles the Saxon language. Shirley Brooks also delighted. John Murray says there has never been

Journal, 1859.

such a book. Mr Langford says there must be a second edition, in 3 vols., and they will print 500: whether Mudie takes more or not, they will have sold all by the end of a month. Lucas delighted with the book, and will review it in the 'Times' the first opportunity.

Letter to John Blackwood, 30th March 1859.

I should like you to convey my gratitude to your reviewer. I see well he is a man whose experience and study enable him to relish parts of my book, which I should despair of seeing recognised by critics in London back drawing-rooms. He has gratified me keenly by laying his finger on passages which I wrote either with strong feeling or from intimate knowledge, but which I had prepared myself to find entirely passed over by reviewers. Surely I am not wrong in supposing him to be a clergyman? There was one exemplary lady Mr Langford spoke of, who, after reading 'Adam,' came the next day and bought a copy both of that and the 'Clerical Scenes.' I wish there may be three hundred matrons as good as she! It is a disappointment to me to find that 'Adam' has given no impulse to the 'Scenes,' for I had sordid desires for money from a second edition, and had dreamed of its coming speedily.

About my new story, which will be a novel as

long as 'Adam Bede,' and a sort of companion picture of provincial life, we must talk when I have the pleasure of seeing you. It will be a work which will require time and labour.

Letter to John Blackwood, 30th March 1859.

Do write me good news as often as you can. I owe thanks to Major Blackwood for a very charming letter.

The other day I received a letter from an old friend in Warwickshire, containing some striking information about the author of 'Adam Bede.' I extract the passage for your amusement:—

Letter to John Blackwood, 10th April 1859

"I want to ask you if you have read 'Adam Bede,' or the 'Scenes of Clerical Life,' and whether you know that the author is Mr Liggins? . . . A deputation of Dissenting parsons went over *to ask him to write for the 'Eclectic,'* and they found him washing his slop-basin at a pump. He has no servant, and does everything for himself; but one of the said parsons said that he inspired them with a reverence that would have made any impertinent question impossible. The son of a baker, of no mark at all in his town, so that it is possible you may not have heard of him. You know he calls himself 'George Eliot.' It sounds strange to hear the 'Westminster' doubting whether he is a woman, when *here he is so well known.* But

Letter to John Blackwood, 10th April 1859.

I am glad it has mentioned him. *They say he gets no profit out of 'Adam Bede,' and gives it freely to Blackwood, which is a shame.* We have not read him yet, but the extracts are irresistible."

Conceive the real George Eliot's feelings, conscious of being a base worldling—not washing his own slop-basin, and *not* giving away his MS.! not even intending to do so, in spite of the reverence such a course might inspire. I hope you and Major Blackwood will enjoy the myth.

Mr Langford sent me a letter the other day from Miss Winkworth, a grave lady, who says she never reads novels—except a few of the most famous, but that she has read 'Adam' three times running. One likes to know such things: they show that the book tells on people's hearts, and may be a real instrument of culture. I sing my Magnificat in a quiet way, and have a great deal of deep, silent joy; but few authors, I suppose, who have had a real success, have known less of the flush and the sensations of triumph that are talked of as the accompaniments of success. I think I should soon begin to believe that *Liggins* wrote my books—it is so difficult to believe what the world does *not* believe, so easy to believe what the world keeps repeating.

The very day you wrote we were driving in an open carriage from Ryde to the Sandrock Hotel, taking in a month's delight in the space of five hours. Such skies—such songs of larks—such beds of primroses! *I* am quite well now—set up by iron and quinine, and polished off by the sea-breezes. I have lost my *young* dislike to the spring, and am as glad of it as the birds and plants are. Mr Lewes has read 'Adam Bede,' and is as dithyrambic about it as others appear to be, so *I* must refresh my soul with it now as well as with the spring-tide. Mr Liggins I remember as a vision of my childhood—a tall, black-coated, genteel young clergyman-in-embryo. Letter to Miss Sara Hennell, 11th April 1859.

Mr Lewes is "making himself into four" in writing answers to advertisements and other exertions which he generously takes on himself to save me. A model husband! Letter to Miss Sara Hennell, 15th April 1859.

We both like your literal title, 'Thoughts in Aid of Faith,' very much, and hope to see a little book under that title before the year is out—a book as thorough and effective in its way as 'Christianity and Infidelity.'

*Re*writing is an excellent process, frequently both for the book and its author; and to prevent you from grudging the toil, I will tell you that so old

Letter to Miss Sara Hennell, 15th April 1859.

a writer as Mr Lewes now *re*writes everything of *importance*, though in all the earlier years of his authorship he would never take that trouble.

We are so happy in the neighbourhood of Mr and Mrs Richard Congreve. She is a sweet, intelligent, gentle woman. I already love her: and his fine beaming face does me good, like a glimpse of an Olympian.

Journal, 1859.

April 17.—I have left off recording the history of 'Adam Bede,' and the pleasant letters and words that came to me—the success has been so triumphantly beyond anything I had dreamed of, that it would be tiresome to put down particulars. Four hundred of the second edition (of 750) sold in the first week, and twenty besides ordered when there was not a copy left in the London house. This morning Hachette has sent to ask my terms for the liberty of translation into French. There was a review in the 'Times' last week, which will naturally give a new stimulus to the sale; and yesterday I sent a letter to the 'Times' denying that Mr Liggins is the author, as the world and Mr Anders had settled it. But I must trust to the letters I have received and preserved for giving me the history of the book if I should live long enough to forget details.

Shall I ever write another book as true as 'Adam Bede'? The weight of the future presses on me, and makes itself felt even more than the deep satisfaction of the past and present. Journal, 1859.

This myth about Liggins is getting serious, and must be put a stop to. We are bound not to allow sums of money to be raised on a false supposition of this kind. Don't you think it would be well for *you* to write a letter to the 'Times,' to the effect that, as you find in some stupid quarters my letter has not been received as a *bonâ-fide* denial, you declare Mr Liggins not to be the author of 'Clerical Scenes' and 'Adam Bede;' further, that any future applications to you concerning George Eliot will not be answered, since that writer is not in need of public benevolence. Such a letter might save us from future annoyance and trouble, for I am rather doubtful about Mr Liggins's character. The last report I heard of him was that he spent his time in smoking and drinking. I don't know whether that is one of the data for the Warwickshire logicians who have decided him to be the author of my books. Letter to John Blackwood, 20th April 1859.

April 29.—To-day Blackwood sent me a letter from Bulwer, which I copy because I have to send back the original, and I like to keep in mind the generous praise of one author for another. Journal, 1859.

Letter from E. B. Lytton to John Blackwood.

"MALVERN, *April* 24, 1859.

"MY DEAR SIR,—I ought long since to have thanked you for 'Adam Bede.' But I never had a moment to look at it, till arriving here, and ordered by the doctors to abstain from all 'work.'

"I owe the author much gratitude for some very pleasing hours. The book indeed is worthy of great admiration. There are touches of beauty in the conception of human character that are exquisite, and much wit and much poetry embedded in the 'dialect,' which nevertheless the author over-uses.

"The style is remarkably good whenever it is English and not provincial — racy, original, and nervous.

"I congratulate you on having found an author of such promise, and published one of the very ablest works of fiction I have read for years.—Yours truly, E. B. L.

"I am better than I was, but thoroughly done up."

Journal, 1859.

April 29.—Finished a story—"The Lifted Veil" —which I began one morning at Richmond as a resource when my head was too stupid for more important work. Journal, 1859.

Resumed my new novel, of which I am going to rewrite the two first chapters. I shall call it provisionally "The Tullivers," for the sake of a title *quelconque*, or perhaps "St Ogg's on the Floss."

Letter to John Blackwood, 29th April 1859.

Thank you for sending me Sir Edward Lytton's letter, which has given me real pleasure. The praise is doubly valuable to me for the sake of the generous feeling that prompted it. I think you judged rightly about writing to the 'Times.' I would abstain from the remotest appearance of a "dodge." I am anxious to know of any *positive* rumours that may get abroad; for while I would willingly, if it were possible—which it clearly is not—retain my *incognito* as long as I live, I can suffer no one to bear my arms on his shield.

There is *one* alteration, or rather an addition—merely of a sentence—that I wish to make in the 12s. edition of 'Adam Bede.' It is a sentence in the chapter where Adam is making the coffin at night, and hears the willow wand. Some readers seem not to have understood what I meant—namely, that it was in Adam's peasant blood and nurture to believe in this, and that he narrated it with awed belief to his dying day. That is not a fancy of my

Letter to John Blackwood, 29th April 1859.

own brain, but a matter of observation, and is, in my mind, an important feature in Adam's character. There is nothing else I wish to touch. I will send you the sentence some day soon, with the page where it is to be inserted.

Journal, 1859.

May 3.—I had a letter from Mrs Richard Congreve, telling me of her safe arrival, with her husband and sister,[1] at Dieppe. This new friend, whom I have gained by coming to Wandsworth, is the chief charm of the place to me. Her friendship has the same date as the success of 'Adam Bede'—two good things in my lot that ought to have made me less sad than I have been in this house.

Letter to Mrs Congreve, 4th May 1859.

Your letter came yesterday at tea-time, and made the evening happier than usual. We had thought of you not a little as we listened to the howling winds, especially as the terrible wrecks off the Irish coast had filled our imaginations disagreeably. *Now* I can make a charming picture of you all on the beach, except that I am obliged to fancy *your* face looking still too languid after all your exertion and sleeplessness. I remember the said face with peculiar vividness, which is very pleasant to me. "Rough" has been the daily companion of our

[1] Miss Emily Bury, now Mrs Geddes.

walks, and wins on our affections, as other fellow mortals do, by a mixture of weaknesses and virtues —the weaknesses consisting chiefly in a tendency to become invisible every ten minutes and in a forgetfulness of reproof, which, I fear, is the usual accompaniment of meekness under it. All this is good discipline for us selfish solitaries, who have been used to stroll along, thinking of nothing but ourselves.

Letter to Mrs Congreve, 4th May 1859.

We walked through your garden to-day, and I gathered a bit of your sweetbrier, of which I am at this moment enjoying the scent as it stands on my desk. I am enjoying, too, another sort of sweetness, which I also owe to you — of that subtle, haunting kind which is most like the scent of my favourite plants—the belief that you do really care for me across the seas there, and will associate me continually with your home. Faith is not easy to me, nevertheless I believe everything you say and write.

Write to me as often as you can—that is, as often as you feel any prompting to do so. You were a dear presence to me, and will be a precious thought to me all through your absence.

Journal, 1859.

May 4.—To-day came a letter from Barbara Bodichon, full of joy in my success, in the certainty

Journal, 1859.

that 'Adam Bede' was mine, though she had not read more than extracts in reviews. This is the first delight in the book as *mine,* over and above the fact that the book is good.

Letter to Madame Bodichon, 5th May 1859.

God bless you, dearest Barbara, for your love and sympathy. You are the first friend who has given any symptom of knowing me—the first heart that has recognised me in a book which has come from my heart of hearts. But keep the secret solemnly till I give you leave to tell it, and give way to no impulses of triumphant affection. You have sense enough to know how important the *incognito* has been, and we are anxious to keep it up a few months longer. Curiously enough my old Coventry friends, who have certainly read the 'Westminster' and the 'Times,' and have probably by this time read the book itself, have given no sign of recognition. But a certain Mr Liggins, whom rumour has fixed on as the author of my books, and whom *they* have believed in, has probably screened me from their vision. I am a very blessed woman, am I not, to have all this reason for being glad that I have lived? I have had no time of exultation—on the contrary, these last months have been sadder than usual to me; and I have thought more of the future and the much work that remains to be done in life than of anything that has been achieved. But I think your letter to-day gave me more joy—more heart-glow—than all the letters or reviews or other testimonies of success that have come to me since the evenings when I read aloud my manuscript to my dear, dear husband, and he laughed and cried alternately, and then rushed to me to kiss me. He is the prime blessing that has made all the rest possible to me, giving me a response to everything I have written—a response that I could confide in, as a proof that I had not mistaken my work.

Letter to Madame Bodichon, 5th May 1859.

You must not think me too soft-hearted, when I tell you that it would make me uneasy to leave Mr Anders without an assurance that his apology is accepted. "Who with repentance is not satisfied," &c.; that doctrine is bad for the sinning, but good for those sinned against. Will you oblige me by allowing a clerk to write something to this effect in the name of the firm?—"We are requested by George Eliot to state, in reply to your letter of the 16th, that he accepts your assurance that the publication of your letter to the reviewer of 'Adam Bede' in the 'Times' was unintentional on your part."

Letter to Major Blackwood, 6th May 1859.

Yes, I *am* assured now that 'Adam Bede' was

Letter to Major Blackwood, 6th May 1859.

worth writing—worth living through long years to write. But now it seems impossible to me that I shall ever write anything so good and true again. I have arrived at faith in the past, but not at faith in the future.

A friend in Algiers[1] has found me out—"will go to the stake on the assertion that I wrote 'Adam Bede'"—simply on the evidence of a few extracts. So far as I know, this is the first case of detection on purely internal evidence. But the secret is safe in that quarter.

I hope I shall have the pleasure of seeing you again during some visit that you will pay to town before very long. It would do me good to have you shake me by the hand as the ascertained George Eliot.

Journal, 1859.

May 9.—We had a delicious drive to Dulwich and back by Sydenham. We staid an hour in the gallery at Dulwich, and I satisfied myself that the St Sebastian is no exception to the usual "petty prettiness" of Guido's conceptions. The Cuyp glowing in the evening sun, the Spanish beggar boys of Murillo, and Gainsborough's portrait of Mrs Sheridan and her sister, are the gems of the gallery. But better than the pictures was the fresh greenth

[1] Madame Bodichon.

of the spring,—the chestnuts just on the verge of their flowering beauty, the bright leaves of the limes, the rich yellow-brown of the oaks, the meadows full of buttercups. We saw for the first time Clapham Common, Streatham Common, and Tooting Common,—the two last like parks rather than commons. Journal, 1859.

May 19.—A letter from Blackwood, in which he proposes to give me another £400 at the end of the year, making in all £1200, as an acknowledgment of 'Adam Bede's' success.

Letter to Miss Sara Hennell, 19th May 1859.

Mrs Congreve is a sweet woman, and I feel that I have acquired a friend in her—after recently declaring that we would never have any *friends* again, only *acquaintances.*

Letter to John Blackwood, 21st May 1859.

Thank you: first, for acting with that fine integrity which makes part of my faith in you; secondly, for the material sign of that integrity. I don't know which of those two things I care for most—that people should act nobly towards me, or that I should get honest money. I certainly care a great deal for the money, as I suppose all anxious minds do that love independence and have been brought up to think debt and begging the two deepest dishonours short of crime.

I look forward with quite eager expectation to

Letter to John Blackwood, 21st May 1859.

seeing you—we have so much to say. Pray give us the first day at your command. The excursion, as you may imagine, is not ardently longed for in this weather, but when "merry May" is quite gone, we may surely hope for some sunshine; and then I have a pet project of rambling along by the banks of a river, not without artistic as well as hygienic purposes.

Pray bring me all the Liggins Correspondence. I have an amusing letter or two to show you,—one from a gentleman who has sent me his works; happily the only instance of the kind. For as Charles Lamb complains, it is always the people whose books *don't* sell who are anxious to send them to one, with their "foolish autographs" inside.

Letter to Miss Sara Hennell, 21st May 1859.

We don't think of going to the festival, not for want of power to enjoy Handel,—there are few things that I care for more in the way of music than his choruses, performed by a grand orchestra, —but because we are neither of us fit to encounter the physical exertion and inconveniences. It is a cruel thing the difficulty and dearness of getting any music in England—concerted music, which is the only music I care for much now. At Dresden we could have thoroughly enjoyable instrumental music every evening for twopence; and I owed so many thoughts and inspirations of feeling to that stimulus.

May 27.—Blackwood came to dine with us on his arrival in London, and we had much talk. A day or two before he had sent me a letter from Professor Aytoun, saying that he had neglected his work to read the first volume of 'Adam Bede;' and he actually sent the other two volumes out of the house to save himself from temptation. Blackwood brought with him a correspondence he has had with various people about Liggins, beginning with Mr Bracebridge, who will have it that Liggins is the author of 'Adam Bede' in spite of all denials. Journal, 1859.

June 5.—Blackwood came, and we concocted two letters to send to the 'Times,' in order to put a stop to the Liggins affair.

The "Liggins business" *does* annoy me, because it subjects you and Mr John Blackwood to the reception of insulting letters, and the trouble of writing contradictions. Otherwise, the whole affair is really a subject for a Molière comedy—"The Wise Men of Warwickshire," who might supersede "The Wise Men of Gotham." Letter to Major Blackwood, 6th June 1859.

The letter you sent me was a very pleasant one from Mrs Gaskell, saying that since she came up to town she has had the compliment paid her of being

Letter to Major Blackwood, 6th June 1859.

suspected to have written 'Adam Bede.' "I have hitherto denied it; but really, I think that, as you want to keep your real name a secret, it would be very pleasant for me to blush acquiescence. Will you give me leave?"

I hope the inaccuracy with which she writes my name is not characteristic of a genius for fiction, though I once heard a German account for the bad spelling in Goethe's early letters by saying that it was "genial"—their word for whatever is characteristic of genius.

Letter to Mrs Congreve, 8th June 1859.

I was glad you wrote to me from Avignon of all the places you have visited, because Avignon is one of my most vivid remembrances from out the dimness of ten years ago. Lucerne would be a strange region to me but for Calame's pictures. Through them I have a vision of it, but of course when I see it 'twill be another Luzern. Mr Lewes obstinately nurses the project of carrying me thither with him, and depositing me within reach of you while he goes to Hofwyl. But at present I say "No." We have been waiting and waiting for the skies to let us take a few days' ramble by the river, but now I fear we must give it up till all the freshness of young summer is gone. July and August are the two months I care least about for leafy scenery.

However, we are kept at home this month partly by pleasures: the Handel Festival, for which we have indulged ourselves with tickets, and the sight of old friends—Mrs Bodichon among the rest, and for her we hope to use your kind loan of a bedroom. We are both of us in much better condition than when you said good-bye to us, and I have many other sources of gladness just now,—so I mean to make myself disagreeable no longer by caring about petty troubles. If one could but order cheerfulness from the druggist's! or even a few doses of coldness and distrust, to prevent one from foolish confidence in one's fellow-mortals! Letter to Mrs Congreve, 8th June 1859.

I want to get rid of this house—cut cables and drift about. I dislike Wandsworth, and should think with unmitigated regret of our coming here if it were not for you. But you are worth paying a price for.

There! I have written about nothing but ourselves this time! *You* do the same, and then I think I will promise . . . not to write again, but to ask you to go on writing to me without an answer.

How cool and idle you are this morning! I am warm and busy, but always at all temperatures—Yours affectionately.

Journal, 1859.

June 20.—We went to the Crystal Palace to hear the "Messiah," and dined afterwards with the Brays and Sara Hennell. I told them I was the author of 'Adam Bede' and Clerical Scenes,' and they seemed overwhelmed with surprise. This experience has enlightened me a good deal as to the ignorance in which we all live of each other.

Letter to Miss Sara Hennell, 24th June 1859.

There is always an after sadness belonging to brief and interrupted intercourse between friends—the sadness of feeling that the blundering efforts we have made towards mutual understanding have only made a new veil between us—still more, the sadness of feeling that some pain may have been given which separation makes a permanent memory. We are quite unable to represent ourselves truly. Why should we complain that our friends see a false image? I say this, because I am feeling painfully this morning, that instead of helping you when you brought before me a matter so deeply interesting to you, I have only blundered, and that I have blundered, as most of us do, from too much egoism and too little sympathy. If my mind had been more open to receive impressions, instead of being in over haste to give them, I should more readily have seen what your object was in giving me that portion of your MS., and we might have gone through the necessary part of it on Tuesday. It seems no use to write this now, and yet I can't help wanting to assure you, that if I am too imperfect to do and feel the right thing at the right moment, I am not without the slower sympathy that becomes all the stronger from a sense of previous mistake. Letter to Miss Sara Hennell, 24th June 1859.

I am told peremptorily that I am to go to Switzerland next month, but now I have read your letter, I can't help thinking more of your illness than of the pleasure in prospect—according to my foolish nature, which is always prone to live in past pain. Letter to Mrs Congreve, 27th June 1859.

We shall not arrive at Lucerne till the 12th, at the earliest, I imagine, so I hope we are secured from the danger of alighting precisely on the days of your absence. That would be cruel, for I shall only be left at Lucerne for three days. You must positively have nothing more interesting to do than to talk to me and let me look at you. Tell your sister I shall be all ears and eyes and no tongue, so she will find me the most *aimable* of conversers.

I think it must be that the sunshine makes your absence more conspicuous, for this place certainly becomes drearier to me as the summer advances.

Letter to Mrs Congreve, 27th June 1859.

The dusty roads are all longer, and the shade is farther off. No more now about anything—except that Mr Lewes commands me to say he has just read the 'Roman Empire of the West' with much interest, and is going now to flesh his teeth in the "Politique" (Auguste Comte's).

Letter to the Brays, Monday evening, end of June 1859.

DEAR FRIENDS,—All three of you—thanks for your packet of heartfelt kindness. That is the best of your kindness—there is no sham in it. It was inevitable to me to have that outburst when I saw you for a little while after the long silence, and felt that I must tell you then or be forestalled, and leave you to gather the truth amidst an inextricable mixture of falsehood. But I feel that the influence of talking about my books, even to you and Mrs Bodichon, has been so bad to me that I should like to be able to keep silence concerning them for evermore. If people were to buzz round me with their remarks, or compliments, I should lose the repose of mind and truthfulness of production, without which no good healthy books can be written. Talking about my books, I find, has much the same malign effect on me as talking of my feelings or my religion.

I should think Sara's version of my brother's words concerning 'Adam Bede' is the correct one

—"*that there are things in it about my father*" (*i.e.*, being interpreted, things my father told us about his early life), not "portrait" of my father. There is not a single portrait in the book, nor will there be in any future book of mine. There are portraits in the 'Clerical Scenes;' but that was my first bit of art, and my hand was not well in. I did not know so well how to manipulate my materials. As soon as the Liggins falsehood is annihilated, of course there will be twenty new ones in its place; and one of the first will be that I was not the sole author. The only safe thing for my mind's health is to shut my ears and go on with my work.

Letter to the Brays, Monday evening, end of June 1859.

Thanks for your letters. They have given me one pleasure—that of knowing that Mr Liggins has not been *greatly* culpable—though Mr Bracebridge's statement, that only "some small sums" have been collected, does not accord with what has been written to Mr Blackwood from other counties. But "Oh, I am sick!" Take no more trouble about me, and let every one believe—as they will, in spite of your kind efforts—*what they like to believe.* I can't tell you how much melancholy it causes me that people are, for the most part, so incapable of comprehending the state of mind which cares for that which is essentially human in all forms of

Letter to Chas. Bray, 5th July 1859.

Letter to Chas. Bray, 5th July 1859.

belief, and desires to exhibit it under all forms with loving truthfulness. Freethinkers are scarcely wider than the orthodox in this matter,—they all want to see themselves and their own opinions held up as the true and the lovely. On the same ground that an idle woman, with flirtations and flounces, likes to read a French novel, because she can imagine herself the heroine, grave people, with opinions, like the most admirable character in a novel to be their mouthpiece. If art does not enlarge men's sympathies, it does nothing morally. I have had heart-cutting experience that *opinions* are a poor cement between human souls: and the only effect I ardently long to produce by my writings is, that those who read them should be better able to *imagine* and to *feel* the pains and the joys of those who differ from themselves in everything but the broad fact of being struggling, erring, human creatures.

Letter to Mrs Congreve, 6th July 1859.

We shall not start till Saturday, and shall not reach Lucerne till the *evening* of the 11th. There is a project of our returning through Holland, but the attractions of Lucerne are sure to keep us there as long as possible. We have given up Zurich in spite of Moleschott and science. The other day I said to Mr Lewes, "Every now and then it comes across me, like the recollection of some precious little store laid by, that there is Mrs Congreve in the world." That is how people talk of you in your absence.

July 9.—We started for Switzerland. Spent a delightful day in Paris. To the Louvre first, where we looked chiefly at the "Marriage at Cana," by Paul Veronese. This picture, the greatest I have seen of his, converted me to high admiration of him. Journal, 1859.

July 12.—Arrived at Lucerne in the evening. Glad to make a home at the charming Schweizerhof on the banks of the Lake. G. went to call on the Congreves, and in the afternoon Mrs Congreve came to chat with us. In the evening we had a boat on the Lake.

July 13.—G. set off for Hofwyl at five o'clock, and the three next days were passed by me in quiet chat with the Congreves and quiet resting on my own sofa.

July 19.—Spent the morning in Bâle, chiefly under the chestnut trees, near the Cathedral, I reading aloud Flourens's sketch of Cuvier's labours. In the afternoon to Paris.

July 21.—Holly Lodge, Wandsworth. Found a charming letter from Dickens, and pleasant letters

Journal, 1859.

from Blackwood: nothing to annoy us. Before we set off we had heard the excellent news that the fourth edition of 'Adam Bede' (5000) had all been sold in a fortnight. The fifth edition appeared last week.

Letter to Mrs Bray 23d July 1859.

We reached here last evening, and though I was a good deal over-done in getting to Lucerne, I have borne the equally rapid journey back without headache—a proof that I am strengthened. I had three quiet days of talk with the Congreves at Lucerne, while Mr Lewes went to Hofwyl. Mrs Congreve is one of those women of whom there are few—rich in intelligence, without pretension, and quivering with sensibility, yet calm and quiet in her manners.

Letter to John Blackwood, 23d July 1859.

I thank you for your offer about the money for 'Adam,' but I have intentions of stern thrift, and mean to want as little as possible. When "Maggie" is done, and I have a month or two of leisure, I should like to transfer our present house, into which we were driven by haste and economy, to some one who likes houses full of eyes all round him. I long for a house with some shade and grass close round it—I don't care how rough—and the sight of Swiss houses has heightened my longing. But at present I say Avaunt to all desires.

While I think of it, let me beg of you to mention to the superintendent of your printing-office, that in case of another reprint of 'Adam,' I beg the word "sperrit" (for "spirit") may be particularly attended to. Adam never said "speerit," as he is made to do in the cheaper edition, at least in one place—his speech at the birthday dinner. This is a small matter: but it is a point I care about. Letter to John Blackwood, 23d July 1859.

Words fail me about the not impossible Pug, for some compunction at having mentioned my unreasonable wish will mingle itself paradoxically with the hope that it may be fulfilled.

I hope we shall have other interviews to remember this time next year, and that you will find me without aggravated symptoms of the "author's malady" —a determination of talk to my own books, which I was alarmingly conscious of when you and the Major were here. After all, I fear authors must submit to be something of monsters—not quite simple, healthy human beings; but I will keep my monstrosity within bounds if possible.

The things you tell me are just such as I need to know—I mean about the help my book is to the people who read it. The weight of my future life, —the self-questioning whether my nature will be Letter to Mrs Bray, 26th July 1859.

Letter to Mrs Bray, 26th July 1859.

able to meet the heavy demands upon it, both of personal duty and intellectual production,—presses upon me almost continually in a way that prevents me even from tasting the quiet joy I might have in the *work done.* Buoyancy and exultation, I fancy, are out of the question when one has lived so long as I have. But I am the better for every word of encouragement, and am helped over many days by such a note as yours. I often think of my dreams when I was four or five and twenty. I thought then how happy fame would make me! I feel no regret that the fame, as such, brings no pleasure; but it *is* a grief to me that I do not constantly feel strong in thankfulness that my past life has vindicated its uses, and given me reason for gladness that such an unpromising woman child was born into the world. I ought not to care about small annoyances, and it is chiefly egoism that makes them annoyances. I had quite an *enthusiastic* letter from Herbert Spencer the other day about 'Adam Bede.' He says he feels the better for reading it—really words to be treasured up. I can't bear the idea of appearing further in the papers. And there is no one now except people who would not be convinced, though one rose from the dead, to whom any statement *apropos* of Liggins would be otherwise than superfluous. I daresay some "investigator" of the Bracebridge order will arise after I am dead and revive the story—and perhaps posterity will believe in Liggins. Why not? A man a little while ago wrote a pamphlet to prove that the Waverley novels were chiefly written, not by Walter Scott, but by Thomas Scott and his wife Elizabeth. The main evidence being that several people thought Thomas cleverer than Walter, and that in the list of the Canadian regiment of Scots to which Thomas belonged, many of the *names* of the Waverley novels occurred—among the rest *Monk*—and in 'Woodstock' there is a *General Monk!* The writer expected to get a great reputation by his pamphlet, and I think it might have suggested to Mr B. his style of critical and historical inference. I must tell you, *in confidence*, that Dickens has written to me the noblest, most touching words about 'Adam'—not hyperbolical compliments, but expressions of deep feeling. He says the reading made an epoch in his life. Letter to Mrs Bray, 26th July 1859.

Pug is come!—come to fill up the void left by false and narrow-hearted friends. I see already that he is without envy, hatred, or malice—that he will betray no secrets, and feel neither pain at my Letter to John Blackwood, 30th July 1859.

Letter to John Blackwood, 30th July 1859.

success nor pleasure in my chagrin. I hope the photograph does justice to his physiognomy. It is expressive: full of gentleness and affection, and radiant with intelligence when there is a savoury morsel in question—a hopeful indication of his mental capacity. I distrust all intellectual pretension that announces itself by obtuseness of palate!

I wish you could see him in his best *pose*,—when I have arrested him in a violent career of carpet-scratching, and he looks at me with fore-legs very wide apart, trying to penetrate the deep mystery of this arbitrary, not to say capricious, prohibition. He is snoring by my side at this moment, with a serene promise of remaining quiet for any length of time: he couldn't behave better if he had been expressly educated for me. I am too lazy a lover of dogs and all earthly things to like them when they give me much trouble, preferring to describe the pleasure other people have in taking trouble.

Alas! the shadow that tracks all earthly good—the possibility of loss. One may lose one's faculties, which will not always fetch a high price; how much more a *Pug* worth unmentionable sums—a PUG which some generous-hearted personage in some other corner of Great Britain than Edinburgh may even now be sending emissaries after, being bent on paying the kindest, most delicate attention to a sensitive mortal not sufficiently reticent of wishes.

Letter to John Blackwood, 30th July 1859.

All I can say of that generous-hearted personage No. 2 is, that I wish he may get—somebody else's Pug, not mine. And all I will say of the sensitive, insufficiently-reticent mortal No. 2 is, that I hope he may be as pleased and as grateful as George Eliot.

Letter to Charles L. Lewes, 30th July 1859.

I look forward to playing duets with you as one of my future pleasures; and if I am able to go on working, I hope we shall afford to have a fine grand piano. I have none of Mozart's Symphonies, so that you can be guided in your choice of them entirely by your own taste. I know Beethoven's Sonata in E flat well; it is a very charming one, and I shall like to hear you play it. That is one of my luxuries—to sit still and hear some one playing my favourite music; so that you may be sure you will find willing ears to listen to the fruits of your industrious practising.

There are ladies in the world, not a few, who play the violin, and I wish I were one of them, for then we could play together sonatas for the piano

Letter to Charles L. Lewes, 30th July 1859.

and violin, which make a charming combination. The violin gives that *keen edge* of tone which the piano wants.

I like to know that you were gratified by getting a watch so much sooner than you expected; and it was the greater satisfaction to me to send it you, because you had earned it by making good use of these precious years at Hofwyl. It is a great comfort to your father and me to think of that, for we, with our old grave heads, can't help talking very often of the need our boys will have for all sorts of good qualities and habits in making their way through this difficult life. It is a world, you perceive, in which cross-bows *will* be *launisch* sometimes, and frustrate the skill of excellent marksmen—how much more of lazy bunglers?

The first volume of the 'Physiology of Common Life' is just published, and it is a great pleasure to see so much of your father's hard work successfully finished. He has been giving a great deal of labour to the numbers on the physiology of the nervous system, which are to appear in the course of two or three months, and he has enjoyed the labour in spite of the drawback of imperfect health, which obliges him very often to leave the desk with a hot and aching head. It is quite my worst trouble that he has so much of this discomfort to bear; and we must all try and make everything else as pleasant to him as we can, to make up for it.

Letter to Charles L. Lewes, 30th July 1859.

Tell Thornton he shall have the book he asks for, if possible—I mean the book of moths and butterflies; and tell Bertie I expect to hear about the wonderful things he has done with his pocket-knife. Tell him he is equipped well enough to become king of a desert island with that pocket-knife of his; and if, as I think I remember, it has a corkscrew attached, he would certainly have more implements than he would need in that romantic position.

We shall hope to hear a great deal of your journey, with all its haps and mishaps. The mishaps are just as pleasant as the haps when they are past—that is one comfort for tormented travellers.

You are an excellent correspondent, so I do not fear you will flag in writing to me; and remember, you are always giving a pleasure when you write to me.

Aug. 11.—Received a letter from an American—Mr J. C. Evans—asking me to write a story for an American periodical. Answered that I could not

Journal, 1859.

write one for less than £1000, since, in order to do it, I must suspend my actual work.

Letter to Madame Bodichon, 11th Aug. 1859.

I do wish much to see more of human life—how can one see enough in the short years one has to stay in the world? But I meant that at present my mind works with the most freedom and the keenest sense of poetry in my remotest past, and there are many strata to be worked through before I can begin to use, *artistically*, any material I may gather in the present. Curiously enough, *apropos* of your remark about 'Adam Bede,' there is much less "out of my own life" in that book—*i.e.*, the materials are much more a combination from imperfectly-known and widely-sundered elements than the 'Clerical Scenes.' I'm so glad you have enjoyed these—so thankful for the words you write me.

Journal, 1859.

Aug. 12.—Mr J. C. Evans wrote again, declaring his willingness to pay the £1000, and asking for an interview to arrange preliminaries.

Aug. 15.—Declined the American proposition, which was to write a story of twelve parts (weekly parts) in the 'New York Century' for £1200.

Letter to Miss Sara Hennell, 15th Aug. 1859.

I have re-read your whole proof, and feel that every serious reader will be impressed with the indications of real truth-seeking and heart-experience in the tone. Beginnings are always troublesome. Even Macaulay's few pages of introduction to his Introduction in the English History are the worst bit of writing in the book. It was no trouble to me to read your proof, so don't talk as if it had been. Letter to Miss Sara Hennell, 15th Aug. 1859.

Aug. 17.—Received a letter from Blackwood, with cheque for £200 for second edition of 'Clerical Scenes.' Journal, 1859.

I'm glad my story cleaves to you. At present I have no hope that it will affect people as strongly as 'Adam' has done. The characters are on a lower level generally, and the environment less romantic. But my stories grow in me like plants, and this is only in the leaf-bud. I have faith that the flower will come. Not enough faith, though, to make me like the idea of beginning to print till the flower is fairly out—till I know the end as well as the beginning. Letter to John Blackwood, 17th Aug. 1859.

Pug develops new charms every day. I think, in the prehistoric period of his existence, before he came to me, he had led a sort of Caspar Hauser life, shut up in a kennel in Bethnal Green; and he has had to get over much astonishment at the sight of cows and other rural objects on a large scale, which he marches up to and surveys with the gravity of

Letter to John Blackwood, 17th Aug. 1859.

an "Own Correspondent," whose business it is to observe. He has absolutely no bark; but, *en revanche,* he sneezes powerfully, and has speaking eyes, so the *media* of communication are abundant. He sneezes at the world in general, and he looks affectionately at me.

I envy you the acquaintance of a genuine non-bookish man like Captain Speke. I wonder when men of that sort will take their place as heroes in our literature, instead of the inevitable "genius"?

Journal, 1859.

Aug. 20.—Letter from the troublesome Mr Quirk of Attleboro, still wanting satisfaction about Liggins. I did not leave it unanswered, because he is a friend of Chrissey's, but G. wrote for me.

Letter to Miss Sara Hennell, 20th Aug. 1859.

Our great difficulty is *time.* I am little better than a sick nigger with the lash behind him at present. If we go to Penmaenmawr we shall travel all through by night, in order not to lose more than one day; and we shall pause at Lichfield on our way back. To pause at Coventry would be a real pleasure to me; but I think, even if we could do it on our way home, it would be better economy to wait until the sense of hurry is past, and make it a little reward for work done. The going to the coast seems to be a wise measure, quite apart from indulgence. We are both so feeble; but otherwise I should have kept my resolution and remained quiet here for the next six months.

Aug. 25.—In the evening of this day we set off on our journey to Penmaenmawr. We reached Conway at half-past three in the morning; and finding that it was hopeless to get a bed anywhere, we walked about the town till the morning began to dawn, and we could see the outline of the fine old castle's battlemented walls. In the morning we went to Llandudno, thinking that might suit us better than Penmaenmawr. We found it ugly and fashionable. Then we went off to Penmaenmawr, which was beautiful to our hearts' content—or rather discontent—for it would not receive us, being already filled with visitors. Back again in despair to Conway, where we got temporary lodgings at one of the numerous Joneses. This particular Jones happened to be honest and obliging, and we did well enough for a few days in our indoor life, but out of doors there were cold winds and rain. One day we went to Abergele and found a solitary house, called Beach House, which it seemed possible we might have at the end of a few days. But no! And the winds were so cold on this northerly coast, that George was not sorry, preferring rather to take

Journal, 1859.

Journal, Aug. 1859.

flight southward. So we set out again on 31st, and reached Lichfield about half-past five. Here we meant to pass the night, that I might see my nieces—dear Chrissey's orphan children—Emily and Kate. I was much comforted by the sight of them, looking happy, and apparently under excellent care in Miss Eborall's school. We slept at the "Swan," where I remember being with my father and mother when I was a little child, and afterwards with my father alone, in our last journey into Derbyshire. The next morning we set off again, and completed our journey to Weymouth. Many delicious walks and happy hours we had in our fortnight there. A letter from Mr Langford informed us that the subscription for the sixth edition of 'Adam Bede' was 1000. Another pleasant incident was a letter from my old friend and schoolfellow, Martha Jackson, asking if the author of 'Adam Bede' was *her* Marian Evans.

Sept. 16.—We reached home, and found letters awaiting us—one from Mr Quirk, finally renouncing Liggins!—with tracts of an ultra-evangelical kind for me, and the Parish Mag., &c., from the Rev. Erskine Clark of St Michael's, Derby, who had written to me to ask me to help him in this sort of work.

I have just been reading, with deep interest and heart-stirring, the article on the Infant Seamstresses in the 'Englishwoman's Journal.' I am one among the grateful readers of that moving description—moving because the writer's own soul was moved by love and pity in the writing of it. These are the papers that will make the 'Journal' a true organ with a *function.* I am writing at the end of the day, on the brink of sleep, too tired to think of anything but that picture of the little sleeping slop-worker who had pricked her tiny finger so. Letter to Madame Bodichon, 17th Sept. 1859.

Sept. 18.—A volume of devotional poetry from the authoress of 'Visiting my Relations,' with an inscription admonishing me not to be beguiled by the love of money. *In much anxiety and doubt about my new novel.* Journal, 1859.

Oct. 7.—Since the last entry in my Journal various matters of interest have occurred. Certain "new" ideas have occurred to me in relation to my novel, and I am in better hope of it. At Weymouth I had written to Blackwood to ask him about terms, supposing I published in 'Maga.' His answer determined me to decline. On Monday, the 26th, we set out on a three days' journey to Lincolnshire and back—very pleasant and successful both as to weather and the object I was in search of. A less

Journal, 1859.

pleasant business has been a correspondence with a *crétin*,—a Warwickshire magistrate, who undertakes to declare the process by which I wrote my books —and who is the chief propagator and maintainer of the story that Liggins is at the bottom of the 'Clerical Scenes' and 'Adam Bede.' It is poor George who has had to conduct the correspondence, making his head hot by it, to the exclusion of more fructifying work. To-day, in answer to a letter from Sara, I have written her an account of my interviews with my Aunt Samuel. This evening comes a letter from Miss Brewster, full of well-meant exhortation.

Letter to Charles L. Lewes, 7th Oct. 1859.

The very best bit of news I can tell you to begin with is that your father's 'Physiology of Common Life' is selling remarkably well, being much in request among medical students. You are not to be a medical student, but I hope, nevertheless, you will by-and-by read the work with interest. There is to be a new edition of the 'Sea-side Studies' at Christmas, or soon after—a proof that this book also meets with a good number of readers. I wish you could have seen to-day, as I did, the delicate spinal cord of a dragon-fly—like a tiny thread with tiny beads on it—which your father had just dissected! He is so wonderfully clever now at the dissection of these delicate things, and has attained this cleverness entirely by devoted practice during the last three years. I hope *you* have some of his resolution and persistent regularity in work. I think you have, if I may judge from your application to music, which I am always glad to read of in your letters. I was a very idle practiser, and I often regret now that when I had abundant time and opportunity for hours of piano playing, I used them so little. I have about eighteen Sonatas and Symphonies of Beethoven, I think, but I shall be delighted to find that you can play them better than I can. I am very sensitive to blunders and wrong notes, and instruments out of tune; but I have never played much from ear, though I used to play from memory a great deal. The other evening Mr Pigott, whom you remember, Mr Redford, another friend of your father's, and Mr Wilkie Collins, dined with us, and we had a charming musical evening: Mr Pigott has a delicious tenor voice, and Mr Redford a fine baritone. The latter sings "Adelaide," that exquisite song of Beethoven's, which I should like you to learn. Schubert's songs, too, I especially delight in; but, as you say, they are difficult.

Letter to Charles L. Lewes, 7th Oct. 1859.

It is pleasant to have to tell you that Mr Bracebridge has been at last awakened to do the right

Letter to Miss Sara Hennell, 10th Oct. 1859.

Letter to Miss Sara Hennell, 10th Oct. 1859.

thing. This morning came a letter enclosing the following to me:—

"Madame, I have much pleasure on receiving your declaration that '&c. &c.,' in replying that I frankly accept your declaration as the truth, and I shall repeat it, if the contrary is again asserted to me."

This is the first symptom we have had from him of common-sense. I am very thankful—for it ends transactions with him.

Mr Lewes is of so sensitive a temperament, and so used to feeling more angry and more glad on my behalf than his own, that he has been made, several mornings, quite unable to go on with his work by this irritating correspondence. It is all my fault, for if he didn't see in the first instance that I am completely upset by anything that arouses unloving emotions, he would never feel as he does about outer sayings and doings. No one is more indifferent than he is to what is said about himself. No more about my business, let us hope, for a long while to come!

The Congreves are settled at home again now—blessing us with the sight of kind faces—Mr Congreve beginning his medical course.

Delicious confusion of ideas! Mr Lewes, walking in Wandsworth, saw a good woman cross over the street to speak to a blind man. She accosted him with, "Well, *I* knew you, *though you are dark!*"

I wish you had read the letter you enclosed to me; it is really curious. The writer, an educated person, asks me to perfect and extend the benefit 'Adam Bede' has "conferred on society" by writing a *sequel* to it, in which I am to tell all about Hetty after her reprieve: "Arthur's efforts to obtain the reprieve, and his desperate ride after obtaining it —Dinah on board the convict ship—Dinah's letters to Hetty—and whatever the author might choose to reveal concerning Hetty's years of banishment. Minor instances of the incompleteness which induces an unsatisfactory feeling may be alleged in the disposal of the *locket and ear-rings*—which everybody expects to reappear—and in the incident of the pink silk neckerchief, of which all would like to hear a little more"!! Letter to John Blackwood, 16th Oct. 1859.

I do feel more than I ought about outside sayings and doings, and I constantly rebuke myself for all that part of my susceptibility, which I know to be weak and egoistic; still what is said about one's art is not merely a personal matter—it touches the very highest things one lives for. *Truth* in art is so startling that no one can believe in it as art, and

Letter to John Blackwood, 16th Oct. 1859.

the specific forms of religious life which have made some of the grandest elements in human history are looked down upon as if they were not within the artist's sympathy and veneration and intensely-dramatic reproduction. "I do well to be angry" on that ground, don't I? The simple fact is, that I never saw anything of my aunt's writing, and Dinah's words came from me "as the tears come because our heart is full, and we can't help them."

If you were living in London instead of at Edinburgh, I should ask you to read the first volume of 'Sister Maggie' at once, for the sake of having your impression, but it is inconvenient to me to part with the MS. The great success of 'Adam' makes my writing a matter of more anxiety than ever. I suppose there is a little sense of responsibility mixed up with a great deal of pride. And I think I should worry myself still more if I began to print before the thing is essentially complete. So on all grounds it is better to wait. How clever and picturesque the "Horse-dealer in Syria" is! I read him with keen interest, only wishing that he saw the seamy side of things rather less habitually. Excellent Captain Speke can't write so well, but one follows him out of grave sympathy. That a man should live through such things as that beetle in his ear! Such papers as that make the *specialité* of 'Blackwood'—one sees them nowhere else.

Oct. 16.—Yesterday came a pleasant packet of letters: one from Blackwood saying that they are printing a seventh edition of 'Adam Bede' (of 2000), and that 'Clerical Scenes' will soon be exhausted. I have finished the first volume of my new novel, 'Sister Maggie;' have got my legal questions answered satisfactorily, and when my headache has cleared off, must go at it full speed. Journal, 1859.

Oct. 25. — The day before yesterday Herbert Spencer dined with us. We have just finished reading aloud 'Père Goriot'—a hateful book. I have been reading lately and have nearly finished Comte's 'Catechism.'

Oct. 28. — Received from Blackwood a cheque for £400, the last payment for 'Adam Bede' in the terms of the agreement. But in consequence of the great success, he proposes to pay me £800 more at the beginning of next year. Yesterday Smith, the publisher, called to make propositions to G. about writing in the 'Cornhill Magazine.'

I beg that you and Major Blackwood will accept my thanks for your proposal to give me a further share in the success of 'Adam Bede,' beyond the terms of our agreement, which are fulfilled by the Letter to John Blackwood, 28th Oct. 1859.

Letter to John Blackwood, 28th Oct. 1859.

second cheque for £400, received this morning. Neither you nor I ever calculated on half such a success, thinking that the book was too quiet, and too unflattering to dominant fashion, ever to be very popular. I hope that opinion of ours is a guarantee that there is nothing hollow or transient in the reception 'Adam' has met with. Sometimes when I read a book which has had a great success, and am unable to see any valid merits of an artistic kind to account for it, I am visited with a horrible alarm lest 'Adam,' too, should ultimately sink into the same class of outworn admirations. But I always fall back on the fact that no shibboleth and no vanity is flattered by it, and that there is no novelty of mere form in it which can have delighted simply by startling.

Journal, 1859.

Nov. 10.—Dickens dined with us to-day, for the first time, and after he left I went to the Congreves', where George joined me, and we had much chat—about George Stephenson, religion, &c.

Letter to Miss Sara Hennell, 11th Nov. 1859.

A very beautiful letter—beautiful in feeling—that I have received from Mrs Gaskell to-day, prompts me to write to you and let you know how entirely she has freed herself from any imputation of being unwilling to accept the truth when it has once clearly presented itself as truth. Since she has known "on authority" that the two books are mine, she has re-read them, and has written to me, apparently on the prompting they gave in that second reading,—very sweet and noble words they are that she has written to me. Yesterday Dickens dined with us, on *his* return from the country. That was a great pleasure to me: he is a man one can thoroughly enjoy talking to—there is a strain of real seriousness along with his keenness and humour. Letter to Miss Sara Hennell, 11th Nov. 1859.

The Liggins affair is concluded so far as any *action* of ours is concerned, since Mr Quirk (the inmost citadel, I presume) has surrendered by writing an apology to Blackwood, saying he now believes he was imposed on by Mr Liggins. As to Miss Martineau, I respect her so much as an authoress, and have so pleasant a recollection of her as a hostess for three days, that I wish that distant impression from herself and her writings to be disturbed as little as possible by mere personal details. Anything she may do, or say, or feel concerning me personally, is a matter of entire indifference: I share her bitterness with a large number of far more blameless people than myself. It can be of no possible benefit to me, or any one else, that I should know more of those things, either past, present, or to come. "I do owe no man anything," Letter to Miss Sara Hennell, 14th Nov. 1859.

Letter to Miss Sara Hennell, 14th Nov. 1859.

except to write honestly and religiously what comes from my inward promptings; and the freer I am kept of all knowledge of that comparatively small circle who mingle personal regards or hatred with their judgment or reception of my writings, the easier it will be to keep my motives free from all indirectness and write truly.

Journal, 1859.

Nov. 18.—On Monday Dickens wrote asking me to give him, after I have finished my present novel, a story to be printed in 'All the Year Round'—to begin four months after next Easter, and assuring me of my own terms. The next day G. had an interview by appointment with Evans (of Bradbury & Evans), and Lucas, the editor of 'Once a Week,' who, after preliminary pressing of G. himself to contribute, put forward their wish that I should give them a novel for their Magazine. They were to write and make an offer, but have not yet done so. We have written to Dickens saying that *time* is an insurmountable obstacle to his proposition, as he puts it.

I am reading Thomas à Kempis.

Nov. 19.—Mr Lockhart Clarke and Mr Herbert Spencer dined with us.

Nov. 22.—We have been much annoyed lately by Newby's advertisement of a book called 'Adam

Bede, Junior,' a sequel; and to-day Dickens has written to mention a story of the tricks which are being used to push the book under the pretence of its being mine. One librarian has been forced to order the book against his will, because the public have demanded it! Dickens is going to put an article on the subject in 'Household Words,' in order to scarify the rascally bookseller. Journal, 1859.

Nov. 23.—We began Darwin's book on 'The Origin of Species' to-night. Though full of interesting matter, it is not impressive, from want of luminous and orderly presentation.

Nov. 24.—This morning I wrote the scene between Mrs Tulliver and Wakem. G. went into town and saw young Evans (of Bradbury & Evans), who agreed that it would be well to have an article in 'Punch' on this scoundrelly business of 'Adam Bede, Junior.' A divine day. I walked out, and Mrs Congreve joined me. Then music, 'Arabian Nights,' and Darwin.

Nov. 25.—I am reading old Bunyan again, after the long lapse of years, and am profoundly struck with the true genius manifested in the simple, vigorous, rhythmic style.

Letter to the Brays, 25th Nov. 1859.

Thanks for 'Bentley.' Some one said the writer of the article on 'Adam Bede' was a Mr Mozeley, a

Letter to the Brays, 25th Nov. 1859.

clergyman, and a writer in the 'Times:' but these reports about authorship are as often false as true. I think it is, on the whole, the best review we have seen, unless we must except the one in the 'Revue des Deux Mondes,' by Emile Montégut. I don't mean to read *any* reviews of my next book; so far as they would produce any effect, they would be confusing. Everybody admires something that somebody else finds fault with; and the miller with his donkey was in a clear and decided state of mind compared with the unfortunate writer who should set himself to please all the world of review writers. I am compelled, in spite of myself, to be annoyed with this business of 'Adam Bede, Junior.' You see I am well provided with thorns in the flesh, lest I should be exalted beyond measure. To part with the copyright of a book which sells 16,000 in one year—to have a Liggins and an unknown writer of one's "Sequel" all to one's self—is excellent discipline.

We are reading Darwin's book on Species, just come out after long expectation. It is an elaborate exposition of the evidence in favour of the Development Theory, and so makes an epoch. Do you see how the publishing world is going mad on periodicals? If I could be seduced by such offers, I might have written three poor novels, and made my fortune in one year. Happily, I have no need to exert myself when I say "Avaunt thee, Satan!" Satan, in the form of bad writing and good pay, is not seductive to me.

Letter to the Brays, 25th Nov. 1859.

Nov. 26.—Letter from Lucas, editor of 'Once a Week,' anxious to come to terms about my writing for said periodical.

Journal, 1859.

It was very pretty and generous of you to send me a nice long letter out of your turn, and I think I shall give you, as a reward, other opportunities of being generous in the same way for the next few months, for I am likely to be a poor correspondent, having my head and hands full.

Letter to Charles L. Lewes, 26th Nov. 1859.

We have the whole of Vilmar's 'Literatur Geschichte,' but not the remainder of the 'Deutsche Humoristik.' I agree with you in liking the history of German literature, especially the earlier ages — the birth-time of the legendary poetry. Have you read the 'Nibelungenlied' yet?

Whereabouts are you in Algebra? It would be very pleasant to study it with you, if I could possibly find time to rub up my knowledge. It is now a good while since I looked into Algebra, but I was very fond of it in old days, though I daresay

Letter to Charles L. Lewes, 26th Nov. 1859.

I never went so far as you have now gone. Tell me your latitude and longitude.

I have no memory of an autumn so disappointing as this. It is my favourite season. I delight especially in the golden and red tints under the purple clouds. But this year the trees were almost stripped of their leaves before they had changed colour — dashed off by the winds and rain. We have had *no* autumnal beauty.

I am writing at night—very tired—so you must not wonder if I have left out words, or been otherwise incoherent.

Journal, 1859.

Nov. 29.—Wrote a letter to the 'Times,' and to Delane about Newby.

Letter to Madame Bodichon, 5th Dec. 1859.

I took no notice of the extract you sent me from a letter of Mrs Gaskell's, being determined not to engage in any writing on the topic of my authorship, except such as was absolutely demanded of us. But since then I have had a very beautiful letter from Mrs Gaskell, and I will quote some of her words, because they do her honour, and will incline you to think more highly of her. She begins in this way: "Since I heard, on authority, that you were the author of 'Scenes of Clerical Life' and 'Adam Bede,' I have read them again, and I must once more tell you how earnestly, fully, and *humbly*

I admire them. I never read anything so complete and beautiful in fiction in my life before." Very sweet and noble of her was it not? She went on to speak of her having held to the notion of Liggins, but she adds, "I was never such a goose as to believe that books like yours were a mosaic of real and ideal." The 'Seth Bede' and 'Adam Bede, Junior' are speculations of those who are always ready to fasten themselves like leeches on a popular fame. Such things must be endured: they are the shadow to the bright fact of selling 16,000 in one year. As to the silly falsehoods and empty opinions afloat in some petty circles, I have quite conquered my temporary irritation about them—indeed, I feel all the more serene now for that very irritation. It has impressed on me more deeply how entirely the rewards of the artist lie apart from everything that is narrow and personal: there is no peace until that lesson is thoroughly learned. I shall go on writing from my inward promptings—writing what I love and believe, what I feel to be true and good, if I can only render it worthily—and then leave all the rest to take its chance: "As it was in the beginning, is now, and ever shall be" with those who are to produce any art that will lastingly touch the generations of men. We have

Letter to Madame Bodichon, 5th Dec. 1859.

Letter to Madame Bodichon, 5th Dec. 1859.

been reading Darwin's book on the 'Origin of Species' just now: it makes an epoch, as the expression of his thorough adhesion, after long years of study, to the Doctrine of Development—and not the adhesion of an anonym like the author of the 'Vestiges,' but of a long-celebrated naturalist. The book is sadly wanting in illustrative facts—of which he has collected a vast number, but reserves them for a future book, of which this smaller one is the *avant coureur*. This will prevent the work from becoming popular as the 'Vestiges' did, but it will have a great effect in the scientific world, causing a thorough and open discussion of a question about which people have hitherto felt timid. So the world gets on step by step towards brave clearness and honesty! But to me the Development Theory, and all other explanations of processes by which things came to be, produce a feeble impression compared with the mystery that lies under the processes. It is nice to think of you reading our great, great favourite Molière, while, for the present, we are not taking him down from the shelves—only talking about him, as we do very often. I get a good deal of pleasure out of the sense that some one I love is reading and enjoying my best-loved writers. I think the "Misanthrope" the finest, most complete production *of its kind* in the world. I know you enjoy the "sonnet" scene, and the one between Arsinoé and Célimène.

In opposition to most people, who love to *read* Shakspeare, I like to see his plays acted better than any others: his great tragedies thrill me, let them be acted how they may. I think it is something like what I used to experience in old days in listening to uncultured preachers—the emotions lay hold of one too strongly for one to care about the medium. Before all other plays I find myself cold and critical, seeing nothing but actors and "properties." I like going to those little provincial theatres. One's heart streams out to the poor devils of actors who get so little clapping, and will go home to so poor a supper. One of my pleasures lately has been hearing repeatedly from my Genevese friends M. and Mme. d'Albert, who were so good to me during my residence with them. M. d'Albert had read the 'Scenes of Clerical Life' before he knew they were mine, and had been so much struck with them that he had wanted to translate them. One likes to feel old ties strengthened by fresh sympathies. The 'Cornhill Magazine' is going to lead off with great spirit, and promises to eclipse all the other new-born periodicals. Mr Lewes is writing a series of

Letter to Miss Sara Hennell, Monday evening, 5th Dec. 1859.

Letter to Miss Sara Hennell, Monday evening, 5th Dec. 1859.

papers for it—"Studies in Animal Life"—which are to be subsequently published in a book. It is quite as well that your book should not be ready for publication just yet. February is a much better time than Christmas. I shall be one of your most eager readers—for every book that comes from the heart of hearts does me good, and I quite share your faith that what you yourself feel so deeply, and find so precious, will find a home in some other minds. Do not suspect that I impose on you the task of writing letters to answer my *dilettante* questions. "Am I on a bed of roses?" I have four children to correspond with—the three boys in Switzerland, and Emily at Lichfield.

Journal, 1859.

Dec. 15.—Blackwood proposes to give me for 'The Mill on the Floss' £2000 for 4000 copies of an edition at 31s. 6d., and after the same rate for any more that may be printed at the same price: £150 for 1000 at 12s.; and £60 for 1000 at 6s. I have accepted.

Dec. 25.—Christmas Day. We all, including Pug, dined with Mr and Mrs Congreve, and had a delightful day. Mr Bridges was there too.

Letter to Mrs Bray, 30th Dec. 1859.

I don't like Christmas to go by without sending you a greeting, though I have really nothing to say beyond that. We spent our Christmas Day with the Congreves, shutting up our house, and taking our servant and Pug with us. And so we ate our turkey and plum-pudding in very social, joyous fashion with those charming friends. Mr Bridges was there too. Letter to Mrs Bray, 30th Dec. 1859.

We are meditating flight to Italy when my present work is done, as our last bit of vagrancy for a long, long while. We shall only stay two months, doing nothing but absorb.

I don't think I have anything else to tell, except that we, being very happy, wish all mortals to be in like condition, and especially the mortals we know in the flesh. Human happiness is a web with many threads of pain in it—that is always *sub auditum*—"Twist ye, twine ye, even so," &c., &c.

I never before had so pleasant a New Year's greeting as your letter containing a cheque for £800, for which I have to thank you to-day. On every ground—including considerations that are not at all of a monetary kind—I am deeply obliged to you and to Major Blackwood for your liberal conduct in relation to 'Adam Bede.' Letter to John Blackwood, 3d Jan. 1860.

As, owing to your generous concession of the copyright of 'Adam Bede,' the three books will be henceforth on the same footing, we shall be delivered from further discussion as to terms.

Letter to John Blackwood, 3d Jan. 1860.

We are demurring about the title. Mr Lewes is beginning to prefer *The House of Tulliver; or, Life on the Floss,* to our old notion of 'Sister Maggie.' *The Tullivers; or, Life on the Floss,* has the advantage of slipping easily off the lazy English tongue, but it is after too common a fashion ('The Newcomes,' 'The Bertrams,' &c., &c.) Then there is *The Tulliver Family; or, Life on the Floss.* Pray meditate and give us your opinion.

I am very anxious that the 'Scenes of Clerical Life' should have every chance of impressing the public with its existence: first, because I think it of importance to the estimate of me as a writer that 'Adam Bede' should not be counted as my only book; and secondly, because there are ideas presented in these stories about which I care a good deal, and am not sure that I can ever embody again. This latter reason is my private affair, but the other reason, if valid, is yours also. I must tell you that I had another cheering letter to-day besides yours: one from a person of mark in your Edinburgh University,[1] full of the very strongest words of sympathy and encouragement, hoping that my life may long be spared "to give pictures of the deeper life of this age." So I sat down to my desk with a

[1] Professor Blackie.

delicious confidence that my audience is not made up of reviewers and literary clubs. If there is any truth in me that the world wants, nothing will hinder the world from drinking what it is athirst for. And if there is no needful truth in me, let me, howl as I may in the process, be hurled into the Domdaniel, where I wish all other futile writers to sink. Letter to John Blackwood, 3d Jan. 1860.

Your description of the "curling" made me envy you the sight.

The sun is shining with us too, and your pleasant letter made it seem to shine more brightly. I am not going to be expansive in this appendix to your father's chapter of love and news, for my head is tired with writing this morning—it is not so young as yours, you know, and, besides, is a feminine head, supported by weaker muscles, and a weaker digestive apparatus than that of a young gentleman with a broad chest and hopeful whiskers. I don't wonder at your being more conscious of your attachment to Hofwyl now the time of leaving is so near. I fear you will miss a great many things in exchanging Hofwyl, with its snowy mountains and glorious spaces, for a very moderate home in the neighbourhood of London. You will have a less various, more arduous life: but the time of *Entbehrung* or Letter to Charles L. Lewes, 4th Jan. 1860.

Letter to Charles L. Lewes, 4th Jan. 1860.

Entsagung must begin, you know, for every mortal of us. And let us hope that we shall all—father and mother and sons—help one another with love.

What jolly times you have had lately! It did us good to read of your merrymaking.

Letter to John Blackwood, 6th Jan. 1860.

'The Mill on the Floss' be it then! The only objections are, that the mill is not *strictly* on the Floss, being on its small tributary, and that the title is of rather laborious utterance. But I think these objections do not deprive it of its advantage over 'The Tullivers; or, Life on the Floss'—the only alternative, so far as we can see. Pray give the casting-vote.

Easter Monday, I see, is on the 8th April, and I wish to be out by the middle or end of March. Illness apart, I intend to have finished Vol. III. by the beginning of that month, and I hope no obstacle will impede the rapidity of the printing.

Journal, 1860.

Jan. 11.—I have had a very delightful letter of sympathy from Professor Blackie of Edinburgh, which came to me on New Year's morning, and a proposal from Blackwood to publish a third edition of 'Clerical Scenes' at 12s. George's article in the 'Cornhill Magazine'—the first of a series of "Studies in Animal Life"—is much admired, and in other ways our New Year opens with happy omens.

Thank you for letting me see the specimen advertisements; they have helped us to come to a decision—namely, for 'The Mill on the Floss.'

Letter to John Blackwood, 12th Jan. 1860.

I agree with you that it will be well not to promise the book in March — not because I do not desire and hope to be ready, but because I set my face against all pledges that I am not *sure* of being able to fulfil. The third volume is, I fancy, always more rapidly written than the rest. The third volume of 'Adam Bede' was written in six weeks, even with headaching interruptions, because it was written under a stress of emotion, which first volumes cannot be. I will send you the first volume of 'The Mill' at once. The second is ready, but I would rather keep it as long as I can. Besides the advantage to the book of being out by Easter, I have another reason for wishing to have done in time for that. We want to get away for two months to Italy, if possible, to feed my mind with fresh thoughts, and to assure ourselves of that fructifying holiday before the boys are about us, making it difficult for us to leave home. But you may rely on it that no amount of horse-power would make me *hurry* over my book, so as not to do my best. If it is written fast, it will be because I can't help writing it fast.

Journal, 1860.

Jan. 16.—Finished my second volume this morning, and am going to send off the MS. of the first volume to-morrow. We have decided that the title shall be 'The Mill on the Floss.' We have been reading 'Humphrey Clinker' in the evenings, and have been much disappointed in it, after the praise of Thackeray and Dickens.

Jan. 26.—Mr Pigott, Mr Redford, and Mr F. Chapman dined with us, and we had a musical evening,—Mrs Congreve and Miss Bury[1] joining us after dinner.

Letter to John Blackwood, 28th Jan. 1860.

Thanks for your letter of yesterday, with the Genevese enclosure. No promise, alas! of smallest watch expressing largest admiration, but a desire for "permission to translate."

I have been invalided for the last week, and, of course, am a prisoner in the castle of Giant Despair, who growls in my ear that 'The Mill on the Floss' is detestable, and that the last volume will be the climax of that general detestableness. Such is the elation attendant on what a self-elected lady correspondent of mine from Scotland calls my "exciting career"!

I have had a great pleasure this week. Dr Inman of Liverpool has dedicated a new book

[1] Mrs Congreve's sister.

('Foundation for a New Theory and Practice of Medicine') "to G. H. Lewes, as an acknowledgment of benefit received from noticing his close observation and clear inductive reasoning in 'Sea-side Studies' and the 'Physiology of Common Life.'" Letter to John Blackwood, 28th Jan. 1860.

That is really gratifying, coming from a *physician* of some scientific mark, who is *not* a personal friend.

Feb. 4.—Came this morning a letter from Blackwood announcing the despatch of the first eight sheets of proof of 'The Mill on the Floss,' and expressing his delight in it. To-night G. has read them, and says—"*Ganz famos!*" Ebenezer! Journal, 1860.

Feb. 23.—Sir Edward Lytton called on us. Guy Darrell *in propriâ personâ.*

Sir Edward Lytton called on us yesterday. The conversation lapsed chiefly into monologue, from the difficulty I found in making him hear, but under all disadvantages I had an agreeable impression of his kindness and sincerity. He thinks the two defects of 'Adam Bede' are the dialect and Adam's marriage with Dinah; but, of course, I would have my teeth drawn rather than give up either. Letter to John Blackwood, 23d Feb. 1860.

Jacobi told Jean Paul that unless he altered the *dénouement* of his Titan, he would withdraw his

Letter to John Blackwood, 23d Feb. 1860.

friendship from him; and I am preparing myself for your lasting enmity on the ground of the tragedy in my third volume. But an unfortunate duck can only lay blue eggs, however much white ones may be in demand.

Journal, 1860.

Feb. 29.—G. has been in the town to-day, and has agreed for £300 for 'The Mill on the Floss' from Harpers of New York. This evening, too, has come a letter from Williams & Norgate, saying that Tauchnitz will give £100 for the German reprint; also, that 'Bede Adam' is translated into Hungarian.

March 5.—Yesterday Mr Lawrence, the portrait painter, lunched with us, and expressed to G. his wish to take my portrait.

March 9.—Yesterday a letter from Blackwood, expressing his strong delight in my third volume, which he had read to the beginning of "Borne along by the Tide." To-day young Blackwood called, and told us, among other things, that the last copies of 'Clerical Scenes' had gone to-day—twelve for export. Letter came from Germany, announcing a translation of G.'s 'Biographical History of Philosophy.'

March 11.—To-day the first volume of the German translation of 'Adam Bede' came. It is done by Dr Frese, the same man who translated the 'Life of Goethe.' Journal, 1860.

March 20.—Professor Owen sent me his 'Palæontology' to-day. Have missed two days of work from headache, and so have not yet finished my book.

March 21.—Finished this morning 'The Mill on the Floss,' writing from the moment when Maggie, carried out on the water, thinks of her mother and brother. We hope to start for Rome on Saturday, 24th.

Magnificat anima mea!

The manuscript of 'The Mill on the Floss' bears the following inscription:—

"To my beloved husband, George Henry Lewes, I give this MS. of my third book, written in the sixth year of our life together, at Holly Lodge, South Field, Wandsworth, and finished 21st March 1860."

Your letter yesterday morning helped to inspire me for the last eleven pages, if they have any inspiration in them. They were written in a *furor*, but I daresay there is not a word different from what it would have been if I had written them at the slowest pace. Letter to John Blackwood, 22d March 1860.

We expect to start on Saturday morning, and to

Letter to John Blackwood, 22d March 1860.

be in Rome by Palm Sunday, or else by the following Tuesday. Of course we shall write to you when we know what will be our address in Rome. In the meantime news will gather.

I don't mean to send 'The Mill on the Floss' to any one, except to Dickens, who has behaved with a delicate kindness in a recent matter, which I wish to acknowledge.

I am grateful and yet rather sad to have finished —sad that I shall live with my people on the banks of the Floss no longer. But it is time that I should go and absorb some new life, and gather fresh ideas.

SUMMARY.

JANUARY 1859 TO MARCH 1860.

Looking for cases of *inundation* in 'Annual Register'—New House—Holly Lodge, Wandsworth—Letter to John Blackwood—George Eliot fears she has not characteristics of "the popular author"—Subscription to 'Adam Bede' 730 copies —Appreciation by a cabinetmaker—Dr John Brown sends 'Rab and his Friends' with an inscription—Letter to Blackwood thereon—Tries to be hopeful—Letters to Miss Hennell —Description of Holly Lodge—Miss Nightingale—Thoughts on death—Scott—Mrs Clarke writes—Mr and Mrs Congreve—Letter to Mrs Bray on effects of anxiety—Mrs Clarke dying—Letter to John Blackwood—Wishes Carlyle to read 'Adam Bede'—'Life of Frederic' painful—Susceptibility to newspaper criticism—Edinburgh more encouraging than London—Letter to Blackwood to stop puffing notices—Letter from E. Hall, working man, asking for cheap editions—Sale of 'Adam Bede'—Death of Mrs Clarke—1800 copies of 'Adam Bede' sold—Letter to Blackwood—Awakening to fame—Letter to Froude—Mrs Poyser quoted in House of Commons by Mr Charles Buxton—Opinions of Charles Reade, Shirley Brooks, and John Murray—Letter to John Blackwood—Warwickshire correspondent insists that Liggins is author of 'Adam Bede'—Not flushed with success—Visit to Isle of Wight—Letter to Miss Hennell on rewriting, and pleasure in Mr and Mrs Congreve—Letter to 'Times' denying that Liggins is the author—Letter to Blackwood—The Liggins myth—Letter from Bulwer—Finished 'The Lifted Veil'—Writing 'The Tullivers'—Mrs Congreve—Letter to Mrs Congreve—Faith in her—Letter from Madame Bodichon—Reply breathing joy in sympathy—Letter to Major Blackwood—Mr Anders's apology for the Liggins business—'Adam Bede' worth writing—Dulwich gallery—Blackwood gives £400 more in acknowledgment of 'Adam Bede's' success—Letter to Miss Hennell on Mrs Congreve—On difficulty of getting cheap music in England—Professor Aytoun on 'Adam Bede'—Letter to Major Blackwood—Liggins—Mrs Gaskell—Letter to Mrs Congreve—Dislike of Wandsworth—To Crystal Palace to hear "Messiah," and reveals herself to Brays as author of 'Adam Bede'—Letter to Brays—Bad effect of talking of her books—Letter to Charles Bray—Melancholy that her writing does not produce effect intended—Letter to Mrs Congreve—To Switzerland by Paris—At Schweizerhof, Lucerne, with Congreves—Mr Lewes goes to

Hofwyl—Return to Richmond by Bâle and Paris—Fourth edition of 'Adam Bede' (5000) sold in a fortnight—Letter to Mrs Bray on Mrs Congreve—On the effect of her books and fame—Herbert Spencer on 'Adam Bede'—Pamphlet to prove that Scott's novels were written by Thomas Scott—Letter from Dickens on 'Adam Bede' referred to—Letter to John Blackwood on "Pug"—Letter to Charles Lewes—'The Physiology of Common Life'—American proposition for a story for £1200—Letter to Mme. Bodichon—Distance from experience artistically necessary—Letter to John Blackwood—Development of stories—Visit to Penmaenmawr—Return by Lichfield to Weymouth—Sixth edition of 'Adam Bede'—Back to Richmond—Anxiety about new novel—Journey to Gainsboro', Lincolnshire—Letter to Miss Hennell—End of Liggins business—Letter to John Blackwood—A correspondent suggests a sequel to 'Adam Bede'—Susceptibility to outside opinion—Seventh edition of 'Adam Bede'—Blackwood proposes to pay £800 beyond the bargain for success of 'Adam Bede'—Dickens dines at Holly Lodge—Letter to Miss Hennell—Quotes letter from Mrs Gaskell—Miss Martineau—Dickens asks for story for 'All the Year Round'—'Adam Bede, Junior'—Reading Darwin on 'Origin of Species'—Bunyan—Letter to Mr Bray—Article on 'Adam Bede' in 'Bentley'—In 'Revue des Deux Mondes,' by Émile Montégut—Reviews generally—16,000 of 'Adam Bede' sold in year—Darwin's book—Letter to Charles Lewes—Mentions fondness of algebra—Letter to Mme. Bodichon quoting Mrs Gaskell's letter—Rewards of the artist lie apart from everything personal—Darwin's book—Molière—Letter to Miss Hennell—Likes to see Shakspeare acted—Hears from M. and Mme. d'Albert—'Cornhill Magazine'—Blackwood's terms for 'Mill on the Floss'—Christmas Day with Congreves—Letter of sympathy from Professor Blackie—Third edition of 'Clerical Scenes'—Letters to Blackwood—Thanks for concession of copyright of 'Adam Bede'—Title of new novel considered—Suggestion of the 'Mill on the Floss' accepted—The third volume of 'Adam Bede' written in six weeks—Depression with the 'Mill'—Sir Edward Lytton—'Adam Bede' translated into Hungarian and German—'Mill on the Floss' finished—Letter to Blackwood—Sad at finishing—Start for Italy.

CHAPTER X.

Italy, 1860. WE have finished our journey to Italy—the journey I had looked forward to for years, rather with the hope of the new elements it would bring to my culture, than with the hope of immediate pleasure. Travelling can hardly be without a continual current of disappointment if the main object is not the enlargement of one's general life, so as to make even weariness and annoyances enter into the sum of benefit. One great deduction to me from the delight of seeing world-famous objects is the frequent double consciousness which tells me that I am not enjoying the actual vision enough, and that when higher enjoyment comes with the reproduction of the scenes in my imagination, I shall have lost some of the details, which impress me too feebly in the present because the faculties are not wrought up into energetic action.

I have no other journal than the briefest record

of what we did each day; so I shall put down my recollections whenever I happen to have leisure and inclination—just for the sake of making clear to myself the impressions I have brought away from our three months' travel. Italy, 1860.

The first striking moment in our journey was when we arrived, I think about eleven o'clock at night, at the point in the ascent of the Mont Cenis where we were to quit the diligences and take to the sledges. After a hasty drink of hot coffee in the roadside inn, our large party—the inmates of three diligences—turned out into the starlight to await the signal for getting into the sledges. That signal seemed to be considerably on in the future—to be arrived at through much confusion of luggage lifting, voices, and leading about of mules. The human bustle and confusion made a poetic contrast with the sublime stillness of the star-lit heavens spread over the snowy table-land and surrounding heights. The keenness of the air contributed strongly to the sense of novelty: we had left our everyday conventional world quite behind us, and were on a visit to Nature in her private home.

Once closely packed in our sledge, congratulating ourselves that after all we were no more squeezed than in our diligence, I gave myself up to as many

Italy, 1860. naps as chose to take possession of me, and actually slept without very considerable interruption till we were near the summit of the mighty pass. Already there was a faint hint of the morning in the starlight which showed us the vast sloping snow-fields as we commenced the descent. I got a few glimpses of the pure far-stretching whiteness before the sharpening edge of cold forced us to close the window. Then there was no more to be seen till it was time to get out of the sledge and ascend the diligence once more: not, however, without a preliminary struggle with the wind, which fairly blew me down on my slippery standing-ground. The rest of our descent showed us fine varied scenes of mountain and ravine till we got down at Susa, where breakfast and the railway came as a desirable variety after our long mountain journey and long fast. One of our companions had been a gigantic French soldier, who had in charge a bag of Government money. He was my *vis-à-vis* for some time, and cramped my poor legs not a little with his precious bag, which he would by no means part from.

The approach to Turin by the railway gave us a grand view of snowy mountains surrounding the city on three sides. A few hours of rest spent there could leave no very vivid impression. A handsome street well broken by architectural details, with a glimpse of snowy mountains at the end of the vista, colonnades on each side, and flags waving their bright colours in sign of political joy—is the image that usually rises before me at the mention of Turin. I fancy the said street is the principal one, but in our walk about the town we saw everywhere a similar character of prosperous well-lodged town existence—only without the colonnades and without the balconies and other details, which make the principal street picturesque. This is the place that Alfieri lived in through many of his young follies, getting tired of it at last for the Piedmontese pettiness of which it was the centre. And now, eighty years later, it is the centre of a widening life which may at last become the life of resuscitated Italy. At the railway station, as we waited to take our departure for Genoa, we had a sight of the man whose name will always be connected with the story of that widening life — Count Cavour — "*imitant son portrait*," which we had seen in the shops, with unusual closeness. A man pleasant to look upon, with a smile half kind, half caustic; giving you altogether the impression that he thinks of "many matters," but thanks heaven and makes

Italy, 1860. no boast of them. He was there to meet the Prince de Carignan, who was going to Genoa on his way towards Florence by the same train as ourselves. The Prince is a notability with a thick waist, bound in by a gold belt, and with a fat face, predominated over by a large moustache—"*Non ragionam di lui.*" The railway journey from Turin was chiefly distinguished by dust; but I slept through the latter half, without prejudice, however, to the satisfaction with which I lay down in a comfortable bedroom in the Hotel Feder.

In Genoa again on a bright, warm, spring morning! I was here eleven years ago, and the image that visit had left in my mind was surprisingly faithful, though fragmentary. The outlook from our hotel was nearly the same as before—over a low building with a colonnade, at the masts of the abundant shipping. But there was a striking change in the interior of the hotel. It was, like the other, a palace adapted to the purposes of an inn—but be-carpeted and be-furnished with an exaggeration of English fashion.

We lost no time in turning out after breakfast into the morning sunshine. George was enchanted with the aspect of the place, as we drove or walked along the streets. It was his first vision of anything corresponding to his preconception of Italy. Italy, 1860. After the Adlergasse in Nürnberg surely no streets can be more impressive than the Strada Nuova and Strada Nuovissima at Genoa. In street architecture I can rise to the highest point of the admiration given to the Palladian style. And here in these chief streets of Genoa the palaces have two advantages over those of Florence: they form a series, creating a general impression of grandeur of which each particular palace gets the benefit; and they have the open gateway, showing the *cortile* within—sometimes containing grand stone staircases. And all this architectural splendour is accompanied with the signs of actual prosperity. Genova la Superba is not a name of the past merely.

We ascended the tower of S. Maria di Carignano to get a panoramic view of the city with its embosoming hills and bay—saw the Cathedral with its banded black-and-white marble—the Churches of the Annunziata and Sant' Ambrogio, with their wealth of gilding and rich pink-brown marbles—the Palazzo Rosso, with its collection of eminently forgettable pictures,—and the pretty gardens of the Palazzo Doria, with their flourishing green close against the sea.

A drive in the direction of the Campo Santo

Italy, 1860. along the dry pebbly bed of the river showed us the terraced hills planted with olives, and many picturesque groups of the common people with mules or on carts; not to mention what gives beauty to every corner of the inhabited world—the groups of children squatting against walls or trotting about by the side of their elders, or grinning together over their play.

One of the personages we were pleased to encounter in the streets here was a quack—a Dulcamara—mounted on his carriage and holding forth with much *brio* before proceeding to take out the tooth of a negro, already seated in preparation.

We left Genoa on the second evening—unhappily a little too long after sundown, so that we did not get a perfect view of the grand city from the sea. The pale starlight could bring out no colour. We had a prosperous passage to Leghorn.

Leghorn on a brilliant warm morning, with five or six hours before us to fill as agreeably as possible! Of course the first thought was to go to Pisa, but the train would not start till eleven; so in the meantime we took a drive about the prosperous-looking town, and saw the great reservoir which receives the water brought from the distant mountains: a beautiful and interesting sight—to look into the glassy depth and see columns and grand arches reflected as if in mockery and frustration of one's desire to see the bottom. But in one corner the light fell so as to reveal that reality instead of the beautiful illusion. On our way back we passed the Hebrew synagogue, and were glad of our coachman's suggestion that we should enter, seeing it was the Jews' Sabbath. Italy, 1860.

At Pisa we took a carriage and drove at once to the cathedral, seeing as we went the well-looking lines of building on each side of the Arno.

A wonderful sight is that first glimpse of the cathedral, with the leaning campanile on one side and the baptistery on the other, green turf below and a clear blue sky above! The structure of the campanile is exquisitely light and graceful—tier above tier of small circular arches, supported by delicate round pillars narrowing gradually in circumference, but very slightly, so that there is no striking difference of size between the base and summit. The campanile is all of white marble, but the cathedral has the bands of black and white, softened in effect by the yellowing which time has given to the white. There is a family likeness among all these structures: they all have the delicate little colonnades and circular arches.

Italy, 1860. But the baptistery has stronger traits of the Gothic style in the pinnacles that crown the encircling colonnade.

After some dusty delay outside the railway station, we set off back again to Livorno, and forthwith got on board our steamboat again — to awake next morning (being Palm Sunday) at Civita Vecchia. Much waiting before we were allowed to land; and again much waiting for the clumsy process of "visiting" our luggage. I was amused while sitting at the *Dogana*, where almost every one was cross and busy, to see a dog making his way quietly out with a bone in his mouth.

Getting into our railway carriage, our *vis-à-vis*— a stout, amiable, intelligent Livornian, with his wife and son, named Dubreux — exclaimed, "Ç'en est fini d'un peuple qui n'est pas capable de changer une bêtise comme ça!" George got into pleasant talk with him, and his son, about Edinburgh and the scientific men there — the son having been there for some time in order to go through a course of practical science. The father was a naturalist— an entomologist, I think.

It was an interesting journey from Civita Vecchia to Rome: at first a scene of rough, hilly character, then a vast plain, frequently marshy, crowded with asphodels, inhabited by buffaloes; here and there a falcon or other slow large-winged bird floating and alighting. Italy, 1860.

At last we came in sight of Rome, but there was nothing imposing to be seen. The chief object was what I afterwards knew to be one of the aqueducts, but which I then, in the vagueness of my conceptions, guessed to be the ruins of baths. The railway station where we alighted looked remote and countrified: only the omnibuses and one family carriage were waiting, so that we were obliged to take our chance in one of the omnibuses—that is, the chance of finding no place left for us in the hotels. And so it was. Every one wanted to go to the Hotel d'Angleterre, and every one was disappointed. We, at last, by help of some fellow-travellers, got a small room *au troisième* at the Hotel d'Amérique; and as soon as that business was settled we walked out to look at Rome—not without a rather heavy load of disappointment on our minds from the vision we had of it from the omnibus windows. A weary length of dirty, uninteresting streets had brought us within sight of the dome of St Peter's, which was not impressive, seen in a peeping, makeshift manner, just rising above the houses; and the

Italy, 1860. Castle of St Angelo seemed but a shabby likeness of the engravings. Not one iota had I seen that corresponded with my preconceptions.

Our hotel was in the Strada Babuino, which leads directly from the Piazza del Popolo to the Piazza di Spagna. We went to the latter for our first walk, and, arriving opposite the high broad flights of stone steps which lead up to the Trinità di Monte, stopped for the first time with a sense that here was something not quite common and ugly. But I think we got hardly any farther, that evening, than the tall column at the end of the Piazza, which celebrates the final settlement by Pius IX. of the Virgin's Immaculate Conception. Oh yes; I think we wandered farther among narrow and ugly streets, and came into our hotel again still with some dejection at the probable relation our "Rome visited" was to bear to our "Rome unvisited."

Discontented with our little room at an extravagant height of stairs and price, we found and took lodgings the next day in the Corso opposite San Carlo, with a well-mannered Frenchman named Peureux and his little dark Italian wife—and so felt ourselves settled for a month. By this time we were in better spirits; for in the morning we had been to the Capitol (Campidoglio, the modern variant for Capitolium), had ascended the tower, and had driven to the Coliseum. The scene, looking along the Forum to the Arch of Titus, resembled strongly that mixture of ruined grandeur with modern life which I had always had in my imagination at the mention of Rome. The approach to the Capitol from the opposite side is also impressive: on the right hand the broad steep flight of steps leading up to the Church and Monastery of Ara Cœli, placed, some say, on the site of the Arx; in the front a less steep flight of steps *à cordon* leading to that lower, flatter portion of the hill which was called the *Intermontium*, and which now forms a sort of piazza, with the equestrian statue of Marcus Aurelius in the centre, and on three sides buildings designed, or rather modified, by Michael Angelo—on the left the Muséum, on the right the Museo dei Conservatori, and, on the side opposite the steps, the building devoted to public offices (Palazzo dei Senatori), in the centre of which stands the tower. On each hand at the summit of the steps are the two Colossi, less celebrated but hardly less imposing in their calm grandeur than the Colossi of the Quirinal. They are strangely streaked and disfigured by the black-

Italy, 1860. ening weather; but their large-eyed, mild might, gives one a thrill of awe, half like what might have been felt by the men of old who saw the divine twins watering their steeds when they brought the news of victory.

Perhaps the world can hardly offer a more interesting outlook than that from the tower of the Capitol. The eye leaps first to the mountains that bound the Campagna—the Sabine and Alban hills and the solitary Soracte farther on to the left. Then wandering back across the Campagna, it searches for the Sister hills, hardly distinguishable now as hills. The Palatine is conspicuous enough, marked by the ruins of the Palace of the Cæsars, and rising up beyond the extremity of the Forum. And now, once resting on the Forum, the eye will not readily quit the long area that begins with the Clivus Capitolinus and extends to the Coliseum—an area that was once the very focus of the world. The Campo Vaccino, the site probably of the Comitium, was this first morning covered with carts and animals, mingling a simple form of actual life with those signs of the highly artificial life that had been crowded here in ages gone by: the three Corinthian pillars at the extremity of the Forum, said to have belonged to the Temple of Jupiter Stator; the grand temple of Antoninus and Faustina; the white arch of Titus; the Basilica of Constantine; the temple built by Adrian, with its great broken granite columns scattered around on the green rising ground; the huge arc of the Coliseum and the arch of Constantine. Italy, 1860.

The scene of these great relics remained our favourite haunt during our stay at Rome; and one day near the end of it we entered the enclosure of the Clivus Capitolinus and the excavated space of the Forum. The ruins on the Clivus—the façade of massive columns on the right, called the temple of Vespasian; the two Corinthian columns, called the temple of Saturn, in the centre, and the arch of Septimius Severus on the left—have their rich colour set off by the luxuriant green, clothing the lower masonry, which formed the foundations of the crowded buildings on this narrow space, and as a background to them all, the rough solidity of the ancient wall forming the back of the central building on the Intermontium, and regarded as one of the few remains of Republican constructions. On either hand, at another angle from the arch, the ancient road forming the double ascent of the Clivus is seen firm and level with its great blocks

Italy, 1860. of pavement. The arch of Septimius Severus is particularly rich in colour; and the poorly executed bas-reliefs of military groups still look out in grotesque completeness of attitude and expression, even on the sides exposed to the weather. From the Clivus, a passage, underneath the present road, leads into the Forum, whose immense, pinkish, granite columns lie on the weather-worn white marble pavement. The column of Phocas, with its base no longer "buried," stands at the extreme corner nearest the Clivus; and the three elegant columns of the temple (say some) of Jupiter Stator, mark the opposite extremity: between lie traces, utterly confused to all but erudite eyes, of marble steps and of pedestals stripped of their marble.

Let me see what I most delighted in, in Rome. Certainly this drive from the Clivus to the Coliseum was, from first to last, one of the chief things; but there are many objects and many impressions of various kinds which I can reckon up as of almost equal interest: the Coliseum itself, with the view from it; the drive along the Appian Way to the tomb of Cecilia Metella, and the view from thence of the Campagna bridged by the aqueduct: the baths of Titus, with the remnants of their arabesques, seen by the light of torches, in the now damp and gloomy spaces; the glimpse of the Tarpeian rock, with its growth of cactus and rough herbage; the grand bare arch brickwork of the Palace of the Cæsars rising in huge masses on the Palatine; the theatre of Marcellus bursting suddenly into view from among the crowded mean houses of the modern city, and still more the temple of Minerva and temple of Nerva, also set in the crowded city of the present; and the exterior of the Pantheon, if it were not marred by the Papal belfries,—these are the traces of ancient Rome that have left the strongest image of themselves in my mind. I ought not to leave out Trajan's column, and the forum in which it stands; though the severe cold tint of the grey granite columns, or fragments of columns, gave this forum rather a dreary effect to me. For vastness there is perhaps nothing more impressive in Rome than the Baths of Caracalla, except the Coliseum; and I remember that it was amongst them that I first noticed the lovely effect of the giant fennel, luxuriant among the crumbling brickwork. Italy, 1860.

Among the ancient sculptures, I think I must place on a level the Apollo, the Dying Gladiator, and the Lateran Antinous: they affected me equally in different ways. After these I delighted in the

Italy, 1860. Venus of the Capitol, and the Kissing Children in the same room; the Sophocles at the Lateran Museum; the Nile; the black laughing Centaur at the Capitol; the Laughing Faun in the Vatican; and the *Sauroktonos,* or Boy with the Lizard, and the sitting statue called Menander. The Faun of Praxiteles, and the old Faun with the infant Bacchus, I had already seen at Munich, else I should have mentioned them among my first favourites. Perhaps the greatest treat we had at the Vatican was the sight of a few statues, including the Apollo, by torchlight—all the more impressive because it was our first sight of the Vatican. Even the mere hurrying along the vast halls, with the fitful torchlight falling on the innumerable statues, and busts, and bas-reliefs, and sarcophagi, would have left a sense of awe at these crowded silent forms which have the solemnity of suddenly arrested life. Wonderfully grand these halls of the Vatican are; and there is but one complaint to be made against the home provided for this richest collection of antiquities—it is, that there is no historical arrangement of them, and no catalogue. The system of classification is based on the history of their collection by the different Popes, so that for every other purpose but that of securing to each

Pope his share of glory, it is a system of helter-skelter. Italy, 1860.

Of Christian Rome, St Peter's is, of course, the supreme wonder. The piazza, with Bernini's colonnades, and the gradual slope upward to the mighty temple, gave me always a sense of having entered some millennial new Jerusalem, where all small and shabby things were unknown. But the exterior of the cathedral itself is even ugly; it causes a constant irritation by its partial concealment of the dome. The first impression from the interior was perhaps at a higher pitch than any subsequent impression either of its beauty or vastness; but then, on later visits, the lovely marble, which has a tone at once subdued and warm, was half-covered with hideous red drapery. There is hardly any detail one cares to dwell on in St Peter's. It is interesting, for once, to look at the mosaic altar-pieces, some of which render with marvellous success such famous pictures as the Transfiguration, the Communion of St Jerome, and the Entombment or Disentombment of St Petronilla. And some of the monuments are worth looking at more than once, the chief glory of that kind being Canova's Lions. I was pleased one day to watch a group of poor people looking with an admiration that had a

Italy, 1860. half-childish terror in it, at the sleeping lion, and with a sort of daring air thrusting their fingers against the teeth of the waking "mane-bearer."

We ascended the dome near the end of our stay, but the cloudy horizon was not friendly to our distant view, and Rome itself is ugly to a bird's-eye contemplation. The chief interest of the ascent was the vivid realisation it gave of the building's enormous size, and after that the sight of the inner courts and garden of the Vatican.

Our most beautiful view of Rome and the Campagna was one we had much earlier in our stay, before the snow had vanished from the mountains; it was from the terrace of the Villa Pamfili Doria.

Of smaller churches, I remember especially Santa Maria degli Angeli, a church formed by Michael Angelo, by additions to the grand hall in the Baths of Diocletian—the only remaining hall of ancient Rome; and the Church of San Clemente, where there is a chapel painted by Masaccio, as well as a perfect specimen of the ancient enclosure near the tribune, called the presbytery, with the *ambones* or pulpits from which the lessons and gospel were read. Santa Maria Maggiore is an exquisitely beautiful basilica, rich in marbles from a pagan temple; and the reconstructed San Paolo fuori le

Mura is a wonder of wealth and beauty, with its lines of white marble columns—if one could possibly look with pleasure at such a perverted appliance of money and labour as a church built in an unhealthy solitude. After St Peter's, however, the next great monument of Christian art is the Sistine Chapel; but since I care for the chapel solely for the sake of its ceiling, I ought rather to number it among my favourite paintings than among the most memorable buildings. Certainly this ceiling of Michael Angelo's is the most wonderful fresco in the world. After it come Raphael's "School of Athens" and "Triumph of Galatea," so far as Rome is concerned. Among oil-paintings there, I like best the Madonna di Foligno, for the sake of the cherub who is standing and looking upward; the Perugino also, in the Vatican, and the pretty Sassoferrato, with the clouds budding angels; at the Barberini Palace, Beatrice Cenci, and Una Schiava, by Titian; at the Sciarra Palace, the Joueurs de Violon, by Raphael, another of Titian's golden-haired women, and a sweet Madonna and Child with a bird, by Fra Bartolomeo; at the Borghese Palace, Domenichino's Chase, the Entombment, by Raphael, and the Three Ages—a copy of Titian, by Sassoferrato. Italy, 1860.

Italy, 1860. We should have regretted entirely our efforts to get to Rome during the Holy Week, instead of making Florence our first resting-place, if we had not had the compensation for wearisome, empty ceremonies and closed museums in the wonderful spectacle of the illumination of St Peter's. That, really, is a thing so wondrous, so magically beautiful, that one can't find in one's heart to say it is not worth doing. I remember well the first glimpse we had, as we drove out towards it, of the outline of the dome like a new constellation on the black sky. I thought *that* was the final illumination, and was regretting our tardy arrival, from the *détour* we had to make, when, as our carriage stopped in front of the cathedral, the great bell sounded, and in an instant the grand illumination flashed out and turned the outline of stars into a palace of gold. Venus looked on palely.

One of the finest positions in Rome is the Monte Cavallo (the Quirinal), the site of the Pope's palace, and of the fountain against which are placed the two Colossi — the Castor and Pollux, ascribed, after a lax method of affiliation, to Phidias and Praxiteles. Standing near this fountain, one has a real sense of being on a hill,—city and distant ridge stretching below. Close by is the Palazzo Rospigliosi, where we went to see Guido's Aurora. Italy, 1860.

Another spot where I was struck with the view of modern Rome (and *that* happened rarely) was at San Pietro in Vincoli, on the Esquiline, where we went to see Michael Angelo's Moses. Turning round before one enters the church, a palm-tree in the high foreground relieves very picturesquely the view of the lower distance. The Moses did not affect me agreeably: both the attitude and the expression of the face seemed to me, in that one visit, to have an exaggeration that strained after effect without reaching it. The failure seemed to me of this kind:—Moses was an angry man trying to frighten the people by his mien, instead of being rapt by his anger, and terrible without self-consciousness. To look at the statue of Christ, after the other works of Michael Angelo at Rome, was a surprise; in this the fault seems to incline slightly to the namby-pamby. The Pietà in St Peter's has real tenderness in it.

The visit to the Farnesina was one of the most interesting among our visits to Roman palaces. It is here that Raphael painted the "Triumph of Galatea," and here this wonderful fresco is still bright upon the wall. In the same room is a colossal head,

Italy, 1860. drawn by Michael Angelo with a bit of charcoal, by way of *carte-de-visite,* one day that he called on Daniele di Volterra, who was painting detestably in this room, and happened to be absent. In the entrance-hall, preceding the Galatea room, are the frescoes by Raphael representing the story of Cupid and Psyche; but we did not linger long to look at them, as they disappointed us.

We visited only four artists' studios in Rome: Gibson's, the sculptor; Frey's, the landscape painter; Riedel's, genre painter, and Overbeck's. Gibson's was entirely disappointing to me, so far as his own sculptures are concerned: except the Cacciatore, which he sent to the Great Exhibition, I could see nothing but feeble imitations of the antique—no spontaneity and no vigour. Miss Hosmer's Beatrice Cenci is a pleasing and new conception; and her little Puck, a bit of humour that one would like to have if one were a grand seigneur.

Frey is a very meritorious landscape painter—finished in execution and poetic in feeling. His Egyptian scenes—the Simoon, the Pair in the Light of Sunset, and the Island of Philæ, are memorable pictures; so is the View of Athens, with its blue island-studded sea. Riedel interested us greatly with his account of the coincidence between the views of light and colours at which he had arrived through his artistic experience, and Goethe's theory of colours, with which he became acquainted only after he had thought of putting his own ideas into shape for publication. He says the majority of painters continue their work when the sun shines from the north—they paint with *blue* light.

But it was our visit to Overbeck that we were most pleased not to have missed. The man himself is more interesting than his pictures: a benevolent calm, and quiet conviction, breathes from his person and manners. He has a thin, rather high-nosed face, with long grey hair, set off by a maroon velvet cap, and a grey scarf over his shoulders. Some of his cartoons pleased me: one large one of our Saviour passing from the midst of the throng, who were going to cast Him from the brow of the hill at Capernaum—one foot resting on a cloud borne up by cherubs; and some smaller round cartoons representing the Parable of the Ten Virgins, and applying it to the function of the artist.

We drove about a great deal in Rome, but were rather afflicted in our drives by the unending walls that enclose everything like a garden, even outside the city gates. First among our charming drives

Italy, 1860. was that to the Villa Pamfili Doria—a place which has the beauties of an English park and gardens, with views such as no English park can show; not to speak of the Columbarium or ancient Roman burying-place, which has been disinterred in the grounds. The compactest of all burying-places must these Columbaria be: little pigeon-holes, tier above tier, for the small urns containing the ashes of the dead. In this one, traces of peacocks and other figures in fresco, ornamenting the divisions between the rows, are still visible. We sat down in the sunshine by the side of the water, which is made to fall in a cascade in the grounds fronting the house, and then spreads out into a considerable breadth of mirror for the plantation on the slope which runs along one side of it. On the opposite side is a broad grassy walk, and here we sat on some blocks of stone, watching the little green lizards. Then we walked on up the slope on the other side, and through a grove of weird ilexes, and across a plantation of tall pines, where we saw the mountains in the far distance. A beautiful spot! We ought to have gone there again.

Another drive was to the Villa Albani, where, again, the view is grand. The precious sculptures once there are all at Munich now; and the most remarkable remnants of the collection are the bas-relief of Antinous, and the Æsop. The Antinous is the least beautiful of all the representations of that sad loveliness that I have seen — be it said in spite of Winckelmann: attitude and face are strongly Egyptian. In an outside pavilion in the garden were some interesting examples of Greek masks. Italy, 1860.

Our journey to Frascati by railway was fortunate. The day was fine, except, indeed, for the half hour that we were on the heights of Tusculum, and longed for a clear horizon. But the weather was so generally gloomy during our stay in Rome, that we were "thankful for small mercies" in the way of sunshine. I enjoyed greatly our excursion up the hill on donkey-back to the ruins of Tusculum —in spite of our loquacious guide, who exasperated George. The sight of the Campagna on one side: and of Mount Algidus, with its snow-capped fellows, and Mount Albano, with Rocca di Papa on its side, and Castel Gandolfo below on the other side, was worth the trouble: to say nothing of the little theatre, which was the most perfect example of an ancient theatre I had then seen in that pre-Pompeian period of my travels. After lunching at Frascati, we strolled out to the Villa Aldobrandini,

Italy, 1860. and enjoyed a brighter view of the Campagna in the afternoon sunlight. Then we lingered in a little croft enclosed by plantations, and enjoyed this familiar-looking bit of grass with wild flowers perhaps more, even, than the greatest novelties. There are fine plantations on the hill behind the villa, and there we wandered till it was time to go back to the railway. A literally grotesque thing in these plantations is the opening of a grotto in the hill-side, cut in the form of a huge Greek comic mask. It was a lovely walk from the town downward to the railway station—between the olive-clad slopes looking toward the illimitable plain. Our best view of the aqueducts was on this journey, but it was the tantalising sort of view one gets from a railway carriage.

Our excursion to Tivoli, reserved till nearly the end of our stay, happened on one of those cruel seductive days that smile upon you at five o'clock in the morning, to become cold and cloudy at eight, and resolutely rainy at ten. And so we ascended the hill through the vast venerable olive grove, thinking what would be the effect of sunshine among those grey fantastically twisted trunks and boughs; and paddled along the wet streets under umbrellas to look at the Temple of the Sibyl, and to descend the ravine of the waterfalls. Yet it was enjoyable; for the rain was not dense enough to shroud the near view of rock and foliage. We looked for the first time at a rock of travertine, with its curious petrified vegetable forms; and lower down at a mighty cavern, under which the smaller cascade rushes—an awful hollow in the midst of huge rocky masses. But—rain, rain, rain! No possibility of seeing the Villa of Hadrian, chief wonder of Tivoli: and so we had our carriage covered up, and turned homeward in despair. Italy, 1860.

The last week of our stay we went for the first time to the picture-gallery of the Capitol, where we saw the famous Guercino—the "Entombment of Petronilla"—which we had already seen in mosaic at St Peter's. It is a stupendous piece of painting, about which one's only feeling is, that it might as well have been left undone. More interesting is the portrait of Michael Angelo by himself—a deeply melancholy face. And there is also a picture of a Bishop by Giovanni Bellini, which arrested us a long while. After these, I remember most distinctly Veronese's Europa, superior to that we afterwards saw at Venice; a delicious mythological Poussin, all light and joy; and a Sebastian by Guido, ex-

Italy, 1860. ceptionally beautiful among the many detestable things of his in this gallery.

The Lateran Museum, also, was a sight we had neglected till this last week, though it turned out to be one of the most memorable. In the classical museum are the great Antinous, a Bacchus, and the Sophocles; besides a number of other remains of high interest, especially in the department of architectural decoration. In the museum of Christian antiquities, there are, besides sculptures, copies of the frescoes in the Catacombs—invaluable as a record of those perishable remains. If we ever go to Rome again, the Lateran Museum will be one of the first places I shall wish to revisit.

We saw the Catacombs of St Calixtus on the Appian Way—the long dark passages, with great oblong hollows in the rock for the bodies long since crumbled, and the one or two openings out of the passages into a rather wider space, called chapels, but no indication of paintings or other detail—our monkish guide being an old man, who spoke with an indistinct grunt that would not have enlightened us if we had asked any questions. In the church through which we entered there is a strangely barbarous reclining statue of St Sebastian, with arrows sticking all over it.

A spot that touched me deeply was Shelley's grave. The English cemetery in which he lies is the most attractive burying-place I have seen. It lies against the old city walls, close to the Porta San Paolo and the pyramid of Caius Cestius—one of the quietest spots of old Rome. And there, under the shadow of the old walls on one side, and cypresses on the other, lies the *Cor cordium*, for ever at rest from the unloving cavillers of this world, whether or not he may have entered on other purifying struggles in some world unseen by us. The grave of Keats lies far off from Shelley's, unshaded by wall or trees. It is painful to look upon, because of the inscription on the stone, which seems to make him still speak in bitterness from his grave.[1] Italy, 1860.

A wet day for the first time since we left Paris! That assists our consciences considerably in urging us to write our letters on this fourth day at Rome, for I will not pretend that writing a letter, even to you, can be anything more alluring than a duty when there is a blue sky over the Coliseum and the Arch of Constantine, and all the other marvels of this marvellous place. Since our arrival in the middle of Sunday, I have been gradually rising from Letter to Mrs Congreve, 4th April 1860.

1 "Here lies one whose name was writ in water."

Letter to Mrs Congreve, 4th April 1860.

the depth of disappointment to an intoxication of delight; and that makes me wish to do for you what no one ever did for me—warn you that you must expect no grand impression on your first entrance into Rome, at least if you enter it from Civita Vecchia. My heart sank, as it would if you behaved shabbily to me, when I looked through the windows of the omnibus as it passed through street after street of ugly modern Rome, and in that mood the dome of St Peter's and the Castle of St Angelo—the only grand objects on our way—could only look disappointing to me. I believe the impression on entering from the Naples side is quite different: there, one must get a glimpse of the broken grandeur and Renaissance splendour that one associates with the word "Rome." So keep up your spirits in the omnibus when your turn comes, and believe that you will mount the Capitol the next morning, as we did, and look out on the Forum and the Coliseum, far on to the Alban mountains, with snowy Apennines behind them, and feel—what I leave you to imagine, because the rain has left off, and my husband commands me to put on my bonnet. (Two hours later.) Can you believe that I have not had a headache since we set out? But I would willingly have endured more than one to be less anxious than I am about Mr Lewes's health. Now that we are just come in from our walk to the Pantheon, he is obliged to lie down with terrible oppression of the head; and since we have been in Rome he has been nearly deaf on one side. That is the dark "crow that flies in heaven's sweetest air" just now: everything else in our circumstances here is perfect. We are glad to have been driven into apartments, instead of remaining at the hotel as we had intended; for we enjoy the abundance of room and the quiet that belong to this mode of life, and we get our cooking and all other comforts in perfection at little more than a third of the hotel prices. Most of the visitors to Rome this season seem to come only for a short stay, and as apartments can't be taken for less than a month, the hotels are full and the lodgings are empty. Extremely unpleasant for the people who have lodgings to let, but very convenient for us, since we get excellent rooms in a good situation for a moderate price. We have a good little landlady, who can speak nothing but Italian, so that she serves as a *parlatrice* for us, and awakens our memory of Italian dialogue—a memory which consists chiefly of recollecting Italian words without knowing their meaning, and English words without knowing the Italian for them.

Letter to Mrs Congreve, 4th April 1860.

Letter to Mrs Congreve, 4th April 1860.

I shall tell you nothing of what we have seen. Have you not a husband who has seen it all, and can tell you much better? Except, perhaps, one sight which might have had some interest for him, namely, Count Cavour, who was waiting with other eminences at the Turin station to receive the Prince de Carignan, the new Viceroy of Tuscany. A really pleasant sight—not the Prince, who is a large stout "moustache," squeezed in at the waist with a gold belt, looking like one of those dressed-up personages who are among the chessmen that the Cavours of the world play their game with. The pleasant sight was Count Cavour, in plainest dress, with a head full of power, mingled with *bonhomie.* We had several fellow-travellers who belonged to Savoy, and were full of chagrin at the prospect of the French annexation. Our most agreeable companion was a Baron de Magliano, a Neapolitan who has married a French wife with a large fortune, and has been living in France for years, but has now left his wife and children behind for the sake of entering the Sardinian army, and, if possible, helping to turn out the Neapolitan Bourbons. I feel some stirrings of the insurrectionary spirit myself when I see the red pantaloons at every turn in the streets of Rome. I suppose Mrs Browning could explain to me that this is part of the great idea nourished in the soul of the modern saviour Louis Napoleon, and that for the French to impose a hateful government on the Romans is the only proper sequence to the story of the French Revolution.

Letter to Mrs Congreve, 4th April 1860.

Oh, the beautiful men and women and children here! Such wonderful babies with wise eyes!—such grand-featured mothers nursing them! As one drives along the streets sometimes, one sees a madonna and child at every third or fourth upper window; and on Monday a little crippled girl seated at the door of a church looked up at us with a face full of such pathetic sweetness and beauty, that I think it can hardly leave me again. Yesterday we went to see dear Shelley's tomb, and it was like a personal consolation to me to see that simple outward sign that he is at rest, where no hatred can ever reach him again. Poor Keats's tombstone, with that despairing bitter inscription, is almost as painful to think of as Swift's.

And what have you been doing, being, or suffering in these long twelve days? While we were standing with weary impatience in the custom-house at Civita Vecchia, Mr Congreve was delivering his third lecture, and you were listening. And what else? *Friday.* Since I wrote my letter we

Letter to Mrs Congreve, 4th April 1860.

have not been able to get near the post-office. Yesterday was taken up with seeing ceremonies, or rather with waiting for them. I knelt down to receive the Pope's blessing, remembering what Pius VII. said to the soldier—that he would never be the worse for the blessing of an old man. But altogether, these ceremonies are a melancholy, hollow business, and we regret bitterly that the Holy Week has taken up our time from better things. I have a cold and headache this morning, and in other ways am not conscious of improvement from the Pope's blessing. I may comfort myself with thinking that the King of Sardinia is none the worse for the Pope's curse. It is farcical enough that the excommunication is posted up at the Church of St John Lateran, out of everybody's way, and yet there are police to guard it.

Italy, 1860.

How much more I have to write about Rome! How I should like to linger over every particular object that has left an image in my memory! But here I am only to give a hasty sketch of what we saw and did at each place at which we paused in our three months' life in Italy.

It was on the 29th of April that we left Rome, and on the morning of the 30th we arrived at Naples—under a rainy sky, alas! but not so rainy as to prevent our feeling the beauty of the city and bay, and declaring it to surpass all places we had seen before. The weather cleared up soon after our arrival at the Hotel des Étrangers, and after a few days it became brilliant, showing us the blue sea, the purple mountains, and bright city, in which we had almost disbelieved as we saw them in the pictures. Hardly anything can be more lovely than Naples seen from Posilipo under a blue sky,—the irregular outline with which the town meets the sea, jutting out in picturesque masses, then lifted up high on a basis of rock, with the grand castle of St Elmo and the monastery on the central height crowning all the rest; the graceful outline of purple Vesuvius rising beyond the Molo, and the line of deeply indented mountains carrying the eye along to the Cape of Sorrento; and last of all, Capri sleeping between sea and sky in the distance. Crossing the promontory of Posilipo, another wonderful scene presents itself: white Nisida on its island rock; the sweep of bay towards Pozzuoli; beyond that, in fainter colours of farther distance, the Cape of Miseno, and the peaks of Ischia. Italy, 1860.

Our first expedition was to Pozzuoli and Miseno, on a bright warm day, with a slip-shod Neapolitan driver, whom I christened Baboon, and who acted

Italy, 1860. as our charioteer throughout our stay at Naples. Beyond picturesque Pozzuoli, jutting out with precipitous piles of building into the sea, lies Baiæ. Here we halted to look at a great circular temple, where there was a wonderful echo that made whispers circulate and become loud on the opposite side to that on which they were uttered. Here, for our amusement, a young maiden and a little old man danced to the sound of a tambourine and fife. On our way to Baiæ we had stopped to see the Lake Avernus, no longer terrible to behold, and the amphitheatre of Cumæ, now grown over with greensward, and fringed with garden stuff.

From Baiæ we went to Miseno—the Misenum where Pliny was stationed with the fleet—and looked out from the promontory on the lovely isles of Ischia and Procida. On the approach to this promontory lies the Piscina Mirabilis, one of the most striking remains of Roman building. It is a great reservoir, into which one may now descend dryshod and look up at the lofty arches festooned with delicate plants, while the sunlight shoots aslant through the openings above. It was on this drive coming back towards Pozzuoli that we saw the Mesembryanthemum in its greatest luxuriance—a star of amethyst with its golden tassel in the centre. The amphitheatre at Pozzuoli is the most interesting in Italy after the Coliseum. The seats are in excellent preservation, and the subterranean structures for water and for the introduction of wild beasts are unique. The temple of Jupiter Serapis is another remarkable ruin, made more peculiar by the intrusion of the water, which makes the central structure, with its great columns an island to be approached by a plank bridge. Italy, 1860.

In the views from Capo di Monte—the king's summer residence—and from St Elmo, one enjoys not only the view towards the sea, but the wide green plain sprinkled with houses and studded with small towns or villages, bounded on the one hand by Vesuvius, and shut in, in every other direction, by the nearer heights close upon Naples, or by the sublimer heights of the distant Apennines. We had the view from St Elmo on a clear, breezy afternoon, in company with a Frenchman and his wife, come from Rome with his family after a two years' residence there—worth remembering for the pretty bondage the brusque, stern, thin father was under to the tiny, sickly-looking boy.

It was a grand drive up to Capo di Monte—between rich plantations, with glimpses, as we went up, of the city lying in picturesque irregu-

Italy, 1860. larity below; and as we went down in the other direction, views of distant mountain rising above some pretty accident of roof or groups of trees in the foreground.

One day we went, from this drive, along the Poggio Reale to the cemetery — the most ambitious burying-place I ever saw, with building after building of elaborate architecture, serving as tombs to various *Arci-confraternità*, as well as to private families, all set in the midst of well-kept gardens. The humblest kind of tombs there, were long niches for coffins in a wall bordering the carriage-road, which are simply built up when the coffin is once in—the inscription being added on this final bit of masonry. The lines of lofty sepulchres suggested to one very vividly the probable appearance of the Appian Way when the old Roman tombs were in all their glory.

Our first visit to the Museo Borbonico was devoted to the sculpture, of which there is a precious collection. Of the famous Balbi family, found at Herculaneum, the mother, in grand drapery, wound round her head and body, is the most unforgettable —a really grand woman of fifty, with firm mouth and knitted brow, yet not unbenignant. Farther on in this transverse hall is a Young Faun with the infant Bacchus—a different conception altogether from the fine Munich statue, but delicious for humour and geniality. Then there is the Aristides —more real and speaking and easy in attitude even than the Sophocles at Rome. Opposite is a lovely Antinous, in no mythological character, but in simple, melancholy beauty. In the centre of the deep recess, in front of which these statues are placed, is the colossal Flora, who holds up her thin dress in too finicking a style for a colossal goddess; and on the floor—to be seen by ascending a platform—is the precious, great mosaic representing the Battle of the Issus, found at Pompeii. It is full of spirit; the *ordonnance* of the figures is very much after the same style as in the ancient bas-reliefs, and the colours are still vivid enough for us to have a just idea of the effect. In the halls on each side of this central one there are various Bacchuses and Apollos, Atlas groaning under the weight of the Globe, the Farnese Hercules, the Toro Farnese, and amongst other things less memorable, a glorious Head of Jupiter. Italy, 1860.

The bronzes here are even more interesting than the marbles. Among them there is Mercury Resting, the Sleeping Faun, the little Dancing Faun, and the Drunken Faun snapping his fingers, of

Italy, 1860. which there is a marble copy at Munich, with the two remarkable Heads of Plato and Seneca.

But our greatest treat at the Museo Borbonico could only be enjoyed after our visit to Pompeii, where we went, unhappily, in the company of some Russians whose acquaintance G. had made at the *table d'hôte.* I hope I shall never forget the solemnity of our first entrance into that silent city, and the walk along the street of tombs. After seeing the principal houses, we went, as a proper climax, to the Forum, where, amongst the lines of pedestals and the ruins of temples and tribunal, we could see Vesuvius overlooking us; then to the two theatres, and finally to the amphitheatre.

This visit prepared us to enjoy the collection of *piccoli bronzi,* of paintings and mosaics, at the Museo. Several of the paintings have considerable positive merit. I remember particularly a large one of Orestes and Pylades, which in composition and general conception might have been a picture of yesterday. But the most impressive collection of remains found at Pompeii and Herculaneum is that of the ornaments, articles of food and domestic utensils, pieces of bread, loaves with the bakers' names on them, fruits, corn, various seeds, paste in the vessel, imperfectly mixed, linen just wrung in washing, eggs, oil consolidated in a glass bottle, wine mixed with the lava, and a piece of asbestos; gold lace, a lens, a lanthorn with sides of talc, gold ornaments of Etruscan character, patty-pans (!), moulds for cakes; ingenious portable cooking apparatus, urn for hot water, portable candelabrum, to be raised or lowered at will, bells, dice, theatre-checks, and endless objects that tell of our close kinship with those old Pompeians. In one of the rooms of this collection there are the Farnese cameos and engraved gems, some of them—especially of the latter—marvellously beautiful, complicated, and exquisitely minute in workmanship. I remember particularly one splendid yellow stone engraved with an elaborate composition of Apollo and his chariot and horses—a masterpiece of delicate form. Italy, 1860.

We left Rome a week ago, almost longing, at last, to come southward in search of sunshine. Every one likes to boast of peculiar experience, and we can boast of having gone to Rome in the very worst spring that has been known for the last twenty years. Here, at Naples, we have had some brilliant days, though the wind is still cold, and rain has often fallen heavily in the night. It is the very best change for us after Rome: there is Letter to Mrs Congreve, 5th May 1860.

Letter to Mrs Congreve, 5th May 1860.

comparatively little art to see, and there is nature in transcendent beauty. We both think it the most beautiful place in the world, and are sceptical about Constantinople, which has not had the advantage of having been seen by us. That is the fashion of travellers, as you know: for you must have been bored many times in your life by people who have insisted on it that you *must* go and see the thing *they* have seen—there is nothing like it. We shall bore you in that way, I daresay—so prepare yourself. Our plan at present is to spend the next week in seeing Pæstum, Amalfi, Castellamare, and Sorrento, and drinking in as much of this Southern beauty, in a quiet way, as our souls are capable of absorbing.

The calm blue sea, and the mountains sleeping in the afternoon light, as we have seen them to-day from the height of St Elmo, make one feel very passive and contemplative, and disinclined to bustle about in search of meaner sights. Yet I confess Pompeii, and the remains of Pompeian art and life in the Museum, have been impressive enough to rival the sea and sky. It is a thing never to be forgotten—that walk through the silent city of the past, and then the sight of utensils, and eatables, and ornaments, and half-washed linen, and hundreds of other traces of life so startlingly like our own in its minutest details, suddenly arrested by the fiery deluge. All that you will see some day, and with the advantage of younger eyes than mine. **Letter to Mrs Congreve, 5th May 1860.**

We expect to reach Florence (by steamboat, alas!) on the 17th, so that if you have the charity to write to me again, address to me there.

We thought the advance to eighteen in the number of hearers was very satisfactory, and rejoiced over it. The most solid comfort one can fall back upon is the thought that the business of one's life—the work at home after the holiday is done—is to help in some small nibbling way to reduce the sum of ignorance, degradation, and misery on the face of this beautiful earth. I am writing at night—Mr Lewes is already asleep, else he would say, "Send my kind regards to them all." We have often talked of you, and the thought of seeing you again makes the South Fields look brighter in our imagination than they could have looked from the dreariest part of the world if you had not been living in them.

The pictures at Naples are worth little: the Marriage of St Catherine, a small picture by Correggio; a Holy Family by Raphael, with a singularly fine St Ann, and Titian's Paul the Third, **Italy, 1860.**

Italy, 1860. are the only paintings I have registered very distinctly in all the large collection. The much-praised frescoes of the dome in a chapel of the Cathedral, and the oil-paintings over the altars, by Domenichino and Spagnoletto, produced no effect on me. Worth more than all these, are Giotto's frescoes in the choir of the little old Church of l'Incoronata, though these are not, I think, in Giotto's ripest manner, for they are inferior to his frescoes in the Santa Croce at Florence — more uniform in the type of face.

We went to a Sunday morning service at the Cathedral, and saw a detachment of silver busts of saints ranged around the tribune—Naples being famous for gold and silver sanctities.

When we had been a week at Naples, we set off in our carriage with Baboon on an expedition to Pæstum, arriving the first evening at Salerno—beautiful Salerno, with a bay as lovely, though in a different way, as the bay of Naples. It has a larger sweep, grander piles of rocky mountain on the north and north-east—then a stretch of low plain, the mountains receding—and finally, on the south, another line of mountain coast extending to the promontory of Sicosa.

From Salerno we started early in the morning

for Pæstum, with no alloy to the pleasure of the journey but the dust, which was capable of making a simoon under a high wind. For a long way we passed through a well-cultivated plain, the mountains on our left, and the sea on our right; but farther on came a swampy unenclosed space of great extent, inhabited by buffaloes, who lay in groups, comfortably wallowing in the muddy water, with their grand stupid heads protruding horizontally. Italy, 1860.

On approaching Pæstum, the first thing one catches sight of is the Temple of Vesta, which is not beautiful either for form or colour, so that we began to tremble lest disappointment were to be the harvest of our dusty journey. But the fear was soon displaced by almost rapturous admiration at the sight of the great Temple of Neptune—the finest thing, I verily believe, that we had yet seen in Italy. It has all the requisites to make a building impressive. First, *form.* What perfect satisfaction and repose for the eye in the calm repetition of those columns—in the proportions of height and length, of front and sides: the right thing is *found* —it is not being sought after in uneasy labour of detail or exaggeration. Next, *colour.* It is built of travertine, like the other two temples; but while

Italy, 1860. they have remained, for the most part, a cold grey, this Temple of Neptune has a rich, warm, pinkish brown, that seems to glow and deepen under one's eyes. Lastly, *position.* It stands on the rich plain, covered with long grass and flowers, in sight of the sea on one hand, and the sublime blue mountains on the other. Many plants caress the ruins: the acanthus is there, and I saw it in green life for the first time; but the majority of the plants on the floor, or bossing the architrave, are familiar to me as home flowers—purple mallows, snapdragons, pink hawkweeds, &c. On our way back we saw a herd of buffaloes clustered near a pond, and one of them was rolling himself in the water like a gentleman enjoying his bath.

The next day we went in the morning from Salerno to Amalfi. It is an unspeakably grand drive round the mighty rocks with the sea below; and Amalfi itself surpasses all imagination of a romantic site for a city that once made itself famous in the world. We stupidly neglected seeing the Cathedral, but we saw a macaroni mill and a paper mill from among the many that are turned by the rushing stream, which, with its precipitous course down the ravine, creates an immense water power; and we climbed up endless steps to the

Capuchin Monastery, to see nothing but a cavern where there are barbarous images, and a small cloister with double Gothic arches. Italy, 1860.

Our way back to La Cava gave us a repetition of the grand drive we had had in the morning by the coast, and beyond that an inland drive of much loveliness, through Claude-like scenes of mountain, trees, and meadows, with picturesque accidents of building, such as single, round towers on the heights. The valley beyond La Cava, in which our hotel lay, is of quite paradisaic beauty: a rich cultivated spot, with mountains behind and before—those in front varied by ancient buildings that a painter would have chosen to place there; and one of pyramidal shape, steep as an obelisk, is crowned by a monastery, famous for its library of precious MSS. and its archives. We arrived too late for everything except to see the shroud of mist gather and gradually envelop the mountains.

In the morning we set off, again in brightest weather, to Sorrento, coasting the opposite side of the promontory to that which we had passed along the day before, and having on our right hand Naples and the distant Posilipo. The coast on this side is less grand than on the Amalfi side; but it is more friendly as a place for residence. The most

Italy, 1860. charming spot on the way to Sorrento, to my thinking, is Vico, which I should even prefer to Sorrento, because there is no town to be traversed before entering the ravine and climbing the mountain in the background. But I will not undervalue Sorrento, with its orange groves embalming the air, its glorious sunsets over the sea, setting the grey olives aglow on the hills above us, its walks among the groves and vineyards out to the solitary coast. One day of our stay there we took donkeys and crossed the mountains to the opposite side of the promontory, and saw the Syren Isles—very palpable unmysterious bits of barren rock now. A great delight to me in all the excursions round about Naples was the high cultivation of the soil, and the sight of the vines, trained from elm to elm, above some other precious crop, carpeting the ground below. On our way back to Naples we visited the silent Pompeii again. That place had such a peculiar influence over me, that I could not even look toward the point where it lay on the plain below Vesuvius without a certain thrill.

Amidst much dust we arrived at Naples again on Sunday morning, to start by the steamboat for Leghorn on the following Tuesday. But before I quit Naples, I must remember the Grotto of Posilipo, a wonderful monument of ancient labour; Virgil's tomb, which repaid us for a steep ascent only by the view of the city and bay; and a villa on the way to Posilipo, with gardens gradually descending to the margin of the sea, where there is a collection of animals, both stuffed and alive. It was there we saw the flying fish with their lovely blue fins. Italy, 1860.

One day and night voyage to Civita Vecchia, and another day and night to Leghorn—wearisome to the flesh that suffers from nausea even on the summer sea! We had another look at dear Pisa under the blue sky, and then on to Florence, which, unlike Rome, looks inviting as one catches sight from the railway of its cupolas and towers and its embosoming hills—the greenest of hills, sprinkled everywhere with white villas. We took up our quarters at the Pension Suisse, and on the first evening we took the most agreeable drive to be had round Florence—the drive to Fiesole. It is in this view that the eye takes in the greatest extent of green billowy hills, besprinkled with white houses looking almost like flocks of sheep: the great silent uninhabited mountains lie chiefly behind; the plain of the Arno stretches far to the right. I think the view from Fiesole the most beautiful of all; but that from San Miniato, where we went the next

Italy, 1860. evening, has an interest of another kind, because here Florence lies much nearer below, and one can distinguish the various buildings more completely. It is the same with Bellosguardo in a still more marked degree. What a relief to the eye and the thought among the huddled roofs of a distant town to see towers and cupolas rising in abundant variety as they do at Florence! There is Brunelleschi's mighty dome, and close by it, with its lovely colours not entirely absorbed by distance, Giotto's incomparable campanile, beautiful as a jewel. Farther on, to the right, is the majestic tower of the Palazzo Vecchio, with the flag waving above it; then the elegant Badia and the Bargello close by; nearer to us the grand campanile of Santo Spirito, and that of Santa Croce; far away, on the left, the cupola of San Lorenzo, and the tower of Santa Maria Novella; and scattered far and near other cupolas and campaniles of more insignificant shape and history.

Even apart from its venerable historical glory, the exterior of the Duomo is pleasant to behold when the wretched unfinished *façade* is quite hidden. The soaring pinnacles over the doors are exquisite: so are the forms of the windows in the great semicircle of the apsis: and on the side where Giotto's campanile is placed, especially, the white marble has taken on so rich and deep a yellow, that the black bands cease to be felt as a fault. The entire view on this side, closed in by Giotto's tower, with its delicate pinkish marble, its delicate Gothic windows with twisted columns, and its tall lightness carrying the eye upward, in contrast with the mighty breadth of the dome, is a thing not easily to be forgotten. The Baptistery, with its paradisaic gates, is close by; but except in those gates, it has no exterior beauty. The interior is almost awful with its great dome covered with gigantic early mosaics — the pale large-eyed Christ surrounded by images of Paradise and Perdition. The interior of the Cathedral is comparatively poor and bare; but it has one great beauty—its coloured lanceolate windows. Behind the high altar is a piece of sculpture — the last under Michael Angelo's hand, intended for his own tomb, and left unfinished. It represents Joseph of Arimathea holding the body of Jesus, with Mary, his mother, on one side, and an apparently angelic form on the other. Joseph is a striking and real figure, with a hood over the head. Italy, 1860.

For external architecture it is the palaces, the old palaces of the fifteenth century, that one must

Italy, 1860. look at in the streets of Florence. One of the finest was just opposite our hotel,—the Palazzo Strozzi, built by Cronaca; perfect in its massiveness, with its iron cressets and rings, as if it had been built only last year. This is the palace that the Pitti was built to outvie (so tradition falsely pretends), and to have an inner court that would contain it. A wonderful union is that Pitti Palace, of cyclopean massiveness with stately regularity. Next to the Pitti, I think, comes the Palazzo Riccardi—the house of the Medici, for size and splendour. Then that unique Laurentian library, designed by Michael Angelo: the books ranged on desks in front of seats, so that the appearance of the library resembles that of a chapel with open pews of dark wood. The precious books are all chained to the desk; and here we saw old manuscripts of exquisite neatness, culminating in the Virgil of the fourth century and the Pandects, said to have been recovered from oblivion at Amalfi, but falsely so said, according to those who are more learned than tradition. Here, too, is a little chapel covered with remarkable frescoes by Benozzo Gozzoli.

Grander still, in another style, is the Palazzo Vecchio, with its unique *cortile*, where the pillars are embossed with arabesque and floral tracery, making a contrast in elaborate ornament with the large simplicity of the exterior building. Here there are precious little works in ivory by Benvenuto Cellini, and other small treasures of art and jewellery, preserved in cabinets in one of the great upper chambers, which are painted all over with frescoes, and have curious inlaid doors showing buildings or figures in wooden mosaic, such as is often seen in great beauty in the stalls of the churches. The great Council Chamber is ugly in its ornaments — frescoes and statues in bad taste all round it. Italy, 1860.

Orcagna's Loggia de' Lanzi is disappointing at the first glance, from its sombre, dirty colour; but its beauty grew upon me with longer contemplation. The pillars and groins are very graceful and chaste in ornamentation. Among the statues that are placed under it there is not one I could admire, unless it were the dead body of Ajax with the Greek soldier supporting it. Cellini's Perseus is fantastic. The Bargello, where we went to see Giotto's frescoes (in lamentable condition) was under repair, but I got glimpses of a wonderful inner court, with heraldic carvings and stone stairs and gallery.

Most of the churches in Florence are hideous

Italy, 1860. on the outside—piles of ribbed brickwork awaiting a coat of stone or stucco—looking like skinned animals. The most remarkable exception is Santa Maria Novella, which has an elaborate facing of black and white marble. Both this church and San Lorenzo were under repair in the interior, unfortunately for us; but we could enter Santa Maria so far as to see Orcagna's frescoes of Paradise and Hell. The Hell has been repainted, but the Paradise has not been maltreated in this way; and it is a splendid example of Orcagna's powers—far superior to his frescoes in the Campo Santo at Pisa. Some of the female forms on the lowest range are of exquisite grace. The splendid chapel in San Lorenzo, containing the tombs of the Medici, is ugly and heavy with all its precious marbles; and the world-famous statues of Michael Angelo on the tombs in another smaller chapel—the Notte, the Giorno, and the Crepuscolo—remained to us as affected and exaggerated in the original as in copies and casts.

The two churches we frequented most in Florence were Santa Croce and the Carmine. In this last are the great frescoes of Masaccio—chief among them the "Raising of the Dead Youth." In the other are Giotto's frescoes revealed from under the whitewash by which they were long covered, like those in the Bargello. Of these the best are the "Challenge to pass through the Fire" in the series representing the history of St Francis, and the rising of some saint (unknown to me) from his tomb, while Christ extends His arms to receive him above, and wondering venerators look on, on each side. There are large frescoes here of Taddeo Gaddi's also, but they are not good: one sees in him a pupil of Giotto, and nothing more. Besides the frescoes, Santa Croce has its tombs to attract a repeated visit: the tombs of Michael Angelo, Dante, Alfieri, and Macchiavelli. Even those tombs of the unknown dead under our feet, with their effigies quite worn down to a mere outline, were not without their interest. I used to feel my heart swell a little at the sight of the inscription on Dante's tomb—"*Onorate l'altissimo poeta.*" Italy, 1860.

In the Church of the Trinità also there are valuable frescoes by the excellent Domenico Ghirlandajo, the master of Michael Angelo. They represent the history of St Francis, and happily the best of them is in the best light: it is the death of St Francis, and is full of natural feeling, with well-marked gradations from deepest sorrow to indifferent spectatorship.

Italy, 1860. The frescoes I cared for most in all Florence were the few of Fra Angelico's that a *donna* was allowed to see in the Convent of San Marco. In the Chapter-house, now used as a guard-room, is a large Crucifixion, with the inimitable group of the fainting mother, upheld by St John and the younger Mary, and clasped round by the kneeling Magdalene. The group of adoring, sorrowing saints on the right hand are admirable for earnest truthfulness of representation. The Christ in this fresco is not good, but there is a deeply impressive original crucified Christ outside in the cloisters: St Dominic is clasping the cross, and looking upward at the agonised Saviour, whose real, pale, calmly enduring face is quite unlike any other Christ I have seen.

I forgot to mention, at Santa Maria Novella, the chapel, which is painted with very remarkable frescoes by Simone Memmi and Taddeo Gaddi. The best of these frescoes is the one in which the Dominicans are represented by black and white dogs—*Domini canes.* The human groups have high merit for conception and life-likeness; and they are admirable studies of costume. At this church, too, in the sacristy, is the "Madonna della Stella,"[1] with an altar-step by Fra Angelico—speci-

[1] Now in cell No. 33 in the Museo di San Marco.

mens of his minuter painting in oil. The inner part of the frame is surrounded with his lovely angels, with their seraphic joy and flower-garden colouring. Italy, 1860.

Last of all the churches, we visited San Michele, which had been one of the most familiar to us on the outside, with its statues in niches, and its elaborate Gothic windows, designed by the genius of Orcagna. The great wonder of the interior is the shrine of white marble made to receive the miracle-working image which first caused the consecration of this mundane building, originally a corn-market. Surely this shrine is the most wonderful of all Orcagna's productions: for the beauty of the reliefs he deserves to be placed along with Nicolo Pisano, and for the exquisite Gothic design of the whole he is a compeer of Giotto.

For variety of treasures the Uffizi Gallery is preeminent among all public sights in Florence; but the variety is in some degree a cause of comparative unimpressiveness, pictures and statues being crowded together and destroying each other's effect. In statuary, it has the great Niobe group; the Venus de Medici; the Wrestlers; the admirable statue of the Knife-Sharpener, supposed to repre-

Italy, 1860. sent the flayer of Marsyas; the Apollino, and the Boy taking a Thorn out of his Foot; with numerous less remarkable antiques. And besides these, it has what the Vatican has not—a collection of early Italian sculpture, supreme among which is Giovanni di Bologna's Mercury.[1] Then there is a collection of precious drawings; and there is the cabinet of gems, quite alone in its fantastic, elaborate minuteness of workmanship in rarest materials; and there is another cabinet containing ivory sculptures, cameos, intaglios, and a superlatively fine Niello, as well as Raffaelle porcelain. The pictures here are multitudinous, and among them there is a generous proportion of utterly bad ones. In the entrance gallery, where the early paintings are, is a great Fra Angelico—a Madonna and Child—a triptych, the two side compartments containing very fine figures of saints, and the inner part of the central frame a series of unspeakably lovely angels.[2] Here I always paused with longing, trying to believe that a copyist there could make an imitation angel good enough to be worth buying. Among the other paintings that remain with me, after my visit to the Uffizi, are the portrait of Leonardo da Vinci, by himself;

[1] Now in the Museo Nazionale.

[2] Now in Sala Lorenzo Monaco, Uffizi.

the portrait of Dante, by Filippino Lippi;[1] the Herodias of Luini; Titian's Venus, in the Tribune; Raphael's Madonna and Child with the Bird; and the portrait falsely called the Fornarina; the two remarkable pictures by Ridolfo Ghirlandajo; and the Salutation by Albertinelli, which hangs opposite; the little prince in pink dress, with two recent teeth, in the next room, by Angelo Bronzino (No. 1155); the small picture of Christ in the Garden, by Lorenzo Credi; Titian's Woman with the Golden Hair, in the Venetian room; Leonardo's Medusa head; and Michael Angelo's ugly Holy Family:—these, at least, rise up on a rapid retrospect. Others are in the background; for example, Correggio's Madonna adoring the infant Christ in the Tribune.

For pictures, however, the Pitti Palace surpasses the Uffizi. Here the paintings are more choice and not less numerous. The "Madonna della Sedia" leaves me, with all its beauty, impressed only by the grave gaze of the Infant; but besides this there is another Madonna of Raphael — perhaps the most beautiful of all his earlier ones — the "Madonna del Granduca," which has the sweet grace

[1] The only portraits of Dante in the Uffizi are No. 1207, in the room opening out of the Tribune—by an unknown painter (Scuola Toscana); and No. 553, in the passage to the Pitti—also by an unknown painter.

Italy, 1860. and gentleness of its sisters without their sheep-like look. Andrea del Sarto is seen here in his highest glory of oil-painting. There are numerous large pictures of his—Assumptions and the like—of great technical merit; but better than all these I remember a Holy Family with a very fine St Ann, and the portraits of himself and his fatal auburn-haired wife. Of Fra Bartolomeo there is a Pietà of memorable expression,[1] a Madonna enthroned with saints, and his great St Mark. Of Titian, a Marriage of St Catherine of supreme beauty; a Magdalen, failing in expression; and an exquisite portrait of the same woman, who is represented as Venus at the Uffizi. There is a remarkable group of portraits by Rubens—himself, his brother, Lipsius, and Grotius—and a large landscape by him. The only picture of Veronese's that I remember here is a portrait of his wife when her beauty was gone. There is a remarkably fine sea piece by Salvator Rosa; a striking portrait of Aretino, and a portrait of Vesalius, by Titian; one of Inghirami by Raphael; a delicious rosy baby—future cardinal—lying in a silken bed;[2] a placid, contemplative young woman, with her finger be-

[1] No. 81. Pitti Gallery.

[2] No. 49, by Tiberio Titti. Pitti Gallery.

tween the leaves of a book, by Leonardo da Vinci;[1] a memorable portrait of Philip II. by Titian; a splendid Judith by Bronzino; a portrait of Rembrandt by himself, &c., &c. Italy, 1860.

Andrea del Sarto is seen to advantage at the Pitti Palace; but his *chef-d'œuvre* is a fresco, unhappily much worn—the "Madonna del Sacco"—in the cloister of the Annunziata.

For early Florentine paintings, the most interesting collection is that of the Accademia. Here we saw a Cimabue, which gave us the best idea of his superiority over the painters who went before him: it is a colossal Madonna enthroned. And on the same wall there is a colossal Madonna by Giotto, which is not only a demonstration that he surpassed his master, but that he had a clear vision of the noble in art. A delightful picture—very much restored, I fear—of the Adoration of the Magi made me acquainted with Gentile da Fabriano. The head of Joseph in this picture is masterly in the delicate rendering of the expression; the three kings are very beautiful in conception; and the attendant group, or rather crowd, shows a remarkable combination of realism with love of the beautiful and splendid.

[1] No. 140. Pitti Gallery.

Italy, 1860. There is a fine Domenico Ghirlandajo—the "Adoration of the Shepherds;" a fine Lippo Lippi; and an Assumption by Perugino, which I like well for its cherubs and angels, and for some of the adoring figures below. In the smaller room there is a lovely Pietà by Fra Angelico; and there is a portrait of Fra Angelico himself by another artist.

One of our drives at Florence, which I have not mentioned, was that to Galileo's Tower, which stands conspicuous on one of the hills close about the town. We ascended it for the sake of looking out over the plain from the same spot as the great man looked from, more than two centuries ago. His portrait is in the Pitti Palace—a grave man with an abbreviated nose, not unlike Mr Thomas Adolphus Trollope.

One fine day near the end of our stay we made an expedition to Siena—that fine old town built on an abrupt height overlooking a wide, wide plain. We drove about a couple of hours or more, and saw well the exterior of the place—the peculiar piazza or campo in the shape of a scallop-shell, with its large old Palazzo *publico*, the Porta Ovile and Porta Romana, the archbishop's palace, and the cemetery. Of the churches we saw only the Cathedral, the Chapel of John the

Baptist, and San Domenico. The cathedral has a highly elaborate Gothic façade, but the details of the upper part are unsatisfactory — a square window in the centre shocks the eye, and the gables are not slim and aspiring enough. The interior is full of interest: there is the unique pavement in a sort of marble Niello, presenting Raffaelesque designs by Boccafumi, carrying out the example of the older portions, which are very quaint in their drawing; there is a picture of high interest in the history of early art—a picture by Guido of Siena, who was rather earlier than Cimabue; fine carved stalls and screens in dark wood; and in an adjoining chapel a series of frescoes by Pinturicchio, to which Raphael is said to have contributed designs and workmanship, and wonderfully illuminated old choir-books. The Chapel of St John the Baptist has a remarkable Gothic façade, and a baptismal font inside, with reliefs wrought by Ghiberti and another Florentine artist. To San Domenico we went for the sake of seeing the famous Madonna by Guido da Siena: I think we held it superior to any Cimabue we had seen. There is a considerable collection of the Siennese artists at the Accademia, but the school had no great genius equal to Giotto to

Italy, 1860. lead it. The Three Graces—an antique to which Canova's modern triad bears a strong resemblance in attitude and style — are also at the Accademia.

An interesting visit we made at Florence was to Michael Angelo's house — Casa Buonarotti — in the Via Ghibellina. This street is striking and characteristic: the houses are all old, with broad eaves, and in some cases with an open upper storey, so that the roof forms a sort of pavilion supported on pillars. This is a feature one sees in many parts of Florence. Michael Angelo's house is preserved with great care by his descendants—only one could wish their care had not been shown in giving it entirely new furniture. However, the rooms are the same as those he occupied, and there are many relics of his presence there—his stick, his sword, and many of his drawings. In one room there is a very fine Titian of small size—the principal figure a woman fainting.

The Last Supper — a fresco believed to be by Raphael—is in a room at the Egyptian Museum.[1] The figure of Peter—of which, apparently, there exist various sketches by Raphael's hand — is memorable.

[1] No. 56 Via de Faenza, Capella di Foligno.

Letter to John Blackwood, 18th May 1860.

Things really look so threatening in the Neapolitan kingdom that we begin to think ourselves fortunate in having got our visit done. Tuscany is in the highest political spirits for the moment, and of course Victor Emanuel stares at us at every turn here, with the most loyal exaggeration of moustache and intelligent meaning. But we are selfishly careless about dynasties just now, caring more for the doings of Giotto and Brunelleschi than for those of Count Cavour. On a first journey to the greatest centres of art, one must be excused for letting one's public spirit go to sleep a little. As for me, I am thrown into a state of humiliating passivity by the sight of the great things done in the far past: it seems as if life were not long enough to learn, and as if my own activity were so completely dwarfed by comparison, that I should never have courage for more creation of my own. There is only one thing that has an opposite and stimulating effect: it is the comparative rarity, even here, of great and truthful art, and the abundance of wretched imitation and falsity. Every hand is wanted in the world that can do a little genuine sincere work.

We are at the quietest hotel in Florence, having sought it out for the sake of getting clear of the

Letter to John Blackwood, 18th May 1860.

stream of English and Americans, in which one finds one's self in all the main tracks of travel, so that one seems at last to be in a perpetual noisy picnic, obliged to be civil, though with a strong inclination to be sullen. My philanthropy rises several degrees as soon as we are alone.

Letter to Major Blackwood, 27th May 1860.

I am much obliged to you for writing at once, and so scattering some clouds which had gathered over my mind in consequence of an indication or two in Mr John Blackwood's previous letter. The 'Times' article arrived on Sunday. It is written in a generous spirit, and with so high a degree of intelligence, that I am rather alarmed lest the misapprehensions it exhibits should be due to my defective presentation, rather than to any failure on the part of the critic. I have certainly fulfilled my intention very badly if I have made the Dodson honesty appear "mean and uninteresting," or made the payment of one's debts appear a contemptible virtue in comparison with any sort of "Bohemian" qualities. So far as my own feeling and intention are concerned, no one class of persons or form of character is held up to reprobation or to exclusive admiration. Tom is painted with as much love and pity as Maggie; and I am so far from hating the Dodsons myself, that I am rather aghast to find them ticketed with such very ugly adjectives. We intend to leave this place on Friday (3d), and in four days after that we shall be at Venice—in a few days from that time at Milan—and then, by a route at present uncertain, at Berne, where we take up Mr Lewes's eldest boy, to bring him home with us.

Letter to Major Blackwood, 27th May 1860.

We are particularly happy in our weather, which is unvaryingly fine without excessive heat. There has been a crescendo of enjoyment in our travels; for Florence, from its relation to the history of Modern Art, has roused a keener interest in us even than Rome, and has stimulated me to entertain rather an ambitious project, which I mean to be a secret from every one but you and Mr John Blackwood.

Any news of 'Clerical Scenes' in its third edition? Or has its appearance been deferred? The smallest details are acceptable to ignorant travellers. We are wondering what was the last good article in 'Blackwood,' and whether Thackeray has gathered up his slack reins in the 'Cornhill.' Literature travels slowly even to this Italian Athens. Hawthorne's book is not to be found here yet in the Tauchnitz edition.

Italy, 1860.

We left Florence on the evening of the 1st of June, by diligence, travelling all night and until

Italy, 1860. eleven the next morning to get to Bologna. I wish we could have made that journey across the Apennines by daylight, though in that case I should have missed certain grand startling effects that came to me in my occasional wakings. Wonderful heights and depths I saw on each side of us by the fading light of the evening. Then in the middle of the night, while the lightning was flashing and the sky was heavy with threatening storm-clouds, I waked to find the six horses resolutely refusing or unable to move the diligence—till at last two meek oxen were tied to the axle, and their added strength dragged us up the hill. But one of the strangest effects I ever saw was just before dawn, when we seemed to be high up on mighty mountains, which fell precipitously and showed us the awful pale horizon far, far below.

The first thing we did at Bologna was to go to the Accademia, where I confirmed myself in my utter dislike of the Bolognese school—the Caraccis and Domenichino *et id genus omne*—and felt some disappointment in Raphael's St Cecilia. The pictures of Francia here, to which I had looked forward as likely to give me a fuller and higher idea of him, were less pleasing to me than the smaller specimens of him that I had seen in the Dresden and other galleries. He seems to me to be more limited even than Perugino: but he is a faithful, painstaking painter, with a religious spirit. Agostino Caracci's Communion of St Jerome is a remarkable picture, with real feeling in it—an exception among all the great pieces of canvas that hang beside it. Domenichino's figure of St Jerome is a direct plagiarism from that of Agostino: but in other points the two pictures are quite diverse. Italy, 1860

The following morning we took a carriage, and were diligent in visiting the churches. San Petronio has the melancholy distinction of an exquisite Gothic façade, which is carried up only a little way above the arches of the doorways: the sculptures on these arches are of wonderful beauty. The interior is of lofty, airy, simple Gothic, and it contains some curious old paintings in the various side-chapels—pre-eminent among which are the great frescoes by the so-called Buffalmacco. The Paradise is distinguished in my memory by the fact that the blessed are ranged in seats like the benches of a church or chapel. At Santa Cecilia—now used as a barrack or guard-room—there are two frescoes by Francia, the Marriage and Burial of St Cecilia, characteristic but miserably injured. At the great Church of San Domenico the object of chief inter-

Italy, 1860. est is the tomb of the said saint by the ever-to-be-honoured Nicolo Pisano. I believe this tomb was his first great work, and very remarkable it is; but there is nothing on it equal to the Nativity on the pulpit at Pisa. On this tomb stands a lovely angel by Michael Angelo. It is small in size, holding a small candlestick, and is a work of his youth: it shows clearly enough how the feeling for grace and beauty was strong in him, only not strong enough to wrestle with his love of the grandiose and powerful.

The ugly, painful, leaning towers of Bologna made me desire not to look at them a second time; but there are fine bits of massive palatial building here and there in the colonnaded streets. We trod the court of the once famous university, where the arms of the various scholars ornament the walls above and below an interior gallery. This building is now, as far as I could understand, a communal school, and the university is transported to another part of the town.

We left Bologna in the afternoon, rested at Ferrara for the night, and passed the Euganean Mountains on our left hand as we approached Padua in the middle of the next day.

After dinner and rest from our dusty journeying,

we took a carriage and went out to see the town, desiring most of all to see Giotto's Chapel. We paused first, however, at the great Church of Sant' Antonio, which is remarkable both externally and internally. There are two side chapels opposite each other, which are quite unique for contrasted effect. On the one hand is a chapel of oblong form, covered entirely with white marble *relievi*, golden lamps hanging from the roof; while opposite is a chapel of the same form, covered with frescoes by Avanzi, the artist who seems to have been the link of genius between Giotto and Masaccio. Close by, in a separate building, is the Capella di San Giorgio, also covered with Avanzi's frescoes; and here one may study him more completely, because the light is better than in the church. He has quite a Veronese power of combining his human groups with splendid architecture. Italy, 1860.

The Arena Chapel stands apart, and is approached at present through a pretty garden. Here one is uninterruptedly with Giotto. The whole chapel was designed and painted by himself alone; and it is said that while he was at work on it, Dante lodged with him at Padua. The nave of the chapel is in tolerably good preservation, but the apsis has

Italy, 1860. suffered severely from damp. It is in this apsis that the lovely Madonna, with the Infant at her breast, is painted in a niche, now quite hidden by some altar-piece or woodwork, which one has to push by in order to see the tenderest bit of Giotto's painting. This chapel must have been a blessed vision when it was fresh from Giotto's hand—the blue vaulted roof; the exquisite bands of which he was so fond, representing inlaid marble, uniting roof and walls and forming the divisions between the various frescoes which cover the upper part of the wall. The glory of Paradise at one end, and the histories of Mary and Jesus on the two sides; and the subdued effect of the series of monochromes representing the Virtues and Vices below.

There is a piazza with a plantation and circular public walk, with wildly affected statues of small and great notorieties, which remains with one as a peculiarity of Padua. In general the town is merely old and shabbily Italian, without anything very specific in its aspect.

From Padua to Venice!

It was about ten o'clock on a moonlight night—the 4th of June—that we found ourselves apparently on a railway in the midst of the sea: we were on the bridge across the Lagoon. Soon we were in a gondola on the Grand Canal, looking out at the moonlit buildings and water. What stillness! What beauty! Looking out from the high window of our hotel on the Grand Canal, I felt that it was a pity to go to bed. Venice was more beautiful than romances had feigned. Italy, 1860.

And that was the impression that remained, and even deepened, during our stay of eight days. That quiet which seems the deeper because one hears the delicious dip of the oar (when not disturbed by clamorous church bells), leaves the eye in full liberty and strength to take in the exhaustless loveliness of colour and form.

We were in our gondola by nine o'clock the next morning, and of course the first point we sought was the Piazza di San Marco. I am glad to find Ruskin calling the Palace of the Doges one of the two most perfect buildings in the world: its only defects, to my feeling, are the feebleness or triviality of the frieze or cornice, and the want of length in the Gothic windows with which the upper wall is pierced. This spot is a focus of architectural wonders: but the palace is the crown of them all. The double tier of columns and arches, with the rich sombreness of their finely

Italy, 1860. outlined shadows, contrast satisfactorily with the warmth and light and more continuous surface of the upper part. Even landing on the Piazzetta, one has a sense, not only of being in an entirely novel scene, but one where the ideas of a foreign race have poured themselves in without yet mingling indistinguishably with the pre-existent Italian life. But this is felt yet more strongly when one has passed along the Piazzetta and arrived in front of San Marco, with its low arches and domes and minarets. But perhaps the most striking point to take one's stand on is just in front of the white marble guard-house flanking the great tower—the guard-house with Sansovino's iron gates before it. On the left is San Marco, with the two square pillars from St Jean d'Acre, standing as isolated trophies; on the right the Piazzetta extends between the Doge's palace and the Palazzo Reale to the tall columns from Constantinople; and in front is the elaborate gateway leading to the white marble Scala dei Giganti, in the courtyard of the Doge's palace. Passing through this gateway and up this staircase, we entered the gallery which surrounds the court on three sides, and looked down at the fine sculptured vase-like wells below. Then into the great Sala, surrounded with the portraits of the Doges: the largest oil-painting here—or perhaps anywhere else—is the "Gloria del Paradiso" by Tintoretto, now dark and unlovely. But on the ceiling is a great Paul Veronese—the "Apotheosis of Venice"—which looks as fresh as if it were painted yesterday, and is a miracle of colour and composition—a picture full of glory and joy of an earthly, fleshly kind, but without any touch of coarseness or vulgarity. Below the radiant Venice on her clouds is a balcony filled with upward-looking spectators; and below this gallery is a group of human figures with horses. Next to this Apotheosis, I admire another Coronation of Venice on the ceiling of another Sala, where Venice is sitting enthroned above the globe with her lovely face in half shadow—a creature born with an imperial attitude. There are other Tintorettos, Veroneses, and Palmas in the great halls of this palace; but they left me quite indifferent, and have become vague in my memory. From the splendours of the palace we crossed the Bridge of Sighs to the prisons, and saw the horrible dark damp cells that would make the saddest life in the free light and air seem bright and desirable.

The interior of St Mark's is full of interest, but not of beauty: it is dark and heavy, and ill-suited

Italy, 1860. to the Catholic worship, for the massive piers that obstruct the view everywhere shut out the sight of ceremony and procession, as we witnessed at our leisure on the day of the great procession of Corpus Christi. But everywhere there are relics of gone-by art to be studied, from mosaics of the Greeks to mosaics of later artists than the Zuccati; old marble statues, embrowned like a meerschaum pipe; amazing sculptures in wood; Sansovino doors, ambitious to rival Ghiberti's; transparent alabaster columns; an ancient Madonna, hung with jewels, transported from St Sophia, in Constantinople; and everywhere the venerable pavement, once beautiful with its starry patterns in rich marble, now deadened and sunk to unevenness like the mud floor of a cabin.

Then outside, on the archway of the principal door, there are sculptures of a variety that makes one renounce the study of them in despair at the shortness of one's time—blended fruits and foliage, and human groups and animal forms of all kinds. On our first morning we ascended the great tower, and looked around on the island-city and the distant mountains and the distant Adriatic. And on the same day we went to see the Pisani palace—one of the grand old palaces that are going to decay. An Italian artist who resides in one part of this palace interested us by his frank manner, and the glimpse we had of his domesticity with his pretty wife and children. After this we saw the Church of San Sebastiano, where Paul Veronese is buried, with his own paintings around, mingling their colour with the light that falls on his tombstone. There is one remarkably fine painting of his here: it represents, I think, some Saints going to Martyrdom, but apart from that explanation, is a composition full of vigorous, spirited figures, in which the central ones are two young men leaving some splendid dwelling, on the steps of which stands the mother, pleading and remonstrating—a marvellous figure of an old woman with a bare neck. Italy, 1860.

But supreme among the pictures at Venice is the "Death of Peter the Martyr,"[1] now happily removed from its original position as an altar-piece, and placed in a good light in the sacristy of San Giovanni and Paolo (or San Zani Polo, as the Venetians conveniently abbreviate it). In this picture, as in that of the Tribute-money at Dresden, Titian seems to have surpassed himself, and to have reached as high a point in expression as in colour. In the same sacristy there was a Crucifixion by

[1] Since burnt.

Italy, 1860. Tintoretto, and a remarkable Madonna with Saints by Giovanni Bellini; but we were unable to look long away from the Titian to these, although we paid it five visits during our stay. It is near this church that the famous equestrian statue stands by Verocchio.

Santa Maria della Salute, built as an *ex voto* by the Republic on the cessation of the plague, is one of the most conspicuous churches in Venice, lifting its white cupolas close on the Grand Canal, where it widens out towards the Giudecca.

Here there are various Tintorettos, but the only one which is not blackened so as to be unintelligible is the *Cena*, which is represented as a bustling supper-party, with attendants and sideboard accessories, in thoroughly Dutch fashion! The great scene of Tintoretto's greatness is held to be the Scuola di San Rocco, of which he had the painting entirely to himself, with his pupils; and here one must admire the vigour and freshness of his conceptions, though I saw nothing that delighted me in expression, and much that was preposterous and ugly. The Crucifixion here is certainly a grand work, to which he seems to have given his best powers; and among the smaller designs, in the two larger halls, there were several of thorough originality—for example, the Annunciation, where Mary is seated in a poor house, with a carpenter's shop adjoining, the Nativity in the upper storey of a stable, of which a section is made so as to show the beasts below, and the Flight into Egypt, with a very charming (European) landscape. In this same building of San Rocco there are some exquisite iron gates, a present from Florence, and some singularly painstaking wood-carving, representing, in one compartment of wainscot, above the seats that surrounded the upper hall, a bookcase filled with old books, an inkstand and pen set in front of one shelf *à s'y méprendre.* Italy, 1860.

But of all Tintoretto's paintings, the best preserved, and perhaps the most complete in execution, is the Miracle of St Mark at the Accademia. We saw it the oftener because we were attracted to the Accademia again and again by Titian's Assumption, which we placed next to Peter the Martyr among the pictures at Venice.

For a thoroughly rapt expression I never saw anything equal to the Virgin in this picture; and the expression is the more remarkable because it is not assisted by the usual devices to express spiritual ecstasy, such as delicacy of feature and temperament or pale meagreness. Then what cherubs and angelic heads bathed in light! The lower part of the picture has no interest; the attitudes are theatrical; and the Almighty above is as unbeseeming as painted Almighties usually are: but the middle group falls short only of the Sistine Madonna.

Among the Venetian painters Giovanni Bellini shines with a mild, serious light that gives one an affectionate respect towards him. In the Church of the Scalzi there is an exquisite Madonna by him—probably his *chef-d'œuvre*—comparable to Raphael's for sweetness.

And Palma Vecchio, too, must be held in grateful reverence for his Santa Barbara, standing in calm, grand beauty above an altar in the Church of Santa Maria Formosa. It is an almost unique presentation of a hero-woman, standing in calm preparation for martyrdom, without the slightest air of pietism, yet with the expression of a mind filled with serious conviction.

We made the journey to Chioggia but with small pleasure, on account of my illness, which continued all day. Otherwise that long floating over the water, with the forts and mountains looking as if they were suspended in the air, would have been very enjoyable. Of all dreamy delights, that of floating in a gondola along the canals and out on the Lagoon is surely the greatest. We were out one night on the Lagoon when the sun was setting, and the wide waters were flushed with the reddened light. I should have liked it to last for hours: it is the sort of scene in which I could most readily forget my own existence, and feel melted into the general life. Italy, 1860.

Another charm of evening time was to walk up and down the Piazza of San Marco as the stars were brightening and look at the grand dim buildings, and the flocks of pigeons flitting about them; or to walk on to the Bridge of La Paglia and look along the dark canal that runs under the Bridge of Sighs—its blackness lit up by a gaslight here and there, and the plash of the oar of blackest gondola slowly advancing.

One of our latest visits was to the Palazzo Mamfrini, where there are still the remains of a magnificent collection of pictures — remains still on sale.

The young proprietor was walking about transacting business in the rooms as we passed through them—a handsome, refined-looking man. The chief treasure left—the Entombment, by Titian—is perhaps a superior duplicate of the one in the Louvre.

Italy, 1860. After this we went to a private house (once the house of Bianca Capello), to see a picture which the joint proprietors are anxious to prove to be a Leonardo da Vinci. It is a remarkable—an unforgettable—picture. The subject is the Supper at Emmaus; and the Christ, with open, almost tearful eyes, with loving sadness spread over the regular beauty of his features, is a masterpiece. This head is *not* like the Leonardo sketch at Milan; and the rest of the picture impressed me strongly with the idea that it is of German, not Italian, origin. Again, the head is not like that of Leonardo's Christ in the National Gallery—it is far finer, to my thinking.

Farewell, lovely Venice! and away to Verona, across the green plains of Lombardy, which can hardly look tempting to an eye still filled with the dreamy beauty it has left behind. Yet I liked our short stay at Verona extremely. The Amphitheatre had the disadvantage of coming after the Coliseum and the Pozzuoli Amphitheatre, and would bear comparison with neither; but the Church of San Zenone was equal in interest to almost any of the churches we had seen in Italy. It is a beautiful specimen of Lombard architecture, undisguised by any modern barbarisms in the interior; and on the walls—now that they have been freed from their coat of whitewash—there are early frescoes of high historical value, some of them—apparently of the Giotto school—showing a remarkable striving after human expression. More than this, there is in one case an under layer of yet older frescoes, partly laid bare, and showing the lower part of figures in mummy-like degradation of drawing: while above these are the upper portion of the later figures in striking juxtaposition with the dead art from which they had sprung with the vitality of a hidden germ. There is a very fine crypt to the church, where the fragments of some ancient [statue] are built in wrong way upwards.

This was the only church we entered at Verona; for we contented ourselves with a general view of the town, driving about to get *coups d'œil* of the fine old walls, the river, the bridges, and surrounding hills, and mounting up to a high terrace for the sake of a bird's-eye view: this, with a passing sight of the famous tombs of the Scaligers, was all gathered in our four or five hours at Verona.

Heavy rain came on our way to Milan, putting an end to the brilliant weather we had enjoyed ever since our arrival at Naples. The line of road lies through a luxuriant country, and I remember

Italy, 1860. the picturesque appearance of Bergamo—half of it on the level, half of it lifted up on the green hill.

In this second visit of mine to Milan, my greatest pleasures were the Brera Gallery and the Ambrosian Library, neither of which I had seen before. The cathedral no longer satisfied my eye in its exterior; and though the interior has very grand effects, there are still disturbing elements.

At the Ambrosian Library we saw MSS. surpassing in interest any even of those we had seen in the Laurentian Library at Florence,—illuminated books, sacred and secular—a little Koran, rolled up something after the fashion of a measuring-tape—private letters of Tasso, Galileo, Lucrezia Borgia, &c.—and a book full of Leonardo da Vinci's engineering designs. Then up-stairs, in the picture-gallery, we saw a delicious Holy Family by Luini, of marvellous perfection in its execution, the Cartoon for Raphael's "School of Athens," and a precious collection of drawings by Leonardo da Vinci and Michael Angelo. Among Leonardo's are amazingly grotesque faces, full of humour; among Michael Angelo's is the sketch of the unfortunate Biagio, who figures with asses' ears in the lower corner of the "Last Judgment."

At the Brera, among a host of pictures to which I was indifferent, there were several things that delighted me. Some of Luini's frescoes—especially the burial or transportation of the body of St Catherine by angels; some single figures of young cherubs, and Joseph and Mary going to their Marriage; the drawing in pastel by Leonardo of the Christ's head, supposed to be a study for the *Cena;* the Luini Madonna among trellises—an exquisite oil-painting; Gentile Bellini's picture of St Mark preaching at Alexandria; and the Sposalizio by Raphael. Italy, 1860.

At the Church of San Maurizio Maggiore we saw Luini's power tested by an abundant opportunity. The walls are almost covered with frescoes by him; but the only remarkable felicity he has is his female figures, which are eminently graceful. He has not power enough for a composition of any high character.

We visited, too, the interesting old Church of Sant' Ambrogio, with its court surrounded by cloisters, its old sculptured pulpit, chair of St Ambrose, and illuminated choir-books; and we drove to look at the line of old Roman columns, which are almost the solitary remnant of antiquity left in this ancient city—ancient, at least, in its name and site.

Italy, 1860. We left Milan for Como on a fine Sunday morning, and arrived at beautiful Bellagio by steamer in the evening. Here we spent a delicious day—going to the Villa Somma Riva in the morning, and in the evening to the Serbellone Gardens, from the heights of which we saw the mountain-peaks reddened with the last rays of the sun. The next day we reached lovely Chiavenna, at the foot of the Splügen Pass, and spent the evening in company with a glorious mountain torrent, mountain peaks, huge boulders, with rippling miniature torrents and lovely young flowers among them, and grassy heights with rich Spanish chestnuts shadowing them. Then, the next morning, we set off by post and climbed the almost perpendicular heights of the Pass—chiefly in heavy rain that would hardly let us discern the patches of snow when we reached the tableland of the summit. About five o'clock we reached grassy Splügen, and felt that we had left Italy behind us. Already our driver had been German for the last long post, and now we had come to an hotel where host and waiters were German. Swiss houses of dark wood, outside staircases and broad eaves, stood on the steep, green, and flowery slope that led up to the waterfall; and the hotel and other buildings of masonry were thoroughly German in their aspect. In the evening we enjoyed a walk between the mountains, whose lower sides down to the torrent bed were set with tall dark pines. But the climax of grand—nay, terrible—scenery came the next day as we traversed the Via Mala. Italy, 1860.

After this came open green valleys, with dotted white churches and homesteads. We were in Switzerland, and the mighty wall of the Valtelline Alps shut us out from Italy on the 21st of June.

Letter to John Blackwood, 23d June 1860, from Berne.

Your letter to Florence reached me duly, and I feel as if I had been rather unconscionable in asking for another before our return; but to us who have been seeing new things every day, a month seems so long a space of time that we can't help fancying there must be a great accumulation of news for us at the end of it.

We had hoped to be at home by the 25th; but we were so enchanted with Venice, that we were seduced into staying there a whole week instead of three or four days, and now we must not rob the boys of their two days' holiday with us.

We have had a wonderful journey. From Florence we went to Bologna, Ferrara, and Padua on our way to Venice; and from Venice we have

Letter to John Blackwood, 23d June 1860, from Berne.

come by Verona, Milan, and Como, and across the Splügen to Zurich, where we spent yesterday chiefly in the company of Moleschott the physiologist—an interview that has helped to sharpen Mr Lewes's appetite for a return to his microscope and dissecting table. We ought to be for ever ashamed of ourselves if we don't work the better for this great holiday. We both feel immensely enriched with new ideas and new veins of interest.

I don't think I can venture to tell you what my great project is by letter, for I am anxious to keep it a secret. It will require a great deal of study and labour, and I am athirst to begin.

As for 'The Mill,' I am in repose about it, now I know it has found its way to the great public. Its comparative rank can only be decided after some years have passed, when the judgment upon it is no longer influenced by the recent enthusiasm about 'Adam,' and by the fact that it has the misfortune to be written by me instead of by Mr Liggins. I shall like to see Bulwer's criticism, if you will be kind enough to send it me; but I particularly wish *not* to see any of the newspaper articles.

SUMMARY.

MARCH TO JUNE 1860.—FIRST JOURNEY TO ITALY.

Crossing Mont Cenis by night in diligence—Turin—Sees Count Cavour—Genoa—Leghorn—Pisa—Civita Vecchia—Disappointment with first sight of Rome—Better spirits after visit to Capitol—View from Capitol—Points most struck with in Rome—Sculpture at Capitol—Sculpture at Vatican first seen by torchlight—St Peter's—Other churches—Sistine Chapel — Paintings — Illumination of St Peter's — Disappointment with Michael Angelo's Moses—Visits to artists' studios—Riedel and Overbeck—Pamfili Doria Gardens—Frascati—Tivoli—Pictures at Capitol—Lateran Museum—Shelley's and Keats's graves—Letter to Mrs Congreve—Pope's blessing—Easter ceremonies—From Rome to Naples—Description—Museo Borbonico—Visit to Pompeii—Solemnity of street of tombs—Letter to Mrs Congreve—From Naples to Salerno and Pæstum—Temple of Vesta—Temple of Neptune fulfils expectations—Amalfi—Drive to Sorrento—Back to Naples—By steamer to Leghorn—To Florence—Views from Fiesole and Bellosguardo—The Duomo—Baptistery—Palaces—Churches—Dante's tomb—Frescoes—Pictures at the Uffizi—Pictures at the Pitti—Pictures at the Accademia—Expedition to Siena—Back to Florence—Michael Angelo's house—Letter to Blackwood—Dwarfing effect of the past—Letter to Major Blackwood on 'Times' criticism of 'The Mill on the Floss,' and first mention of an Italian novel—Leave Florence for Bologna—Churches and pictures—To Padua by Ferrara—The Arena Chapel—Venice by moonlight—Doge's Palace—St Mark's—Pictures—Scuola di San Rocco—Accademia—Gondola to Chioggia—From Venice to Verona—Milan—Brera Gallery and Ambrosian Library—Disappointment with cathedral—Bellagio—Over Splügen to Switzerland — Letter to Blackwood — Saw Moleschott at Zurich—Home by Berne and Geneva.

CHAPTER XI.

July 1.—We found ourselves at home again, after three months of delightful travel. From Berne we brought our eldest boy Charles, to begin a new period in his life, after four years at Hofwyl. During our absence 'The Mill on the Floss' came out (April 4), and achieved a greater success than I had ever hoped for it. The subscription was 3600 (the number originally printed was 4000); and shortly after its appearance, Mudie having demanded a second thousand, Blackwood commenced striking off 2000 more, making 6000. While we were at Florence I had the news that these 6000 were all sold, and that 500 more were being prepared. From all we can gather, the votes are rather on the side of 'The Mill' as a better book than 'Adam.' Journal, 1860.

We reached home by starlight at one o'clock this morning; and I write in haste, fear, and trembling Letter to Madame Bodichon, 1st July 1860.

Letter to Madame Bodichon, 1st July 1860.

lest you should already be gone to Surrey. You know what I should like — that you and your husband should come to us the first day possible, naming any hour and conditions. We would arrange meals and everything else as would best suit you. Of course I would willingly go to London to see *you,* if you could not come to me. But I fear lest neither plan should be practicable, and lest this letter should have to be sent after you. It is from your note only that I have learned your loss.[1] It has made me think of you with the sense that there is more than ever a common fund of experience between us. But I will write nothing more now. I am almost ill with fatigue, and have only courage to write at all, because of my anxiety not to miss you.

Affectionate regards from both of *us* to both of *you.*

Letter to Miss Sara Hennell, 2d July 1860.

I opened your letters and parcel a little after one o'clock on Sunday morning, for that was the unseasonable hour of our return from our long, long journey. Yesterday was almost entirely employed in feeling very weary indeed, but this morning we are attacking the heap of small duties that always lie before one after a long absence.

[1] Death of Madame Bodichon's father.

It is pleasant to see your book[1] fairly finished after all delays and anxieties; but I will say nothing to you about *that* until I have read it. I shall read it the first thing before plunging into a course of study which will take me into a different region of thought.

Letter to Miss Sara Hennell, 2d July 1860.

We have had an unspeakably delightful journey—one of those journeys that seem to divide one's life in two, by the new ideas they suggest and the new veins of interest they open. We went to Geneva, and spent two days with my old kind friends the D'Alberts—a real pleasure to me, especially as Mr Lewes was delighted with "Maman" as I used to call Madame d'Albert. She is as bright and upright as ever: the ten years have only whitened her hair—a change which makes her face all the softer in colouring.

Letter to John Blackwood, 3d July 1860.

We did not reach home till past midnight on Saturday, when you, I suppose, had already become used to the comfort of having fairly got through your London season. Self-interest, rightly understood of course, prompts us to a few virtuous actions in the way of letter-writing to let the few people we care to hear from know at once of our whereabouts; and you are one of the first among the few.

[1] 'Thoughts in Aid of Faith.'

Letter to John Blackwood, 3d July 1860.

At Berne Mr Lewes supped with Professors Valentin and Schiff, two highly distinguished physiologists, and I was much delighted to find how much attention and interest they had given to his views in the 'Physiology of Common Life.'

A French translation of Adam Bede,' by a Genevese gentleman[1] well known to me, is now in the press; and the same translator has undertaken 'The Mill on the Floss.' He appears to have rendered 'Adam' with the most scrupulous care. I think these are all the incidents we gathered on our homeward journey that are likely to interest you.

Letter to Miss Sara Hennell, 7th July 1860.

I have finished my first rather rapid reading of your book, and now I thank you for it: not merely for the special gift of the volume and inscription, but for that of which many others will share the benefit with me—the "thoughts" themselves.

So far as my reading in English books of similar character extends, yours seems to me quite unparalleled in the largeness and insight with which it estimates Christianity as an "organised experience" —a grand advance in the moral development of the race.

I especially delight in the passage, p. 105, beginning, "And how can it be otherwise," and ending

[1] M. d'Albert.

with, "formal rejection of it."[1] On this and other supremely interesting matters of thought—perhaps I should rather say of experience—your book has shown me that we are much nearer to each other than I had supposed. At p. 174, again, there is a passage beginning, "These sentiments," and ending with "heroes,"[2] which, for me, expresses the

Letter to Miss Sara Hennell, 7th July 1860.

1 "And how can it be otherwise than real to us, this belief that has nourished the souls of us all, and seems to have moulded actually anew their internal constitution, as well as stored them up with its infinite variety of external interests and associations! What other than a very real thing has it been in the life of the world—sprung out of, and again causing to spring forth, such volumes of human emotion—making a current, as it were, of feeling, that has drawn within its own sphere all the moral vitality of so many ages! In all this reality of influence there is indeed the testimony of Christianity having truly formed an integral portion of the organic life of humanity. The regarding it as a mere excrescence, the product of morbid fanatical humours, is a reaction of judgment, that, it is to be hoped, will soon be seen on all hands to be in no way implied of necessity in the formal rejection of it."—'Thoughts in Aid of Faith,' p. 105.

2 "These sentiments, which are born within us, slumbering as it were in our nature, ready to be awakened into action immediately they are roused by hint of corresponding circumstances, are drawn out of the whole of previous human existence. They constitute our treasured inheritance out of all the life that has been lived before us, to which no age, no human being who has trod the earth and laid himself to rest, with all his mortal burden, upon her maternal bosom, has failed to add his contribution. No generation has had its engrossing conflict, sorely battling out the triumphs of mind over material force, and through forms of monstrous abortions concurrent with its birth, too hideous for us now to bear in contemplation, moulding the early intelligence by every struggle, and winning its gradual powers,—no single soul has borne itself through its personal trial,—without

Letter to Miss Sara Hennell, 7th July 1860.

one-half of true human piety. That thought is one of my favourite altars where I oftenest go to contemplate, and to seek for invigorating motive.

Of the work as a whole I am quite incompetent to judge on a single cursory reading. I admire—I respect—the breadth and industry of mind it exhibits; and I should be obliged to give it a more thorough study than I can afford at present before I should feel warranted to urge, in the light of a criticism, my failure to perceive the logical consistency of your language in some parts with the position you have adopted in others. In many instances your meaning is obscure to me, or at least lies wrapped up in more folds of abstract phraseology than I have the courage or the industry to open for myself. I think you told me that some one had found your treatment of great questions "cold-blooded." I am all the more delighted to find, for my own part, an unusual fulness of sympathy and heart experience breathing throughout

bequeathing to us of its fruit. There is not a religious thought that we take to ourselves for secret comfort in our time of grief, that has not been distilled out of the multiplicity of the hallowed tears of mankind; not an animating idea is there for our fainting courage that has not gathered its inspiration from the bravery of the myriad armies of the world's heroes."—'Thoughts in Aid of Faith,' p. 174.

Letter to Miss Sara Hennell, 7th July 1860.

your book. The ground for that epithet perhaps lay in a certain professorial tone which could hardly be avoided, in a work filled with criticism of other people's theories, except by the adoption of a simply personal style of presentation, in which you would have seemed to be looking up at the oracles, and trying to reconcile their doctrines for your own behoof, instead of appearing to be seated in a chair above them. But you considered your own plan more thoroughly than any one else can have considered it for you; and I have no doubt you had good reasons for preferring the more impersonal style.

Mr Lewes sends his kind regards, and when Du Bois Reymond's book on Johannes Müller, with other preoccupations of a like thrilling kind, no longer stand in the way, he will open *his* copy of the 'Thoughts in Aid of Faith.' He has felt a new interest aroused towards it since he has learned something about it from me and the reviewer in the 'Westminster.'

Madame Bodichon, who was here the other day, told me that Miss Nightingale and Miss Julia Smith had mentioned their pleasure in your book; but you will hear further news of all that from themselves.

Letter to John Blackwood, 9th July 1860.

I return Sir Edward Lytton's critical letter, which I have read with much interest. On two points I recognise the justice of his criticism. First, that Maggie is made to appear too passive in the scene of quarrel in the Red Deeps. If my book were still in MS. I should—now that the defect is suggested to me — alter, or rather expand, that scene. Secondly, that the tragedy is not adequately prepared. This is a defect which I felt even while writing the third volume, and have felt ever since the MS. left me. The *Epische Breite* into which I was beguiled by love of my subject in the two first volumes, caused a want of proportionate fulness in the treatment of the third, which I shall always regret.

The other chief point of criticism—Maggie's position towards Stephen—is too vital a part of my whole conception and purpose for me to be converted to the condemnation of it. If I am wrong there—if I did not really know what my heroine would feel and do under the circumstances in which I deliberately placed her—I ought not to have written this book at all, but quite a different book, if any. If the ethics of art do not admit the truthful presentation of a character essentially noble, but liable to great error—error that is anguish to its own nobleness—then, it seems to me, the ethics of art are too narrow, and must be widened to correspond with a widening psychology.

Letter to John Blackwood, 9th July 1860.

But it is good for me to know how my tendencies as a writer clash with the conclusions of a highly accomplished mind, that I may be warned into examining well whether my discordance with those conclusions may not arise rather from an idiosyncrasy of mine, than from a conviction which is argumentatively justifiable.

I hope you will thank Sir Edward on my behalf for the trouble he has taken to put his criticism into a form specific enough to be useful. I feel his taking such trouble to be at once a tribute and a kindness. If printed criticisms were usually written with only half the same warrant of knowledge, and with an equal sincerity of intention, I should read them without fear of fruitless annoyance.

Letter to Mrs Bray, 10th July 1860.

The little envelope with its address of "Marian" was very welcome, and as Mr Lewes is sending what a Malapropian friend once called a "missile" to Sara, I feel inclined to slip in a word of gratitude—less for the present than for the past goodness, which came back to me with keener remem-

Letter to Mrs Bray, 10th July 1860.

brance than ever when we were at Genoa and at Como — the places I first saw with you. How wretched I was then—how peevish, how utterly morbid! And how kind and forbearing you were under the oppression of my company. I should like you now and then to feel happy in the thought that you were always perfectly good to me. That I was not good to you, is my own disagreeable affair: the bitter taste of that fact is mine, not yours.

Don't you remember Bellagio? It is hardly altered much except in the hotels, which the eleven years have wondrously multiplied and bedizened for the accommodation of the English. But if I begin to recall the things we saw in Italy, I shall write as long a letter as Mr Lewes's, which, by-the-by, now I have read it, seems to be something of a "missile" in another sense than the Malapropian. But Sara is one of the few people to whom candour is acceptable as the highest tribute. And private criticism has more chance of being faithful than public. We must have mercy on critics who are obliged to make a figure in printed pages. They must by all means say striking things. Either we should not read printed criticisms at all (*I don't*), or we should read them with the constant remembrance that they are a fugitive kind of work which, in the present stage of human nature, can rarely engage a very high grade of conscience or ability. The fate of a book, which is not entirely ephemeral, is never decided by journalists or reviewers of any but an exceptional kind. Tell Sara her damnation—if it ever comes to pass—will be quite independent of Nationals and Westminsters. Let half-a-dozen competent people read her book, and an opinion of it will spread quite apart from either praise or blame in reviews and newspapers. Letter to Mrs Bray, 10th July 1860.

Our big boy is a great delight to us, and makes our home doubly cheery. It is very sweet as one gets old to have some young life about one. He is quite a passionate musician, and we play Beethoven duets with increasing appetite every evening. The opportunity of hearing some inspiring music is one of the chief benefits we hope for to counterbalance our loss of the wide common and the fields. Letter to Mrs Bray, Tuesday evening, July 1860.

We shall certainly read the parts you suggest in the 'Education of the Feelings,'[1] and I daresay I shall read a good deal more of it, liking to turn over the leaves of a book which I read first in our old drawing-room at Foleshill, and then lent to my Letter to Mrs Bray, 14th July 1860.

[1] 'Education of the Feelings.' By Charles Bray. Published 1839.

Letter to Mrs Bray, 14th July 1860.

sister, who, with a little air of maternal experience, pronounced it "very sensible."

There is so much that I want to do every day—I had need cut myself into four women. We have a great extra interest and occupation just now in our big boy Charley, who is looking forward to a Government examination, and wants much help and sympathy in music and graver things. I think we are quite peculiarly blest in the fact that this eldest lad seems the most entirely lovable human animal of seventeen and a half that I ever met with or heard of: he has a sweetness of disposition which is saved from weakness by a remarkable sense of duty.

We are going to let our present house, if possible—that is, get rid of it altogether on account of its inconvenient situation: other projects are still in a floating, unfixed condition. The water did not look quite so green at Como—perhaps, as your remark suggests, because there was a less vivid green to be reflected from my personality as I looked down on it. I am eleven years nearer to the sere and yellow leaf, and my feelings are even more autumnal than my years. I have read no reviews of the 'Mill on the Floss' except that in the 'Times' which Blackwood sent me to Florence. I abstain not from superciliousness, but on a calm consideration of the probable proportion of benefit on the one hand, and waste of thought on the other. It was certain that in the notices of my first book, after the removal of my *incognito*, there would be much *ex post facto* wisdom, which could hardly profit me since *I* certainly knew who I was beforehand, and knew also that no one else knew who had not been told.

Letter to Mrs Bray, 14th July 1860.

We are quite uncertain about our plans at present. Our second boy, Thornie, is going to leave Hofwyl, and to be placed in some more expensive position, in order to the carrying on of his education in a more complete way, so that we are thinking of avoiding for the present any final establishment of ourselves, which would necessarily be attended with additional outlay. Besides, these material cares draw rather too severely on my strength and spirits. But until Charlie's career has taken shape we frame no definite projects.

Letter to Chas. Bray, 18th July 1860.

If Cara values the article on Strikes in the 'Westminster Review,' she will be interested to know—if she has not heard it already—that the writer is *blind*. I dined with him the other week, and could hardly keep the tears back as I sat at table with him. Yet he is cheerful and animated, accepting

Letter to Miss Sara Hennell, 6th Aug. 1860.

Letter to Miss Sara Hennell, 6th Aug. 1860.

with graceful quietness all the minute attentions to his wants that his blindness calls forth. His name is Fawcett, and he is a Fellow of Trinity Hall, Cambridge. I am sitting for my portrait—for the last time, I hope—to Lawrence, the artist who drew that chalk-head of Thackeray, which is familiar to you.

Letter to Madame Bodichon, Friday, Aug. 1860.

I know you will rejoice with us that Charley has won his place at the Post Office, having been at the head of the list in the examination. The dear lad is fairly launched in life now.

Letter to Madame Bodichon, Saturday evening, Aug. 1860.

I am thoroughly vexed that we didn't go to Lawrence's to-day. We made an effort, but it was raining too hard at the only time that would serve us to reach the train. That comes of our inconvenient situation, so far off the railway; and alas! no one comes to take our house off our hands. We may be forced to stay here after all.

One of the things I shall count upon, if we are able to get nearer London, is to see more of your schools and other good works. That would help me to do without the fields for many months of the year.

Letter to Miss Sara Hennell, 27th Aug. 1860.

I am very sorry that anything I have written should have pained you. *That,* certainly, is the result I should seek most to avoid in the very slight communication which we are able to keep up—

necessarily under extremely imperfect acquaintance with each other's present self.

Letter to Miss Sara Hennell, 27th Aug. 1860.

My first letter to you about your book, after having read it through, was as simple and sincere a statement of the main impressions it had produced on me, as I knew how to write in few words. My second letter, in which I unhappily used a formula in order to express to you, in briefest phrase, my difficulty in discerning the justice of your *analogical* argument, *as I understood it,* was written from no other impulse than the desire to show you that I did not neglect your abstract just sent to me. The said formula was entirely deprived of its application by the statement in your next letter, that you used the word "essence" in another sense than the one hitherto received in philosophical writing, on the question as to the nature of our knowledge; and the explanation given of your meaning in your last letter shows me—unless I am plunging into further mistake—that you mean nothing but what I fully believe. My offensive formula was written under the supposition that your conclusion meant something which it apparently did *not* mean. It is probable enough that I was stupid; but I should be distressed to think that the discipline of life had been of so little use to me, as to leave me with a

Letter to Miss Sara Hennell, 27th Aug. 1860.

tendency to leap at once to the attitude of a critic, instead of trying first to be a learner from every book written with sincere labour.

Will you tell Mr Bray that we are quitting our present house in order to be *nearer* town for Charlie's sake, who has an appointment in the Post Office, and our time will be arduously occupied during the next few weeks in arrangements to that end, so that our acceptance of the pleasant proposition to visit Sydenham for a while is impossible. We have advertised for a house near Regent's Park, having just found a gentleman and lady ready to take our present one off our hands. They want to come in on quarter-day, so that we have no time to spare.

I have been reading this morning for my spiritual good Emerson's 'Man the Reformer,' which comes to me with fresh beauty and meaning. My heart goes out with venerating gratitude to that mild face, which I daresay is smiling on some one as beneficently as it one day did on me years and years ago.

Do not write again about opinions on large questions, dear Sara. The liability to mutual misconception which attends such correspondence—especially in my case, who can only write with brevity and haste—makes me dread it greatly; and I think there is no benefit derivable to you to compensate for the presence of that dread in me. You do not know me well enough as I *am* (according to the doctrine of development which you have yourself expounded), to have the materials for interpreting my imperfect expressions.

Letter to Miss Sara Hennell, 27th Aug. 1860.

I think you would spare yourself some pain if you would attribute to your friends a larger comprehension of ideas, and a larger acquaintance with them, than you appear to do. I should imagine that many of them, or at least *some* of them, share with you, much more fully than you seem to suppose, in the interest and hope you derive from the doctrine of development, with its geometrical progression towards fuller and fuller being. Surely it is a part of human piety we should all cultivate, not to form conclusions, on slight and dubious evidence, as to other people's "tone of mind," or to regard particular mistakes as a proof of general moral incapacity to understand us. I suppose such a tendency (to large conclusions about others) is part of the original sin we are all born with, for I have continually to check it in myself.

Letter to John Blackwood, 28th Aug. 1860.

I think I must tell you the secret, though I am distrusting my power to make it grow into a published fact. When we were in Florence, I was rather fired with the idea of writing a historical

Letter to John Blackwood, 28th Aug. 1860.

romance—scene, Florence; period, the close of the fifteenth century, which was marked by Savonarola's career and martyrdom. Mr Lewes has encouraged me to persevere in the project, saying that I should probably do something in historical romance rather different in character from what has been done before. But I want first to write another English story, and the plan I should like to carry out is this: to publish my next English novel when my Italian one is advanced enough for us to begin its publication a few months afterwards in 'Maga.' It would appear without a name in the Magazine, and be subsequently reprinted with the name of "George Eliot." I need not tell you the wherefore of this plan. You know well enough the received phrases with which a writer is greeted when he does something else than what was expected of him. But just now I am quite without confidence in my future doings, and almost repent of having formed conceptions which will go on lashing me now until I have at least tried to fulfil them.

I am going to-day to give my last sitting to Lawrence, and we were counting on the Major's coming to look at the portrait and judge of it. I hope it will be satisfactory, for I am quite set against going through the same process a second time.

We are a little distracted just now with the prospect of removal from our present house, which some obliging people have at last come to take off our hands.

Letter to Madame Bodichon, 5th Sept. 1860.

My fingers have been itching to write to you for the last week or more, but I have waited and waited, hoping to be able to tell you that we had decided on our future house. This evening, however, I have been reading your description of Algiers, and the desire to thank you for it moves me too strongly to be resisted. It is admirably written, and makes me *see* the country. I am so glad to think of the deep draughts of life you get from being able to spend half your life in that fresh grand scenery. It must make London and English green fields all the more enjoyable in their turn.

As for us, we are preparing to renounce the delights of roving, and to settle down quietly, as old folks should do, for the benefit of the young ones. We have let our present house.

Is it not cheering to have the sunshine on the corn, and the prospect that the poor people will not have to endure the suffering that comes on them from a bad harvest? The fields that were so sadly beaten down a little while ago on the way to town are now standing in fine yellow shocks.

Letter to Madame Bodichon, 5th Sept. 1860.

I wish you could know how much we felt your kindness to Charley. He is such a dear good fellow that nothing is thrown away upon him.

Write me a scrap of news about yourself, and tell me how you and the doctor are enjoying the country. I shall get a breath of it in that way. I think I love the fields and shudder at the streets more and more every month.

Journal, 1860.

Sept. 27.—To-day is the third day we have spent in our new home here at 10 Harewood Square. It is a furnished house, in which we do not expect to stay longer than six months at the utmost. Since our return from Italy I have written a slight tale, 'Mr David Faux, Confectioner' ('Brother Jacob')—which G. thinks worth printing.

Letter to John Blackwood, 27th Sept. 1860.

The precious cheque arrived safely to-day. I am much obliged to you for it, and also for the offer to hasten further payments. I have no present need of that accommodation, as we have given up the idea of buying the house which attracted us, dreading a step that might fetter us to town, or to a more expensive mode of living than might ultimately be desirable. I hope Mr Lewes will bring us back a good report of Major Blackwood's progress towards re-established health. In default of a visit from him, it was very agreeable to have him represented by his son,[1] who has the happy talent of making a morning call one of the easiest, pleasantest things in the world.

Letter to John Blackwood, 27th Sept. 1860.

I wonder if you know who is the writer of the article in the 'North British,' in which I am reviewed along with Hawthorne. Mr Lewes brought it for me to read this morning, and it is so unmixed in its praise, that if I had any friends I should be uneasy lest a friend should have written it.

Letter to Mrs Congreve, 16th Oct. 1860.

Since there is no possibility of my turning in to see you on my walk as in the old days, I cannot feel easy without writing to tell you my regret that I missed you when you came. In changing a clearer sky for a foggy one, we have not changed our habits, and we walk after lunch as usual; but I should like very much to stay indoors any day with the expectation of seeing you, if I could know beforehand of your coming. It is rather sad not to see your face at all from week to week, and I hope you know that I feel it so. But I am always afraid of falling into a disagreeable urgency of invitation, since we have nothing to offer beyond the familiar well-worn entertainment of our own society. I hope you and Mr Congreve are quite well now and free from cares. Emily, I suppose, is gone with the

[1] Mr William Blackwood.

Letter to Mrs Congreve, 16th Oct. 1860.

sunshine of her face to Coventry. There is sadly little sunshine except that of young faces just now. Still we are flourishing in spite of damp and dismalness. We were glad to hear that the well written article in the 'Westminster' on the "Essays and Reviews" was by your friend Mr Harrison.[1] Though I don't quite agree with his view of the case, I admired the tone and style of the writing greatly.

Letter to Mrs Congreve, 19th Oct. 1860.

There is no objection to Wednesday but this—that it is our day for hearing a course of lectures, and the lecture begins at eight. Now, since you can't come often, we want to keep you as long as we can, and we have a faint hope that Mr Congreve might be able to come from his work and dine with us and take you home. But if that were impossible, could you not stay all night? There is a bed ready for you. Think of all that, and if you can manage to give us the longer visit, choose another day when our evening will be unbroken. I will understand by your silence that you can only come for a shorter time, and that you abide by your plan of coming on Wednesday. I am really quite hungry for the sight of you.

[1] Mr Frederic Harrison, the now well-known writer, and a member of the Positivist body.

I agree with you in preferring to put simply "New Edition"; and I see, too, that the practice of advertising numbers is made vulgar and worthless by the doubtful veracity of some publishers, and the low character of the books to which they affix this supposed guarantee of popularity. *Magna est veritas*, &c. I can't tell you how much comfort I feel in having publishers who believe that.

Letter to John Blackwood, 2d Nov. 1860.

You have read the hostile article in the 'Quarterly,' I daresay. I have not seen it; but Mr Lewes's report of it made me more cheerful than any review I have heard of since 'The Mill' came out. You remember Lord John Russell was once laughed at immensely for saying that he felt confident he was right, because all parties found fault with him. I really find myself taking nearly the same view of my position, with the Freethinkers angry with me on one side and the writer in the 'Quarterly' on the other—*not* because my representations are untruthful, but because they are impartial—because I don't *load* my dice so as to make their side win. The parenthetical hint that the classical quotations in my books might be "more correctly printed," is an amusing sample of the grievance that belongs to review-writing in general, since there happens to be only *one* classical quotation in them all—the

Greek one from the Philoctetes in "Amos Barton." By-the-by, will you see that the readers have not allowed some error to creep into that solitary bit of pedantry?

Letter to Miss Sara Hennell, 13th Nov. 1860.

I understand your paradox of "expecting disappointments," for that is the only form of hope with which I am familiar. I should like, for your sake, that you should rather see us in our *own* house than in this; for I fear your carrying away a general sense of *yellow* in connection with us—and I am sure that is enough to set you against the thought of us. There are some staring yellow curtains which you will hardly help blending with your impression of our moral sentiments. In our own drawing-room I mean to have a paradise of greenness. I have lately re-read your 'Thoughts,' from the beginning of the "Psychical Essence of Christianity" to the end of the "History of Philosophy," and I feel my original impression confirmed —that the "Psychical Essence" and "General Review of the Christian System" are the most valuable portions. I think you once expressed your regret that I did not understand the analogy you traced between Feuerbach's theory and Spencer's. I don't know what gave you that impression, for *I* never said so. I see your meaning distinctly in that parallel. If you referred to something in Mr Lewes's letter, let me say, once for all, that you must not impute *my* opinions to *him* nor *vice versâ*. The intense happiness of our union is derived in a high degree from the perfect freedom with which we each follow and declare our own impressions. In this respect I know *no* man so great as he—that difference of opinion rouses no egoistic irritation in him, and that he is ready to admit that another argument is the stronger the moment his intellect recognises it. I am glad to see Mr Bray contributing his quota to the exposure of that odious trickery—spirit-rapping. It was not headache that I was suffering from when Mr Bray called, but extreme languor and unbroken fatigue from morning to night—a state which is always accompanied in me, psychically, by utter self-distrust and despair of ever being equal to the demands of life. We should be very pleased to hear some news of Mr and Mrs Call. I feel their removal from town quite a loss to us.

Letter to Miss Sara Hennell, 13th Nov. 1860.

Nov. 28.—Since I last wrote in this Journal, I have suffered much from physical weakness, accompanied with mental depression. The loss of the country has seemed very bitter to me, and my want of health and strength has prevented me

Journal, 1860.

Journal, 28th Nov. 1860.

from working much — still worse, has made me despair of ever working well again. I am getting better now by the help of tonics, and shall be better still if I could gather more bravery, resignation, and simplicity of striving. In the meantime my cup is full of blessings: my home is bright and warm with love and tenderness, and in more material, vulgar matters we are very fortunate.

Last Tuesday — the 20th — we had a pleasant evening. Anthony Trollope dined with us, and made me like him very much by his straightforward wholesome *Wesen.* Afterwards Mr Helps came in, and the talk was extremely agreeable. He told me the Queen had been speaking to him in great admiration of my books—especially 'The Mill on the Floss.' It is interesting to know that Royalty can be touched by that sort of writing, and I was grateful to Mr Helps for his wish to tell me of the sympathy given to me in that quarter.

To-day I have had a letter from M. d'Albert, saying that at last the French edition of 'Adam Bede' is published. He pleases me very much by saying that he finds not a sentence that he can retrench in the first volume of 'The Mill.'

I am engaged now in writing a story—the idea

of which came to me after our arrival in this house, and which has thrust itself between me and the other book I was meditating. It is 'Silas Marner, the Weaver of Raveloe.' I am still only at about the 62d page, for I have written slowly and interruptedly. Journal, 28th Nov. 1860.

The sight of sunshine usually brings you to my mind, because you are my latest association with the country; but I think of you much oftener than I see the sunshine, for the weather in London has been more uninterruptedly dismal than ever for the last fortnight. Nevertheless *I* am brighter; and since I believe your goodness will make that agreeable news to you, I write on purpose to tell it. Quinine and steel have at last made me brave and cheerful, and I really don't mind a journey up-stairs. If you had not repressed our hope of seeing you again until your sister's return, I should have asked you to join us for the Exeter Hall performance of the "Messiah" this evening, which I am looking forward to with delight. The Monday Popular Concerts at St James's Hall are our easiest and cheapest pleasures. I go in my bonnet; we sit in the shilling places in the body of the hall, and hear to perfection for a shilling! That is agreeable when one hears Beethoven's quartetts Letter to Mrs Congreve, 7th Dec. 1860 and sonatas. Pray bear in mind that these things are to be had when you are more at liberty.

Journal, 1860.

Dec. 17.—We entered to-day our new home—16 Blandford Square—which we have taken for three years, hoping by the end of that time to have so far done our duty by the boys as to be free to live where we list.

Letter to Miss Sara Hennell, 20th Dec. 1860.

Your vision of me as "settled" was painfully in contrast with the fact. The last virtue human beings will attain, I am inclined to think, is scrupulosity in promising and faithfulness in fulfilment. We are still far off our last stadium of development, and so it has come to pass, that though we were in the house on Monday last, our curtains are not up and our oil-cloth is not down. Such is life, seen from the furnishing point of view! I can't tell you how hateful this sort of time-frittering work is to me, who every year care less for houses and detest shops more. To crown my sorrows, I have lost my pen—my old favourite pen, with which I have written for eight years,—at least it is not forthcoming. We have been reading the proof of Mr Spencer's second part, and I am supremely gratified by it, because he brings his argument to a point which I did not anticipate from him. It is, as he says, a result of his riper thought. After all the bustle of Monday, I went to hear Sims Reeves sing "Adelaide"—that *ne plus ultra* of passionate song,—and I wish you had been there for one quarter of an hour, that you might have heard it too.

The bright point in your letter is, that you are in a happy state of mind yourself. For the rest we must wait and not be impatient with those who have their inward trials, though everything outward seems to smile on them. It seems to those who are differently placed that the time of freedom from strong ties and urgent claims must be very precious for the ends of self-culture and good helpful work towards the world at large. But it hardly ever is so. As for the forms and ceremonies, I feel no regret that any should turn to them for comfort if they can find comfort in them; sympathetically I enjoy them myself. But I have faith in the working out of higher possibilities than the Catholic or any other Church has presented; and those who have strength to wait and endure are bound to accept no formula which their whole souls—their intellect as well as their emotions—do not embrace with entire reverence. The "highest calling and election" is to *do without opium*, and live through all our pain with conscious, clear-eyed endurance.

Letter to Madame Bodichon, 26th Dec. 1860.

Letter to Madame Bodichon, 26th Dec. 1860.

We have no sorrow just now, except my constant inward "worrit" of unbelief in any future of good work on my part. Everything I do seems poor and trivial in the doing; and when it is quite gone from me, and seems no longer my own, then I rejoice in it and think it fine. That is the history of my life.

I have been wanting to go to your school again, to refresh myself with the young voices there, but I have not been able to do it. My walks have all been taken up with shopping errands of late; but I hope to get more leisure soon.

We both beg to offer our affectionate remembrances to the doctor. Get Herbert Spencer's new work—the two first quarterly parts. It is the best thing he has done.

Journal, 1860.

Dec. 31.—This year has been marked by many blessings, and above all, by the comfort we have found in having Charles with us. Since we set out on our journey to Italy on 25th March, the time has not been fruitful in work: distractions about our change of residence have run away with many days; and since I have been in London my state of health has been depressing to all effort.

May the next year be more fruitful!

I am writing a story which came *across* my other plans by a sudden inspiration. I don't know at present whether it will resolve itself into a book short enough for me to complete before Easter, or whether it will expand beyond that possibility. It seems to me that nobody will take any interest in it but myself, for it is extremely unlike the popular stories going; but Mr Lewes declares that I am wrong, and says it is as good as anything I have done. It is a story of old-fashioned village life, which has unfolded itself from the merest millet-seed of thought. I think I get slower and more timid in my writing, but perhaps worry about houses and servants and boys, with want of bodily strength, may have had something to do with that. I hope to be quiet now. Letter to John Blackwood, 12th Jan. 1861.

Feb. 1.—The first month of the New Year has been passed in much bodily discomfort—making both work and leisure heavy. I have reached page 209 of my story, which is to be in one volume, and I want to get it ready for Easter, but I dare promise myself nothing with this feeble body. Journal, 1861.

The other day I had charming letters from M. and Mme. d'Albert, saying that the French 'Adam' goes on very well, and showing an appreciation of 'The Mill' which pleases me.

Letter to Mrs Congreve, 6th Feb. 1861.

I was feeling so ill on Friday and Saturday, that I had not spirit to write and thank you for the basket of eggs—an invaluable present. I was particularly grateful this morning at breakfast, when a fine large one fell to my share.

On Saturday afternoon we were both so utterly incapable, that Mr Lewes insisted on our setting off forthwith into the country. But we only got as far as Dorking, and came back yesterday. I felt a new creature as soon as I was in the country; and we had two brilliant days for rambling and driving about that lovely Surrey. I suppose we must keep soul and body together by occasional flights of this sort; and don't you think an occasional flight to town will be good for you?

Letter to Miss Sara Hennell, 8th Feb. 1861.

I have destroyed almost all my friends' letters to me, because they were only intended for my eyes, and could only fall into the hands of persons who knew little of the writers, if I allowed them to remain till after my death. In proportion as I love every form of piety—which is venerating love—I hate hard curiosity; and, unhappily, my experience has impressed me with the sense that hard curiosity is the more common temper of mind. But enough of that. The reminders I am getting from time to time of Coventry distress have made me think very often yearningly and painfully of the friends who are more immediately affected by it, and I often wonder if more definite information would increase or lessen my anxiety for them. Send me what word you can from time to time, that there may be some reality in my image of things round your hearth. Letter to Miss Sarah Hennell, 8th Feb. 1861.

I send you by post to-day about 230 pages of MS. I send it because in my experience printing and its preliminaries have always been rather a slow business; and as the story—if published at Easter at all—should be ready by Easter week, there is no time to lose. We are reading 'Carlyle's Memoirs' with much interest; but so far as we have gone, he certainly does seem to me something of a "Sadducee"—a very handsome one, judging from the portrait. What a memory and what an experience for a novelist! But somehow experience and finished faculty rarely go together. Dearly beloved Scott had the greatest combination of experience and faculty—yet even he never made the most of his treasures, at least in his *mode* of presentation. Send us better news of Major Blackwood if you can. We feel so old and rickety ourselves, that we have a peculiar interest in invalids. Mr Lewes is going to lecture for the Post Office this evening, by Letter to John Blackwood, 15th Feb. 1861.

Mr Trollope's request. I am rather uneasy about it, and wish he were well through the unusual excitement.

Letter to Mrs Congreve, 16th Feb. 1861.

I have been much relieved by Mr Lewes having got through his lecture at the Post Office[1] with perfect ease and success, for I had feared the unusual excitement for him. *I* am better. I have not been working much lately—indeed this year has been a comparatively idle one. I think my *malaise* is chiefly owing to the depressing influence of town air and town scenes. The Zoological Gardens are my one outdoor pleasure now, and we can take it several times a-week, for Mr Lewes has become a fellow.

My love is often visiting you. Entertain it well.

Letter to Miss Sara Hennell, 20th Feb. 1861.

I am glad to hear that Mr Maurice impressed you agreeably. If I had strength to be adventurous on Sunday, I should go to hear him preach as well as others. But I am unequal to the least exertion or irregularity. My only pleasure away from our own hearth is going to the Zoological Gardens. Mr Lewes is a fellow, so we turn in there several times a-week; and I find the birds and beasts there most congenial to my spirit. There is a Shoebill, a great bird of grotesque ugliness, whose

[1] Lecture on Cell Forms.

top-knot looks brushed up to a point with an exemplary deference to the demands of society, but who, I am sure, has no idea that he looks the handsomer for it. I cherish an unrequited attachment to him. Letter to Miss Sara Hennell, 20th Feb. 1861.

If you are in London this morning, in this fine dun-coloured fog, you know how to pity me. But I feel myself wicked for implying that I have any grievances. Only last week we had a circular from the clergyman at Attleboro, where there is a considerable population entirely dependent on the ribbon trade, telling us how the poor weavers are suffering from the effects of the Coventry strike. And these less known undramatic tales of want win no wide help, such as has been given in the case of the Hartley colliery accident. Letter to Mrs Congreve, 23d Feb. 1861.

Your letter was a contribution towards a more cheerful view of things, for whatever may be the minor evils you hint at, I know that Mr Congreve's better health and the satisfaction you have in his doing effective work will outweigh them. We have had a Dr Wyatt here lately—an Oxford physician—who was much interested in hearing of Mr Congreve again—not only on the ground of Oxford remembrances, but from having read his writings.

Letter to Mrs Congreve, 23d Feb. 1861.

I was much pleased with the affectionate respect that was expressed in all the notices of Mr Clough[1] that I happened to see in the newspapers. They were an indication that there must be a great deal of private sympathy to soothe poor Mrs Clough, if any soothing is possible in such cases. That little poem of his which was quoted in the 'Spectator' about parted friendships touched me deeply.

You may be sure we are ailing, but I am ashamed of dwelling on a subject that offers so little variety.

Letter to John Blackwood, 24th Feb. 1861.

I don't wonder at your finding my story, as far as you have read it, rather sombre: indeed, I should not have believed that any one would have been interested in it but myself (since Wordsworth is dead) if Mr Lewes had not been strongly arrested by it. But I hope you will not find it at all a sad story, as a whole, since it sets—or is intended to set—in a strong light the remedial influences of pure, natural human relations. The Nemesis is a very mild one. I have felt all through as if the story would have lent itself best to metrical rather than to prose fiction, especially in all that relates to the psychology of Silas; except that, under that treatment, there could not be an equal play of humour. It came to me first of all quite suddenly, as a sort

[1] Arthur Hugh Clough—the Poet.

of legendary tale, suggested by my recollection of having once, in early childhood, seen a linen weaver with a bag on his back; but as my mind dwelt on the subject, I became inclined to a more realistic treatment.

Letter to John Blackwood, 24th Feb. 1861.

My chief reason for wishing to publish the story now, is, that I like my writings to appear in the order in which they are written, because they belong to successive mental phases, and when they are a year behind me, I can no longer feel that thorough identification with them which gives zest to the sense of authorship. I generally like them better at that distance, but then I feel as if they might just as well have been written by somebody else. It would have been a great pleasure to me if Major Blackwood could have read my story. I am very glad to have the first part tested by the reading of your nephew and Mr Simpson, and to find that it can interest them at all.

March 10.—Finished 'Silas Marner,' and sent off the last thirty pages to Edinburgh.

Journal, 1861.

Your letter came to me just as we were preparing to start in search of fresh air and the fresh thoughts that come with it. I hope you never doubt that I feel a deep interest in knowing all facts that touch you nearly. I should like to think

Letter to the Brays, 19th March 1861, from Hastings.

Letter to the Brays, 19th March 1861, from Hastings.

that it was some small comfort to Cara and you to know that wherever I am there is one among that number of your friends — necessarily decreasing with increasing years—who enter into your present experience with the light of memories; for kind feeling can never replace fully the sympathy that comes from memory. My disposition is so faultily anxious and foreboding, that I am not likely to forget anything of a saddening sort.

Tell Sara we saw Mr William Smith, author of 'Thorndale,' a short time ago, and he spoke of her and her book with interest: he thought her book "suggestive." He called on us during a visit to London, made for the sake of getting married. The lady is, or rather was, a Miss Cumming, daughter of a blind physician of Edinburgh. He said they had talked to each other for some time of the "impossibility" of marrying, because they were both too poor. "But," he said, "it is dangerous, Lewes, to talk even of the impossibility." The difficulties gradually dwindled, and the advantages magnified themselves. She is a nice person, we hear; and I was particularly pleased with *him*,—he is modest to diffidence, yet bright and keenly awake.

I am just come in from our first good blow on the beach, and have that delicious sort of numbness in arms and legs that comes from walking hard in a fresh wind.

Letter to the Brays, 19th March 1861, from Hastings.

'Silas Marner' is in one volume. It was quite a sudden inspiration that came across me, in the midst of altogether different meditations.

Letter to John Blackwood, 30th March 1861.

The latest number I had heard of was 3300, so that your letter brought me agreeable information. I am particularly gratified, because this spirited subscription must rest on my character as a writer generally, and not simply on the popularity of 'Adam Bede.' There is an article on 'The Mill' in 'Macmillan's Magazine' which is worth reading. I cannot, of course, agree with the writer in all his regrets: if I could have done so, I should not have written the book I did write, but quite another. Still it is a comfort to me to read any criticism which recognises the high responsibilities of literature that undertakes to represent life. The ordinary tone about art is that the artist may do what he will, provided he pleases the public.

I am very glad to be told—whenever you can tell me—that the Major is not suffering heavily. I know so well the preciousness of those smiles that tell one the mind is not held out of all reach of soothing.

We are wavering whether we shall go to Florence

this spring, or wait till the year and other things are more advanced.

Letter to Mrs Peter Taylor, 1st April 1861.

It gave me pleasure to have your letter, not only because of the kind expressions of sympathy it contains, but also because it gives me an opportunity of telling you, after the lapse of years, that I remember gratefully how you wrote to me with generous consideration and belief at a time when most persons who knew anything of me were disposed (naturally enough) to judge me rather severely. Only a woman of rare qualities would have written to me as you did on the strength of the brief intercourse that had passed between us.

It was never a trial to me to have been cut off from what is called the world, and I think I love none of my fellow-creatures the less for it: still I must always retain a peculiar regard for those who showed me any kindness in word or deed at that time, when there was the least evidence in my favour. The list of those who did so is a short one, so that I can often and easily recall it.

For the last six years I have ceased to be "Miss Evans" for any one who has personal relations with me—having held myself under all the responsibilities of a married woman. I wish this to be distinctly understood; and when I tell you that we have a great boy of eighteen at home who calls me "mother," as well as two other boys, almost as tall, who write to me under the same name, you will understand that the point is not one of mere egoism or personal dignity, when I request that any one who has a regard for me will cease to speak of me by my maiden name.

Letter to Mrs Peter Taylor, 1st April 1861.

Letter to John Blackwood, 4th April 1861.

I am much obliged to you for your punctuality in sending me my precious cheque. I prize the money fruit of my labour very highly as the means of saving us dependence, or the degradation of writing when we are no longer able to write well, or to write what we have not written before.

Mr Langford brought us word that he thought the total subscription (including Scotland and Ireland) would mount to 5500. That is really very great. And letters drop in from time to time giving me words of strong encouragement—especially about 'The Mill;' so that I have reason to be cheerful, and to believe that where one has a large public, one's words must hit their mark. If it were not for that, special cases of misinterpretation might paralyse me. For example, pray notice how one critic attributes to me a disdain for Tom; as if it were not *my* respect for Tom which infused itself into my reader,—as if he could have respected Tom

Letter to John Blackwood, 4th April 1861.

if I had not painted him with respect; the exhibition of the right on both sides being the very soul of my intention in the story. However, I ought to be satisfied if I have roused the feeling that does justice to both sides.

Letter to Mrs Peter Taylor, 6th April 1861.

I feel more at ease in omitting formalities with you than I should with most persons, because I know you are yourself accustomed to have other reasons for your conduct than mere fashion, and I believe you will understand me without many words when I tell you what Mr Lewes felt unable to explain on the instant when you kindly expressed the wish to see us at your house—namely, that I have found it a necessity of my London life to make the rule of *never* paying visits. Without a carriage, and with my easily perturbed health, London distances would make any other rule quite irreconcilable for me with any efficient use of my days; and I am obliged to give up the *few* visits which would be really attractive and fruitful in order to avoid the *many* visits which would be the reverse. It is only by saying, "I never pay visits," that I can escape being ungracious or unkind—only by renouncing all social intercourse but such as comes to our own fireside, that I can escape sacrificing the chief objects of life.

I think it very good of those with whom I have much fellow-feeling, if they will let me have the pleasure of seeing them without their expecting the usual reciprocity of visits; and I hope I need hardly say that you are among the visitors who would be giving me pleasure in this way. I think your imagination will supply all I have left unsaid—all the details that run away with our hours when our life extends at all beyond our own homes, and I am not afraid of your misinterpreting my stay-at-home rule into churlishness. Letter to Mrs Peter Taylor, 6th April 1861.

We went to hear Beethoven's "Mass in D" last night, and on Wednesday to hear Mendelssohn's "Walpurgis Nacht," and Beethoven's "Symphony in B," so that we have had two musical treats this week; but the enjoyment of such things is much diminished by the gas and bad air. Indeed our long addiction to a quiet life, in which our daily walk amongst the still grass and trees was a *fête* to us, has unfitted us for the sacrifices that London demands. Don't think about reading 'Silas Marner' just because it is come out. I hate *obligato* reading and *obligato* talk about my books. *I never send them to any one,* and never wish to be spoken to about them, except by an unpremeditated spontaneous prompting. They are written out of my Letter to Miss Sara Hennell, 13th April 1861.

Letter to Miss Sara Hennell, 13th April 1861.

deepest belief, and as well as I can, for the great public — and every sincere strong word will find its mark in that public. Perhaps the annoyance I suffered [referring to the Liggins affair] has made me rather morbid on such points; but apart from my own weaknesses, I think the less an author hears about himself the better. Don't mistake me: I am writing a general explanation, *not* anything applicable to you.

Journal, 1861.

April 19.—We set off on our second journey to Florence, through France and by the Cornice Road. Our weather was delicious, a little rain, and we suffered neither from heat nor from dust.

Letter to Charles L. Lewes, 25th April 1861.

We have had a paradisaic journey hitherto. It does one good to look at the Provençals—men and women. They are quite a different race from the Northern French—large, round-featured, full-eyed, with an expression of *bonhomie,* calm and suave. They are very much like the pleasantest Italians. The women at Arles and Toulon are remarkably handsome. On Tuesday morning we set out about ten on our way to Nice, hiring a carriage and taking post-horses. The sky was grey, and after an hour or so we had rain: nevertheless our journey to Vidauban, about half-way to Nice, was enchanting. Everywhere a delicious plain, covered with bright green corn, sprouting vines, mulberry-trees, olives, and here and there meadows sprinkled with buttercups, made the nearer landscapes, and, in the distance, mountains, of varying outline. *Mutter* felt herself in a state of perfect bliss from only looking at this peaceful, generous nature,—and you often came across the green blades of corn, and made her love it all the better. We had meant to go on to Fréjus that night, but no horses were to be had; so we made up our minds to rest at Vidauban, and went out to have a stroll before our six o'clock dinner. Such a stroll! The sun had kindly come out for us, and we enjoyed it all the more for the greyness of the morning. There is a crystally clear river flowing by Vidauban, called the Argent: it rushes along between a fringe of aspens and willows; and the sunlight lay under the boughs, and fell on the eddying water, making Pater and me very happy as we wandered. The next morning we set off early, to be sure of horses before they had been used up by other travellers. The country was not quite so lovely, but we had the sunlight to compensate until we got past Fréjus, where we had our first view of the sea since Toulon, and where the scenery changes to the entirely mountainous, the road winding above gorges of pine-clad masses for a long way. To

Letter to Charles L. Lewes, 25th April 1861.

Letter to Charles L. Lewes, 25th April 1861.

heighten the contrast, a heavy storm came, which thoroughly laid the dust for us, if it had no other advantage. The sun came out gloriously again before we reached Cannes, and lit up the yellow broom, which is now in all its splendour, and clothes vast slopes by which our road wound. We had still a four hours' journey to Nice, where we arrived at six o'clock, with headaches that made us glad of the luxuries to be found in a great hotel.

Journal, 1861.

May 5.—Dear Florence was lovelier than ever on this second view, and ill-health was the only deduction from perfect enjoyment. We had comfortable quarters in the Albergo della Vittoria, on the Arno; we had the best news from England about the success of 'Silas Marner;' and we had long letters from our dear boy to make us feel easy about home.

Letter to John Blackwood, 5th May 1861.

Your pleasant news had been ripening at the Post Office several days before we enjoyed the receipt of it; for our journey lasted us longer than we expected, and we didn't reach this place till yesterday evening. We have come with *vetturino* from Toulon—the most delightful (and the most expensive) journey we have ever had. I daresay you know the Cornice: if not, *do* know it some time, and bring Mrs Blackwood that way into Italy. Meanwhile I

Letter to John Blackwood, 5th May 1861.

am glad to think that you are having a less fatiguing change to places where you can "carry the comforts o' the Sautmarket" with you, which is not quite the case with travellers along the Mediterranean coast. I hope I shall soon hear that you are thoroughly set up by fresh air and fresh circumstances, along with pleasant companionship.

Except a thunderstorm, which gave a grand variety to the mountains, and a little gentle rain, the first day from Toulon, which made the green corn all the fresher, we have had unbroken sunshine, without heat and without dust. I suppose this season and late autumn must be the perfect moments for taking this supremely beautiful journey. We must be for ever ashamed of ourselves if we don't work the better for it.

It was very good of you to write to me in the midst of your hurry, that I might have good news to greet me. It really did lighten our weariness, and make the noisy streets that prevented sleep more endurable. I was amused with your detail about Professor Aytoun's sovereigns. There can be no great paintings of misers under the present system of paper-money—cheques, bills, scrip, and the like: nobody can handle that dull property as men handled the glittering gold.

Letter to Charles L. Lewes, 17th May 1861.

The Florentine winds, being of a grave and earnest disposition, have naturally a disgust for trivial *dilettanti* foreigners, and seize on the peculiarly feeble and worthless with much virulence. In consequence we had a sad history for nearly a week—Pater doing little else than nurse me, and I doing little else but feel eminently uncomfortable, for which, as you know, I have a faculty "second to none." I feel very full of thankfulness for all the creatures I have got to love—all the beautiful and great things that are given me to know; and I feel, too, much younger and more hopeful, as if a great deal of life and work were still before me. Pater and I have had great satisfaction in finding our impressions of admiration more than renewed in returning to Florence: the things we cared about when we were here before seem even more worthy than they did in our memories. We have had delightful weather since the cold winds abated; and the evening lights on the Arno, the bridges, and the quaint houses, are a treat that we think of beforehand.

Your letters, too, are thought of beforehand. We long for them, and when they come they don't disappoint us: they tell us everything, and make us feel at home with you after a fashion. I confess to some dread of Blandford Square in the abstract. I fear London will seem more odious to me than ever; but I think I shall bear it with more fortitude. After all, that is the best place to live in where one has a strong reason for living.

Letter to Charles L. Lewes, 17th May 1861.

We have been industriously foraging in old streets and old books. I feel very brave just now, and enjoy the thought of work—but don't set your mind on my doing just what I have dreamed. It may turn out that I can't work freely and fully enough in the medium I have chosen, and in that case I must give it up: for I will never write anything to which my whole heart, mind, and conscience don't consent, so that I may feel that it was something—however small—which wanted to be done in this world, and that I am just the organ for that small bit of work.

Letter to John Blackwood, 19th May 1861.

I am very much cheered by the way in which 'Silas' is received. I hope it has made some slight pleasure for you too, in the midst of incomparably deeper feelings of sadness.[1] Your quiet tour among the lakes was the best possible thing for you. What place is not better "out of the season"?—although I feel I am almost wicked in my hatred of being where there are many other people enjoy-

[1] The death of Major Blackwood.

Letter to John Blackwood, 19th May 1861.

ing themselves. I am very far behind Mr Buckle's millennial prospect, which is, that men will be more and more congregated in cities and occupied with human affairs, so as to be less and less under the influence of Nature—*i.e.*, the sky, the hills, and the plains; whereby superstition will vanish, and statistics will reign for ever and ever.

Mr Lewes is kept in continual distraction by having to attend to my wants—going with me to the Magliabecchian library, and poking about everywhere on my behalf—I having very little self-help about me of the pushing and inquiring kind.

I look forward with keen anxiety to the next outbreak of war—longing for some turn of affairs that will save poor Venice from being bombarded by those terrible Austrian forts.

Thanks for your letters: we both say, "More—give us more."

Letter to Charles L. Lewes, 27th May 1861.

Florence is getting hot, and I am the less sorry to leave it because it has agreed very ill with the dear Paterculus. This evening we have been mounting to the top of Giotto's tower—a very sublime getting up-stairs indeed—and our muscles are much astonished at the unusual exercise; so you must not be shocked if my letter seems to be written with dim faculties as well as with a dim light.

We have seen no one but Mrs Trollope and her pretty little girl Beatrice, who is a musical genius. She is a delicate fairy, about ten years old, but sings with a grace and expression that make it a thrilling delight to hear her. Letter to Charles L. Lewes, 27th May 1861.

We have had glorious sunsets, shedding crimson and golden lights under the dark bridges across the Arno. All Florence turns out at eventide, but we avoid the slow crowds on the Lung' Arno, and take our way "up all manner of streets."

May and June.—At the end of May Mr T. Trollope came back and persuaded us to stay long enough to make the expedition to Camaldoli and La Vernia in his company. We arrived at Florence on the 4th May, and left it on the 7th June—thirty-four days of precious time spent there. Will it be all in vain? Our morning hours were spent in looking at streets, buildings, and pictures, in hunting up old books, at shops or stalls, or in reading at the Magliabecchian Library. Alas! I could have done much more if I had been well; but that regret applies to most years of my life. Returned by Lago Maggiore and the St Gothard; reached home June 14. Blackwood having waited in town to see us, came to lunch with us, and asked me if I would go to dine at Greenwich on the following Monday, to which I said Journal. 1861.

Journal 1861.

"yes," by way of exception to my resolve that I will go nowhere for the rest of this year. He drove us there with Colonel Stewart, and we had a pleasant evening—the sight of a game at golf in the Park, and a hazy view of the distant shipping, with the Hospital finely broken by trees in the foreground. At dinner Colonel Hamley and Mr Skene joined us: Delane, who had been invited, was unable to come. The chat was agreeable enough, but the sight of the gliding ships darkening against the dying sunlight made me feel chat rather importunate.

June 16.—This morning, for the first time, I feel myself quietly settled at home. I am in excellent health, and long to work steadily and effectively. If it were possible that I should produce *better* work than I have yet done! At least there is a possibility that I may make greater efforts against indolence and the despondency that comes from too egoistic a dread of failure.

June 19.—This is the last entry I mean to make in my old book in which I wrote for the first time at Geneva in 1849. What moments of despair I passed through after that—despair that life would ever be made precious to me by the consciousness that I lived to some good purpose! It was that sort of despair that sucked away the sap of half the hours which might have been filled by energetic youthful activity; and the same demon tries to get hold of me again whenever an old work is dismissed and a new one is being meditated. Journal, 1861.

Some of one's first thoughts on coming home after an absence of much length are about the friends one had left behind—what has happened to them in the meantime, and how are they now? And yet, though we came home last Friday evening, I have not had the quiet moment for writing these thoughts until this morning. I know I need put no questions to you, who always divine what I want to be told. We have had a perfect journey except as regards health—a large, large exception. The cold winds alternating with the hot sun, or some other cause, laid very unkind hold on Mr Lewes early after our arrival at Florence, and he was ailing with sore throat and cough continually, so that he has come back looking thin and delicate, though the ailments seem to be nearly passed away. Letter to Miss Sara Hennell, 19th June 1861.

I wish you could have shared the pleasures of our last expedition from Florence—to the Monasteries of Camaldoli and La Vernia: I think it was just the sort of thing you would have entered into

Letter to Miss Sara Hennell, 19th June 1861.

with thorough zest. Imagine the Franciscans of La Vernia, which is perched upon an abrupt rock rising sheer on the summit of a mountain, turning out at midnight (and when there is deep snow for their feet to plunge in), and chanting their slow way up to the little chapel perched at a lofty distance above their already lofty monastery! This they do every night throughout the year in all weathers.

Give my loving greeting to Cara and Mr Bray, and then sit down and write me one of your charming letters, making a little picture of everybody and everything about you. God bless you—is the old-fashioned summing up of sincere affection, without the least smirk of studied civility.

Letter to Miss Sara Hennell, 12th July 1861.

Your letter gave me a pleasant vision of Sunday sunshine on the flowers, and you among them, with your eyes brightened by busy and enjoyable thoughts.

Yes; I hope we are well out of that phase in which the most philosophic view of the past was held to be a smiling survey of human folly, and when the wisest man was supposed to be one who could sympathise with no age but the age to come.

When I received your Monday packet, I was

fresh from six quarto volumes on the history of the monastic orders, and had just begun a less formidable modern book on the same subject — Montalembert's 'Monks of the West.' Our reading, you see, lay in very different quarters, but I fancy our thoughts sometimes touched the same ground. I am rather puzzled and shocked, however, by your high admiration of the Articles on the Study of History in the 'Cornhill.' I should speak with the reserve due to the fact that I have only read the second article; and this, I confess, did not impress me as exhibiting any mastery of the question, while its tone towards much abler thinkers than the writer himself is to me extremely repulsive. Such writing as, "We should not be called upon to believe that every crotchet which tickled the insane vanity of a conceited Frenchman was an eternal and self-evident truth," is to me simply disgusting, though it were directed against the Father of lies. It represents no fact except the writer's own desire to be bitter, and is worthily finished by the dull and irreverent antithesis of "the eternal truth and infernal lie."

Letter to Miss Sara Hennell, 12th July 1861.

I quite agree with you—so far as I am able to form a judgment—in regarding Positivism as one-sided; but Comte was a great thinker, nevertheless,

Letter to Miss Sara Hennell, 12th July 1861.

and ought to be treated with reverence by all smaller fry.

I have just been reading the Survey of the Middle Ages contained in the fifth volume of the 'Philosophie Positive,' and to my apprehension few chapters can be fuller of luminous ideas. I am thankful to learn from it. There may be more profundity in the 'Cornhill's' exposition than I am able to penetrate, or possibly the first article may contain weightier matter than the second.

Mrs Bodichon is near us now, and one always gets good from contact with her healthy practical life. Mr Lewes is gone to see Mrs Congreve and carry his net to the Wimbledon ponds. I hope he will get a little strength as well as grist for his microscope.

Letter to Mrs Congreve, 18th July 1861.

The English 'Imitation' I told you of, which is used by the Catholics, is Challoner's. I have looked into it again since I saw you, and I think if you want to give the book away, this translation is as good as any you are likely to get among current editions. If it were for yourself, an old bookstall would be more likely to furnish what you want. Don't ever think of me as valuing either you or Mr Congreve less instead of more. You naughtily implied something of that kind just when you were running away from me. How could any goodness become less precious to me unless my life had ceased to be a growth, and had become mere shrinking and degeneracy? I always imagine that if I were near you now, I should profit more by the gift of your presence—just as one feels about all past sunlight. Letter to Mrs Congreve, 18th July 1861.

July 24.—Walked with George over Primrose Hill. We talked of Plato and Aristotle. Diary, 1861.

July 26.—In the evening went to see Fechter as Hamlet, and sat next to Mrs Carlyle.

July 30.—Read little this morning—my mind dwelling with much depression on the probability or improbability of my achieving the work I wish to do. I struck out two or three thoughts towards an English novel. I am much afflicted with hopelessness and melancholy just now, and yet I feel the value of my blessings.

Thornie, our second boy, is at home from Edinburgh for his holidays, and I am apt to give more thought than is necessary to any little change in our routine. We had a treat the other night which I wished you could have shared with us. We saw Fechter in "Hamlet." His conception of the part is very nearly that indicated by the critical observations in 'Wilhelm Meister,' and the result is deeply Letter to Miss Sara Hennell, 30th July 1861.

Letter to Miss Sara Hennell, 30th July 1861.

interesting—the naturalness and sensibility of the *Wesen* overcoming in most cases the defective intonation. And even the intonation is occasionally admirable—for example, "And for my soul, what can he do to that?" &c., is given by Fechter with perfect simplicity, whereas the herd of English actors imagine themselves in a pulpit when they are saying it. *Apropos* of the pulpit, I had another failure in my search for edification last Sunday. Mme. Bodichon and I went to Little Portland Street Chapel, and lo! instead of James Martineau there was a respectable old Unitarian gentleman preaching about the dangers of ignorance and the satisfaction of a good conscience, in a tone of amiable propriety which seemed to belong to a period when brains were untroubled by difficulties, and the lacteals of all good Christians were in perfect order. I enjoyed the fine selection of Collects he read from the Liturgy. What an age of earnest faith, grasping a noble conception of life and determined to bring all things into harmony with it, has recorded itself in the simple, pregnant, rhythmical English of those Collects and of the Bible! The contrast when the good man got into the pulpit and began to pray in a borrowed, washy lingo—extempore in more sense than one!

Aug. 1.—Struggling constantly with depression. Diary, 1861.

Aug. 2.—Read Boccaccio's capital story of Fra Cipolla—one of his few good stories—and the little Hunchback in the 'Arabian Nights,' which is still better.

Aug. 10.—Walked with G. We talked of my Italian novel. In the evening, Mr Pigott and Mr Redford.

Aug. 12.—Got into a state of so much wretchedness in attempting to concentrate my thoughts on the construction of my story, that I became desperate, and suddenly burst my bonds, saying, I will not think of writing!

That doctrine which we accept rather loftily as a commonplace when we are quite young—namely, that our happiness lies entirely within, in our own mental and bodily state which determines for us the influence of everything outward—becomes a daily lesson to be learned, and learned with much stumbling as we get older. And until we know our friends' private thoughts and emotions, we hardly know what to grieve or rejoice over for them. Letter to Miss Sara Hennell, 12th Aug. 1861.

Aug. 17.—Mr Pigott and Mr Redford came, who gave us some music. Diary, 1861.

Aug. 20.—This morning I conceived the plot of my novel with new distinctness.

Diary, 1861.

Aug. 24.—Mr Pigott and Mr Redford came, and we had music. These have been placid, ineffective days—my mind being clouded and depressed.

Aug. 26.—Went with Barbara to her school, and spent the afternoon there.

Aug. 31.—In the evening came Mr Pigott and Mr Redford, and we had some music.

Letter to Charles L. Lewes, 11th Sept. 1861, from Malvern.

Your letter was a great delight to us, as usual; and the cheque, too, was welcome to people under hydropathic treatment, which appears to stimulate waste of coin as well as of tissue. Altogether we are figures in keeping with the landscape when it is well damped or "packed" under the early mist.

We thought rather contemptuously of the hills on our arrival; like travelled people, we hinted at the Alps and Apennines, and smiled with pity at our long-past selves that had felt quite a thrill at the first sight of them. But now we have tired our limbs by walking round their huge shoulders, we begin to think of them with more respect. We simply looked at them at first; we feel their presence now, and creep about them with due humility —whereby, you perceive, there hangs a moral. I do wish you could have shared for a little while with us the sight of this place. I fear you have never seen England under so loveable an aspect.

On the south-eastern side, where the great green hills have their longest slope, Malvern stands well nestled in fine trees—chiefly "sounding sycamores,"—and beyond there stretches to the horizon, which is marked by a low, faint line of hill, a vast level expanse of grass and corn fields, with hedgerows everywhere plumed with trees, and here and there a rolling mass of wood: it is one of the happiest scenes the eyes can look on—*freundlich*, according to the pretty German phrase. On the opposite side of this main range of hills, there is a more undulated and more thickly wooded country which has the sunset all to itself, and is bright with departing lights when our Malvern side is in cold evening shadow. We are so fortunate as to look out over the wide south-eastern valley from our sitting-room window.

Letter to Charles L. Lewes, 11th Sept. 1861, from Malvern.

Our landlady is a quaint old personage, with a strong Cheshire accent. She is, as she tells us, a sharp old woman, and "can see most things pretty quick;" and she is kind enough to communicate her wisdom very freely to us less crisply-baked mortals.

Sept. 11.—Yesterday we returned from Malvern (having gone there on 4th). During our stay I read Mrs Jameson's book on the 'Legends of the Mon-

Diary, 1861.

Diary, 1861. astic Orders,' corrected the 1st vol. of 'Adam Bede' for the new edition, and began Marchese's 'Storia di San Marco.'

Letter to Miss Sara Hennell, 18th Sept. 1861. I enter into your and Cara's furniture adjusting labours and your enjoyment of church and chapel afterwards. One wants a temple besides the out-door temple—a place where human beings do not ramble apart, but *meet* with a common impulse. I hope you have some agreeable lens through which you can look at circumstances—good health, at least. And really I begin to think people who are robust are in a position to pity all the rest of the world—except, indeed, that there are certain secrets taught only by pain, which are, perhaps, worth the purchase.

Diary, 1861. *Sept.* 23.—I have been unwell ever since we returned from Malvern, and have been disturbed from various causes in my work, so that I have scarcely done anything except correct my own books for a new edition. To-day I am much better, and hope to begin a more effective life to-morrow.

Sept. 28.—In the evening Mr Spencer, Mr Pigott, and Mr Redford came. We talked with Mr Spencer about his chapter on the Direction of Force—*i.e.*, line of least resistance.

Sept. 29 (Sunday).—Finished correcting 'Silas Marner.' I have thus corrected all my books for a new and cheaper edition, and feel my mind free for other work. Walked to the Zoo with the boys. Diary, 1861

Oct. 3.—To-day our new grand piano came—a great addition to our pleasures.

Oct. 4.—My mind still worried about my plot—and without any confidence in my ability to do what I want.

Oct. 5.—In the evening Mr Redford and Mr Spencer came, and we had much music.

Letter to Miss Sara Hennell, 6th Oct. 1861.

We are enjoying a great pleasure—a new grand piano,—and last evening we had a Beethoven night. We are looking out for a violinist: we have our violincello, who is full of sensibility, but with no negative in him—*i.e.*, no obstinate sense of time—a man who is all assent and perpetual *rallentando.* We can enjoy the pleasure the more, because Mr Lewes's health is promising.

Oct. 7.—Began the first chapter of my novel (Romola). Diary, 1861.

Oct. 9.—Read Nerli.

Oct. 11.—Nardi's 'History of Florence.' In the afternoon walked with Barbara, and talked with her from lunch till dinner-time.

Diary, 1861. *Oct.* 12.—In the evening we had our usual Saturday mixture of visitors, talk, and music: an agreeable addition being Dr M'Donnell of Dublin.

Oct. 14.—Went with Barbara to her school to hear the children sing.

Oct. 18.—Walked with G. and Mr Spencer to Hampstead, and continued walking for more than five hours. In the evening we had music. Mrs Bodichon and Miss Parkes were our additional visitors.

Letter to Mrs Congreve, 23d Oct. 1861. I am rather jealous of the friends who get so much of you—especially when they are so unmeritorious as to be evangelical and spoil your rest. But I will not grumble. I am in the happiest, most contented mood, and have only good news to tell you. I have hardly any trouble nearer to me than the American War and the prospects of poor cotton weavers. While you were shivering at Boulogne, we were walking fast to avoid shivering at Malvern, and looking slightly blue after our sitz baths. Nevertheless that discipline answered admirably, and Mr Lewes's health has been steadily improving since our Malvern expedition. As for me, imagine what I must be to have walked for five hours the other day! Or, better still, imagine me always cheerful, and infer the altered condition of my mucous membrane. The difference must be there; for it is not in my moral sentiments or in my circumstances,—unless, indeed, a new grand piano, which tempts me to play more than I have done for years before, may be reckoned an item important enough to have contributed to the change. We talk of you very often, and the image of you is awakened in my mind still oftener. You are associated by many subtle, indescribable ties with some of my most precious and most silent thoughts. I am so glad you have the comfort of feeling that Mr Congreve is prepared for his work again. I am hoping to hear, when we see you, that the work will be less and less fagging, now the introductory years are past. Letter to Mrs Congreve, 23d Oct. 1861.

Charley is going to Switzerland for his holiday next month. We shall enjoy our dual solitude; yet the dear boy is more and more precious to us from the singular rectitude and tenderness of his nature. Make signs to us as often as you can. You know how entirely Mr Lewes shares my delight in seeing you and hearing from you.

Oct. 28 *and* 30.—Not very well. Utterly desponding about my book. Diary, 1861.

Oct. 31.—Still with an incapable head—trying to write, trying to construct, and unable.

Diary, 1861. *Nov.* 6.—So utterly dejected, that in walking with G. in the Park, I almost resolved to give up my Italian novel.

Nov. 10 (Sunday).—New sense of things to be done in my novel, and more brightness in my thoughts. Yesterday I was occupied with ideas about my next English novel; but this morning the Italian scenes returned upon me with fresh attraction. In the evening read 'Monteil.' A marvellous book; crammed with erudition, yet not dull or tiresome.

Nov. 14.—Went to the British Museum reading-room for the first time—looking over costumes.

Nov. 20.—Mrs Congreve, Miss Bury, and Mr Spencer to lunch.

Letter to Miss Sara Hennell, 22d Nov. 1861.

Your loving words of remembrance find a very full answer in my heart—fuller than I can write. The years seem to *rush* by now, and I think of death as a fast approaching end of a journey—double and treble reason for loving as well as working while it is day. We went to see Fechter's Othello the other night. It is lamentably bad. He has not weight and passion enough for deep tragedy; and, to my feeling, the play is so degraded by his representation, that it is positively demoralising—as, indeed, all tragedy must be when it fails to move pity and terror. In this case it seems to move only titters among the smart and vulgar people who always make the bulk of a theatre audience. We had a visit from our dear friend Mrs Congreve on Wednesday—a very infrequent pleasure now; for between our own absences from home and hers, and the fatigue of London journeying, it is difficult for us to manage meetings. Mr Congreve is, as usual, working hard in his medical studies — toiling backward and forward daily. What courage and patience are wanted for every life that aims to produce anything! Letter to Miss Sara Hennell, 22d Nov. 1861.

Nov. 30.—In the evening we had Wilkie Collins, Mr Pigott, and Mr Spencer, and talked without any music. Journal, 1861.

Dec. 3-7.—I continued very unwell until Saturday, when I felt a little better. In the evening Dr Baetcke, Mr Pigott, and Mr Redford.

Miss Marshall came to see us yesterday. That is always a pleasure to me, not only from the sense I have of her goodness, but because she stirs so many remembrances. The first time I saw her was at Rufa's[1] wedding; and don't you remember the evening we spent at Mrs Dobson's? How young we all were then—how old now! She says Letter to Miss Sara Hennell, 6th Dec. 1861.

[1] Mrs Charles Hennell (now Mrs Call).

Letter to Miss Sara Hennell, 6th Dec. 1861.

you are all under the impression that Mr Lewes is still very ailing. Thank all good influences, it is not so. He has been mending ever since we went to Malvern, and is enjoying life and work more than he has done before for nearly a year. He has long had it in his mind to write a history of science —a great, great undertaking, which it is happiness to both of us to contemplate as possible for him. And now he is busy with Aristotle, and works with all the zest that belongs to fresh ideas. Strangely enough, after all the ages of writing about Aristotle, there exists no fair appreciation of his position in natural science.

I am particularly grumbling and disagreeable to myself just now, and I think no one bears physical pain so ill as I do, or is so thoroughly upset by it mentally.

Bulwer has behaved very nicely to me, and I have a great respect for the energetic industry with which he has made the most of his powers. He has been writing diligently in very various departments for more than thirty years, constantly improving his position, and profiting by the lessons of public opinion and of other writers.

I'm sorry you feel any degeneracy in Mr George Dawson. There was something very winning about him in old days, and even what was not winning, but the reverse, affected me with a sort of kindly pity. With such a gift of tongue as he had, it was inevitable that speech should outrun feeling and experience, and I could well imagine that his present self might look back on that self of 21-27 with a sort of disgust. It so often happens that others are measuring us by our past self while we are looking back on that self with a mixture of disgust and sorrow. It would interest me a good deal to know just how Mr Dawson preaches now. Letter to Miss Sara Hennell, 6th Dec. 1861.

I am writing on my knees with my feet on the fender, and in that attitude I always write very small,—but I hope your sight is not teazed by small writing.

Give my best love to Cara, and sympathy with her in the pleasure of grasping an old friend by the hand, and having long talks after the distance of years. I know Mr Bray will enjoy this too—and the new house will seem more like the old one for this warming.

Dec. 8 (Sunday).—G. had a headache, so we walked out in the morning sunshine. I told him my conception of my story, and he expressed great delight. Shall I ever be able to carry out my Journal, 1861.

Journal, 1861.

ideas? Flashes of hope are succeeded by long intervals of dim distrust. Finished the 8th vol. of Lastri, and began the 9th chapter of Varchi, in which he gives an accurate account of Florence.

Dec. 12.—Finished writing my plot, of which I must make several other draughts before I begin to write my book.

Dec. 13.—Read Poggiana. In the afternoon walked to Molini's and brought back Savonarola's 'Dialogus de Veritate Prophetica,' and 'Compendium Revelationum,' for £4!

Dec. 14.—In the evening came Mr Huxley, Mr Pigott, and Mr Redford.

Dec. 17.—Studied the topography of Florence.

Letter to Mrs Peter Taylor, 31st Dec. 1861.

It was pleasant to have a greeting from you at this season when all signs of human kindness have a double emphasis. As one gets older, epochs have necessarily some sadness, even for those who have, as I have, much family joy. The past, that one would like to mend, spreads behind one so lengthily, and the years of retrieval keep shrinking—the terrible *peau de chagrin* whose outline narrows and narrows with our ebbing life.

I hardly know whether it would be agreeable to you, or worth your while, ever to come to us on a Saturday evening, when we are always at home to any friend who may be kind enough to come to us. It would be very pleasant to us if it were pleasant to you.

During the latter half of 1861, I find the following amongst the books read: 'Histoire des Ordres Religieux,' Sacchetti's 'Novelle,' Sismondi's 'History of the Italian Republics,' 'Osservatore Fiorentino,' Tennemann's 'History of Philosophy,' T. A. Trollope's 'Beata,' Sismondi's 'Le Moyen Age Illustré,' 'The Monks of the West,' 'Introduction to Savonarola's Poems,' by Audin de Réans, Renan's 'Études d'Histoire Religieuse,' Virgil's 'Eclogues,' Buhle's 'History of Modern Philosophy,' Hallam on the Study of Roman Law in the Middle Ages, Gibbon on the Revival of Greek Learning, Nardi, Bulwer's 'Rienzi,' Burlamacchi's 'Life of Savonarola,' Pulci, Villari's 'Life of Savonarola,' Mrs Jameson's 'Sacred and Legendary Art,' 'Hymni and Epigrammati' of Marullus, Politian's 'Epistles,' Marchese's Works, Tiraboschi, Rock's 'Hierurgia,' Pettigrew 'On Medical Superstition,' Manni's 'Life of Burchiello,' Machiavelli's Works, Ginguené, Muratori 'On Proper Names,' Cicero 'De Officiis,' Petrarch's Letters, Craik's 'History of English Literature,' 'Conti Carnivaleschi,' Letters of Filelfo, Lastri and Varchi, Heeren on the Fifteenth Century.

SUMMARY.

JULY 1860 TO DECEMBER 1861.

Return from Italy to Wandsworth, accompanied by Charles Lewes—'Mill on the Floss' success—6000 sold—Letter to John Blackwood—French translation of 'Adam Bede,' by M. d'Albert of Geneva—Letter to Miss Hennell on her 'Thoughts in Aid of Faith'—Letter to John Blackwood on Sir Edward Lytton's criticism of 'The Mill on the Floss'—Letter to Mrs Bray, recalling feelings on journey to Italy in 1849—Letter to Miss Sara Hennell—Article on Strikes, by Henry Fawcett, in 'Westminster'—Sitting to Lawrence for portrait—Letter to Madame Bodichon—Interest in her schools—Letter to Miss Hennell, explaining criticism of 'Thoughts in aid of Faith'—Reading Emerson's 'Man the Reformer'—Deprecates writing about opinions on large questions in letters—Letter to John Blackwood—Italian novel project—Letter to Madame Bodichon—Love of the country—Removal to 10 Harewood Square—'Brother Jacob' written—Letter to Mrs Congreve—Frederic Harrison's article in 'Westminster' on "Essays and Reviews"—Letter to John Blackwood—Religious party standpoint—Classical quotations—Letter to Miss Hennell on re-reading 'Thoughts in Aid of Faith'—Tribute to Mr Lewes's dispassionate judgment—Suffering from loss of the country—Independence secured—Anthony Trollope and Arthur Helps—Queen's admiration of 'Mill on the Floss'—Writing 'Silas Marner,' a sudden inspiration—Letter to Mrs Congreve—Monday Popular Concerts—Moved to 16 Blandford Square—Waste of time in furnishing—Letter to Madame Bodichon—On religious forms and ceremonies—Herbert Spencer's new work, the best thing he has done—Letter to John Blackwood—'Silas Marner'—Letters to Mrs Congreve—Zoological Gardens—Visit to Dorking—Letter to John Blackwood—Scott—Letters to Miss Hennell—Private correspondence—Letter to Mrs Congreve—Arthur Clough's death—Letter to John Blackwood—'Silas Marner'—Books belong to successive mental phases—'Silas Marner' finished—Visit to Hastings—Letter to Charles Bray—Marriage of Mr William Smith—Letter to John Blackwood—Subscription to 'Silas Marner' 3300—Article in 'Macmillan' on 'The Mill'—Letter to Mrs Peter Taylor—Position—Letter to John Blackwood—Total Subscription to 'Silas Marner' 5500—Criticism on 'The Mill'—Letter to Mrs P. Taylor—Never pays visits—Letter to Miss Hennell—Hearing Beethoven and Mendelssohn music—Start on second journey to Italy—Letter to Charles Lewes, describing drive from Toulon to Nice—Arrival at Florence—Letter to John Blackwood—No painting of misers with paper money—Letter to Charles Lewes—Feels hopeful about future work—Letter to John Blackwood—Italian novel simmering—Letter to Charles Lewes—Beatrice Trollope—Expedition to Camaldoli and La Vernia with Mr T. A. Trollope—Return home by Lago Maggiore and St Gothard—Dinner at Greenwich with John Blackwood, Colonel Hamley, &c.—Reflections on waste of youth—Letters to Miss Hennell describing La Vernia—Improvement in general philosophic attitude—Articles on Study of History in the 'Cornhill'—Positivism one-sided—Admiration of Comte—Letter to Miss Hennell—Fechter in "Hamlet"—The Liturgy of the English Church—Depression—Musical Evenings with Mr Pigott and Mr

Redford—Trip to Malvern—Letter to Miss Hennell—New grand piano—Began 'Romola'—Saturday visitors—Letter to Mrs Congreve—Better spirits—Renewed depression—Letter to Miss Hennell—Time flying—Fechter as Othello—Letter to Miss Hennell—Lewes busy with Aristotle—Bulwer — George Dawson — Reading towards 'Romola'—Letter to Mrs Peter Taylor on the Past—Books read.

CHAPTER XII.

January 1.—Mr Blackwood sent me a note enclosing a letter from Montalembert about 'Silas Marner.' *I began again my novel of 'Romola.'* Journal, 1862.

It is not unlikely that our thoughts and wishes met about New Year's day, for I was only prevented from writing to you in that week by the fear of saying decidedly that we could *not* go to you, and yet finding afterwards that a clear sky, happening to coincide with an absence of other hindrances, would have made that pleasure possible for us. I think we believe in each other's thorough affection, and need not dread misunderstanding. But you must not write again, as you did in one note, a sort of apology for coming to us when you were tired, as if we didn't like to see you anyhow and at any time! And we especially like to think that our house can be a rest to you. Letter to Mrs Congreve, 7th Jan. 1862.

For the first winter in my life I am hardly ever

Letter to Mrs Congreve, 7th Jan. 1862.

free from cold. As soon as one has departed with the usual final stage of stuffiness, another presents itself with the usual introduction of sore throat. And Mr Lewes just now is a little ailing. But we have nothing serious to complain of.

You seemed to me so bright and brave the last time I saw you, that I have had cheerful thoughts of you ever since. Write to me always when anything happens to you, either pleasant or sad, that there is no reason for my not knowing, so that we may not spend long weeks in wondering how all things are with you.

And do come to us whenever you can, without caring about my going to you, for this is too difficult for me in chill and doubtful weather. Are you not looking anxiously for the news from America?

Letter to Mrs Bray, 13th Jan. 1862.

As for the brain being useless after fifty, that is no general rule: witness the good and hard work that has been done in plenty after that age. I wish I could be inspired with just the knowledge that would enable me to be of some good to you. I feel so ignorant and helpless. The year *is* opening happily for us, except—alas! the exception is a great one—in the way of health. Mr Lewes is constantly ailing, like a delicate headachy woman. But we have abundant blessings.

I hope you are able to enjoy Max Müller's great and delightful book during your imprisonment. It tempts me away from other things. I have read most of the numbers of 'Orley Farm,' and admire it very much, with the exception of such parts as I have read about Moulder & Co. Anthony Trollope is admirable in the presentation of even average life and character, and he is so thoroughly whole-some-minded that one delights in seeing his books lie about to be read. Have you read 'Beata' yet—the first novel written by his brother at Florence, who is our especial favourite? Do read it when you can, if the opportunity has not already come. I am going to be taken to a pantomime in the day-time, like a good child, for a Christmas treat, not having had my fair share of pantomime in the world.

Letter to Miss Sara Hennell, 14th Jan. 1862.

Jan. 18 (Saturday).—We had an agreeable evening. Mr Burton[1] and Mr Clark[2] of Cambridge made an acceptable variety in our party.

Journal, 1862.

Jan. 19-20.—Head very bad—producing terrible depression.

[1] Now Sir Frederic Burton, Director of the National Gallery, to whom we are indebted for the drawing of George Eliot now in the National Portrait Gallery, South Kensington, and who was a very intimate and valued friend of Mr and Mrs Lewes.

[2] Mr W. G. Clark, late Public Orator at Cambridge, well known as a scholar, and for his edition of Shakespeare in conjunction with Mr Aldis Wright.

Journal, 1862.

Jan. 23.—Wrote again, feeling in brighter spirits. Mr Smith the publisher called and had an interview with G. He asked if I were open to "a magnificent offer." This made me think about money —but it is better for me not to be rich.

Jan. 26 (Sunday).—Detained from writing by the necessity of gathering particulars: 1st, about Lorenzo de Medici's death; 2d, about the possible retardation of Easter; 3d, about Corpus Christi day; 4th, about Savonarola's preaching in the Quaresima of 1492. Finished 'La Mandragola'—second time reading for the sake of Florentine expressions—and began 'La Calandra.'

Jan. 31.—Have been reading some entries in my note-book of past times in which I recorded my *malaise* and despair. But it is impossible to me to believe that I have ever been in so unpromising and despairing a state as I now feel. After writing these words I read to G. the Proem and opening scene of my novel, and he expressed great delight in them.

Letter to Miss Sara Hennell, 3d Feb. 1862.

I was taken to see my pantomime. How pretty it is to see the theatre full of children! Ah, what I should have felt in my real child days to have been let into the further history of Mother Hubbard and her Dog!

George Stephenson is one of my great heroes: has he not a dear old face?

I think yours is the instinct of all delicate natures—not to speak to authors about their writings. It is better for us all to hear as little about ourselves as possible; to do our work faithfully, and be satisfied with the certainty that if it touches many minds, it cannot touch them in a way quite aloof from our intention and hope. **Letter to Mrs Peter Taylor, 3d Feb. 1862.**

Feb. 7.—A week of February already gone! I have been obliged to be very moderate in work from feebleness of head and body; but I have re-written, with additions, the first chapter of my book. **Journal, 1862.**

I am wondering whether you could spare me, *for a few weeks*, the "Tempest" music, and any other vocal music of that or of a kindred species? I don't want to buy it until our singers have experimented upon it. Don't think of sending me anything that you are using at all, but if said music be lying idle, I should be grateful for the loan. We have several operas—"Don Giovanni," "Figaro," the "Barbiere," "Flauto Magico," and also the music of "Macbeth;" but I think that is all our stock of concerted vocal music. **Letter to Mrs Bray, 8th Feb. 1862.**

Feb. 11.—We set off to Dorking. The day was lovely, and we walked through Mr Hope's park to **Journal, 1862.**

Journal, 1862.

Betchworth. In the evening I read aloud Sybel's 'Lectures on the Crusades.'

Feb. 12.—The day was grey, but the air was fresh and pleasant. We walked to Wootton Park—Evelyn's Wootton,—lunched at a little roadside inn there, and returned to Dorking to dine. During stay at Dorking finished the first twelve cantos of Pulci.

Feb. 13.—Returned home.

Letter to Madame Bodichon, 15th Feb. 1862.

I think it is a reasonable law that the one who takes wing should be the first to write—not the bird that stays in the old cage, and may be supposed to be eating the usual seed and groundsel, and looking at the same slice of the world through the same wires.

I think the highest and best thing is rather to suffer with real suffering than to be happy in the imagination of an unreal good. I would rather know that the beings I love are in some trouble, and suffer because of it, even though I can't help them, than be fancying them happy when they are not so, and making myself comfortable on the strength of that false belief. And so I am impatient of all ignorance and concealment. I don't say "that is wise," but simply "that is my nature." I can enter into what you have felt, for serious illness, such as seems to bring death near, makes one feel the simple human brother- and sister-hood so strongly, that those we were apt to think almost indifferent to us before, touch the very quick of our hearts. I suppose if we happened only to hold the hand of a hospital patient when she was dying, her face, and all the memories along with it, would seem to lie deeper in our experience than all we knew of many old friends and blood relations.

Letter to Madame Bodichon, 15th Feb. 1862.

We have had no troubles but the public troubles—anxiety about the war with America, and sympathy with the poor Queen. My best consolation is that an example on so tremendous a scale (as the war) of the need for the education of mankind through the affections and sentiments, as a basis for true development, will have a strong influence on all thinkers, and be a check to the arid narrow antagonism which, in some quarters, is held to be the only form of liberal thought.

George has fairly begun what we have long contemplated as a happiness for him—a History of Science, and has written so thorough an analysis and investigation of Aristotle's Natural Science, that he feels it will make an epoch for the men who are interested at once in the progress of modern science and in the question how far Aristotle went both in the observation of facts and in their theoretic combination—a question never yet

Letter to Madame Bodichon, 15th Feb. 1862.

cleared up after all these ages. This work makes him "very jolly," but his dear face looks very pale and narrow. Those only can thoroughly feel the meaning of death who know what is perfect love.

God bless you—that is not a false word, however many false ideas may have been hidden under it. No,—not false ideas, but temporary ones—caterpillars and chrysalids of future ideas.

Journal, 1862.

Feb. 17.—I have written only the two first chapters of my novel besides the Proem, and I have an oppressive sense of the far-stretching task before me, health being feeble just now. I have lately read again with great delight Mrs Browning's "Casa Guidi Windows." It contains, amongst other admirable things, a very noble expression of what I believe to be the true relation of the religious mind to the past.

Feb. 26.—I have been very ailing all this last week, and have worked under impeding discouragement. I have a distrust in myself, in my work, in others' loving acceptance of it, which robs my otherwise happy life of all joy. I ask myself, without being able to answer, whether I have ever before felt so chilled and oppressed. I have written now about sixty pages of my romance. Will it ever be finished? Ever be worth anything?

Feb. 27.—George Smith, the publisher, brought the proof of G.'s book, 'Animal Studies,' and laid before him a proposition to give me £10,000 for my new novel—*i.e.*, for its appearance in the 'Cornhill,' and the entire copyright at home and abroad. Journal, 1862.

March 1.—The idea of my novel appearing in the 'Cornhill' is given up, as G. Smith wishes to have it commenced in May, and I cannot consent to begin publication until I have seen nearly to the end of the work.

We had agreeable weather until yesterday, which was wet and blustering, so that we could only snatch two short walks. Pater is better, I think; and I, as usual, am impudently flourishing in country air and idleness. On Friday Mr Bone, our landlord, drove us out in his pony carriage, to see the "meet" of the stag-hounds, and on Saturday ditto to see the fox-hunters; so you perceive we have been leading rather a grand life. **Letter to Charles L. Lewes, 10th March 1862, from Englefield Green.**

March 11.—On Wednesday last, the 5th, G. and I set off to Englefield Green, where we have spent a delightful week at the Barley Mow Inn. I have finished Pulci there, and read aloud the 'Château d'If.' Journal, 1862.

We returned from our flight into the country yesterday, not without a sigh at parting with the pure air and the notes of the blackbirds for the usual **Letter to Miss Sara Hennell, 12th March 1862.**

canopy of smoke and the sound of cab wheels. I am not going out again, and our life will have its old routine—lunch at half-past one, walk till four, dinner at five.

Journal, 1862.

March 24.—After enjoying our week at Egham, I returned to protracted headache. Last Saturday we received as usual, and our party was joined by Mr and Mrs Noel. I have begun the fourth chapter of my novel, but have been working under a weight.

Letter to Miss Sara Hennell, 27th March 1862.

I congratulate you on being out of London, which is more like a pandemonium than usual. The fog and rain have been the more oppressive because I have seen them through Mr Lewes's almost constant discomfort. I think he has had at least five days of sick headache since you saw him. But then he is better tempered and more cheerful *with* headache than most people are without it; and in that way he lightens his burthen. Have you noticed in the 'Times' Mr Peabody's magnificent deed?—the gift of £150,000 for the amelioration (body and soul, I suppose) of the poorer classes in London. That is a pleasant association to have with an American name.

April 1.—Much headache this last week.

April 2.—Better this morning; writing with enjoyment. At the seventy-seventh page. Read Juvenal this morning and Nisard.

April 16.—As I had been ailing for a fortnight or more, we resolved to go to Dorking, and set off to-day. Journal, 1862.

May 6.—We returned from Dorking after a stay of three weeks, during which we have had delicious weather.

Our life is the old accustomed duet this month. We enjoy an interval of our double solitude. Doesn't the spring look lovelier every year to eyes that want more and more light? It was rather saddening to leave the larks and all the fresh leaves to come back to the rolling of cabs and "the blacks;" but in compensation we have all our conveniences about us. Letter to Mrs Bray, May 1862.

May 23.—Since I wrote last, very important decisions have been made. I am to publish my novel of 'Romola' in the 'Cornhill Magazine' for £7000, paid in twelve monthly payments. There has been the regret of leaving Blackwood, who has written me a letter in the most perfect spirit of gentlemanliness and good feeling. Journal, 1862.

May 27.—Mr Helps, Mr Burton, and Mr T. A. Trollope dined with us.

May 31.—Finished the second part, extending to page 183.

June 30.—I have at present written only the

Journal, 1862.

scene between Romola and her brother in San Marco towards Part IV. This morning I had a delightful generous letter from Mr Anthony Trollope about 'Romola.'

July 6.—The past week has been unfruitful from various causes. The consequence is, that I am no further on in my MS., and have lost the excellent start my early completion of the third part had given me.

July 10.—A dreadful palsy has beset me for the last few days. I have scarcely made any progress. Yet I have been very well in body. I have been reading a book often referred to by Hallam—Meiners's 'Lives of Mirandola and Politian.' They are excellent. They have German industry, and are succinctly and clearly written.

Letter to Miss Sara Hennell, 12th Sept. 1862, from Littlehampton.

Imagine me—not fuming in imperfect resignation under London smoke, but—with the wide sky of the coast above me, and every comfort positive and negative around me, even to the absence of staring eyes and crinolines. Worthing was so full that it rejected us, and, to our great good fortune, sent us here. We were pleased to hear that you had seen Mr Spencer. We always feel him particularly welcome when he comes back to town; there is no one like him for talking to about certain things.

You will come and dine or walk with us whenever you have nothing better to do in your visit to town. I take that for granted. We lie, you know, on the way *between* the Exhibition and Mr Noel's.

Journal, 1862.

Sept. 23.—Returned from our stay in the country, first at the Beach Hotel, Littlehampton, and for the last three days at Dorking.

Sept. 26.—At page 62, Part VI. Yesterday a letter came from Mr T. A. Trollope, full of encouragement for me. *Ebenezer.*

Oct. 2.—At page 85. Scene between Tito and Romola.

Letter to Mrs Congreve, 2d Oct. 1862.

Welcome to your letter, and welcome to the hope of seeing you again! I have an engagement on Monday from lunch till dinner. Apart from that, I know of nothing that will take us farther than for our daily walk, which, you know, begins at two. But we will alter the order of any day for the sake of seeing you. Mr Lewes's absence of a fortnight at Spa was a great success. He has been quite brilliant ever since. Ten days ago we returned from a stay of three weeks in the country—chiefly at Littlehampton—and we are both very well. Everything is prosperous with us; and we are so far from griefs, that if we had a wonderful emerald ring, we should perhaps be wise to throw it away as a propitiation of the envious gods.

So much in immediate reply to your kind anxiety. Everything else when we meet.

Journal, 1862.

Oct. 31.—Finished Part VII., having determined to end at the point where Romola has left Florence.

Nov. 14.—Finished reading 'Boccacio' through for the second time.

Nov. 17.—Read the 'Orfeo' and 'Stanze' of Poliziano. The latter are wonderfully fine for a youth of sixteen. They contain a description of a Palace of Venus, which seems the suggestion of Tennyson's Palace of Art in many points.

Letter to Miss Sara Hennell, 26th Nov. 1862.

I wish I knew that this birthday has found you happier than any that went before. There are so many things—best things—that only come when youth is past, that it may well happen to many of us to find ourselves happier and happier to the last. We have been to a Monday Pop. this week to hear Beethoven's Septett, and an amazing thing of Bach's, played by the amazing Joachim. But there is too much "Pop." for the thorough enjoyment of the chamber music they give. You will be interested to know that there is a new muster of scientific and philosophic men lately established, for the sake of bringing people who care to know and speak the truth, as well as they can, into regular communication. Mr Lewes was at the first meeting at Clunn's Hotel on Friday last. The plan is to meet and dine moderately and cheaply, and no one is to be admitted who is not "thorough" in the sense of being free from the suspicion of temporising and professing opinions on official grounds. The plan was started at Cambridge. Mr Huxley is president, and Charles Kingsley is vice. If they are sufficiently rigid about admissions, the club may come to good—bringing together men who think variously, but have more hearty feelings in common than they give each other credit for. Mr Robert Chambers (who lives in London now) is very warm about the matter. Mr Spencer, too, is a member.

Letter to Miss Sara Hennell, 26th Nov. 1862.

Pray don't ever ask me again not to rob a man of his religious belief, as if you thought my mind tended to such robbery. I have too profound a conviction of the efficacy that lies in all sincere faith, and the spiritual blight that comes with no-faith, to have any negative propagandism in me. In fact, I have very little sympathy with Free-thinkers as a class, and have lost all interest in mere antagonism to religious doctrines. I care only to know, if possible, the lasting meaning that lies in all religious doctrine from the beginning till

Letter to Madame Bodichon, 26th Nov. 1862.

Letter to Madame Bodichon, 26th Nov. 1862.

now. That speech of Carlyle's,[1] which sounds so odious, must, I think, have been provoked by something in the *manner* of the statement to which it came as an answer—else it would hurt me very much that he should have uttered it.

You left a handkerchief at our house. I will take care of it till next summer. I look forward with some longing to that time when I shall have lightened my soul of one chief thing I wanted to do, and be freer to think and feel about other people's work. We shall see you oftener, I hope, and have a great deal more talk than ever we have had before to make amends for our stinted enjoyment of you this summer.

God bless you, dear Barbara. You are very precious to us.

Journal, 1862.

Nov. 30 (Sunday).—Finished Part VIII. Mr Burton came.

Dec. 16.—In the evening Browning paid us a visit for the first time.

Dec. 17.—At p. 22 only. I am extremely spiritless, dead, and hopeless about my writing. The long state of headache has left me in depression and incapacity. The constantly heavy-clouded, and

[1] Some general remark of Carlyle's—Madame Bodichon cannot remember exactly what it was.

often wet, weather tends to increase the depression. I am inwardly irritable, and unvisited by good thoughts. Reading the 'Purgatorio' again, and the 'Compendium Revelationum' of Savonarola. After this record, I read aloud what I had written of Part IX. to George, and he, to my surprise, entirely approved of it. Journal, 1862.

Dec. 24.—Mrs F. Malleson brought me a beautiful plant as a Christmas offering. In the evening we went to hear the "Messiah" at Her Majesty's Theatre.

I am very sensitive to words and looks and all signs of sympathy, so you may be sure that your kind wishes are not lost upon me. Letter to Mrs Peter Taylor, 24th Dec. 1862.

As you will have your house full, the wish for a "Merry Christmas" may be literally fulfilled for you. We shall be quieter, with none but our family trio, but that is always a happy one. We are going to usher in the day by hearing the "Messiah" to-night at Her Majesty's.

Evening will be a pleasanter time for a little genial talk than "calling hours;" and if you will come to us without ceremony, you will hardly run the risk of not finding us. We go nowhere except to concerts.

We are longing to run away from London, but I

Letter to Mrs Peter Taylor, 24th Dec. 1862.

daresay we shall not do so before March. Winter is probably yet to come, and one would not like to be caught by frost and snow away from one's own hearth.

Always believe, without my saying it, that it gladdens me to know when anything I do has value for you.

Letter to Miss Sara Hennell, 26th Dec. 1862.

It is very sweet to me to have any proof of loving remembrance. That would have made the book-marker precious even if it had been ugly. But it is perfectly beautiful—in colour, words, and symbols. Hitherto I have been discontented with the Coventry book-marks; for at the shop where we habitually see them they have all got—"Let the people praise Thee, O God," on them, and nothing else. But I can think of no motto better than those three words. I suppose no wisdom the world will ever find out will make Paul's words obsolete —"Now abide," &c., "but the greatest of these is Charity." Our Christmas, too, has been quiet. Mr Lewes, who talks much less about goodness than I do, but is always readier to do the right thing, thinks it rather wicked for us to eat our turkey and plum-pudding without asking some forlorn person to eat it with us. But I'm afraid we were glad, after all, to find ourselves alone with "the boy." On Christmas Eve a sweet woman, remembering me as you have done, left a beautiful plant at the door, and after that we went to hear the "Messiah" at Her Majesty's. We felt a considerable *minus* from the absence of the organ, contrary to advertisement: nevertheless it was good to be there. What pitiable people those are who feel no poetry in Christianity! Surely the acme of poetry hitherto is the conception of the suffering Messiah, and the final triumph, "He shall reign for ever and for ever." The Prometheus is a very imperfect foreshadowing of that symbol wrought out in the long history of the Jewish and Christian ages.

Letter to Miss Sara Hennell, 26th Dec. 1862.

Mr Lewes and I have both been in miserable health during all this month. I have had a fortnight's incessant *malaise* and feebleness; but as I had had many months of tolerable health, it was my turn to be uncomfortable. If my book-marker were just a little longer, I should keep it in my beautiful Bible in large print, which Mr Lewes bought for me in prevision for my old age. He is not fond of reading the Bible himself, but "sees no harm" in my reading it.

Letter to the Brays, 29th Dec. 1862.

I am not quite sure what you mean by "charity" when you call it humbug. If you mean that atti-

Letter to the Brays, 29th Dec. 1862.

tude of mind which says, "I forgive my fellow-men for not being as good as I am," I agree with you in hoping that it will vanish, as also the circumstantial form of almsgiving. But if you are alluding to anything in my letter, I meant what charity meant in the elder English, and what the translators of the Bible meant in their rendering of the thirteenth chapter of 1st Corinthians — *Caritas,* the highest love or fellowship, which I am happy to believe that no philosophy will expel from the world.

Journal, 1862.

Dec. 31 (last day of the kind old year).—Clear and pleasantly mild. Yesterday a pleasant message from Mr Hannay about 'Romola.' We have had many blessings this year. Opportunities which have enabled us to acquire an abundant independence; the satisfactory progress of our two eldest boys; various grounds of happiness in our work; and ever-growing happiness in each other. I hope with trembling that the coming year may be as comforting a retrospect,— with trembling because my work is not yet done. Besides the finishing of 'Romola,' we have to think of Thornie's passing his final examination, and, in case of success, his going out to India; of Bertie's leaving Hofwyl; and of our finding a new residence. I have had more than my average amount of comfortable health until this last month, in which I have been constantly ailing, and my work has suffered proportionately.

Letter to Miss Sara Hennell, 2d Feb. 1863.

The letter with the one word in it, like a whisper of sympathy, lay on my plate when I went down to lunch this morning. The generous movement that made you send it has gladdened me all day. I have had a great deal of pretty encouragement from immense big-wigs—some of them saying 'Romola' is the finest book they ever read; but the opinion of big-wigs has one sort of value, and the fellow-feeling of a long-known friend has another. One can't do quite well without both. *En revanche*, I am a feeble wretch, with eyes that threaten to get bloodshot on the slightest provocation. We made a rush to Dorking for a day or two, and the quiet and fresh air seemed to make a new creature of me; but when we get back to town, town-sensations return.

Letter to Miss Sara Hennell, 9th March 1863.

That scheme of a sort of Philosophical Club that I told you of went to pieces before it was finished, like a house of cards. So it will be to the end, I fancy, with all attempts at combinations that are not based either on material interests or on opinions that are not merely opinions but *religion*. Doubtless you have been interested in the Colenso correspondence, and perhaps in Miss Cobbe's rejoinder

Letter to Miss Sara Hennell, 9th March 1863.

to Mrs Stowe's remonstrating answer to the women of England. I was glad to see how free the answer was from all tartness or conceit. Miss Cobbe's introduction to the new edition of Theodore Parker is also very honourable to her—a little too metaphorical here and there, but with real thought and good feeling.

Letter to Mrs Congreve, 18th April 1863.

It is a comfort to hear of you again, and to know that there is no serious trouble to mar the spring weather for you. I must carry that thought as my consolation for not seeing you on Tuesday,—not quite a sufficient consolation, for my eyes desire you very much after these long months of almost total separation. The reason I cannot have that pleasure on Tuesday is that, according to a long-arranged plan, I am going on Monday to Dorking again for a fortnight. I should be still more vexed to miss you if I were in better condition, but at present I am rather like a shell-less lobster, and inclined to creep out of sight. I shall write to you, or try to see you, as soon as I can after my return. I wish you could have told me of a more decided return to ordinary health in Mr Congreve, but I am inclined to hope that the lecturing may rather benefit than injure him, by being a moral tonic. How much there is for us to talk about!

But only to look at dear faces that one has seen so little of for a long while, seems reason enough for wanting to meet. Mr Lewes is better than usual just now, and you must not suppose that there is anything worse the matter with me than you have been used to seeing in me. Please give my highest regards to Mr Congreve, and love to Emily, who, I hope, has quite got back the roses which had somewhat paled. My pen straggles as if it had a stronger will than I. **Letter to Mrs Congreve, 18th April 1863.**

Glad you enjoyed 'Esmond.' It is a fine book. Since you have been interested in the historical suggestions, I recommend you to read Thackeray's 'Lectures on the English Humourists,' which are all about the men of the same period. There is a more exaggerated estimate of Swift and Addison than is implied in 'Esmond;' and the excessive laudation of men who are considerably below the tip-top of human nature, both in their lives and genius, rather vitiates the Lectures, which are otherwise admirable, and are delightful reading. **Letter to Charles L. Lewes, 28th April 1863, from Dorking.**

The wind is high and cold, making the sunshine seem hard and unsympathetic.

May 6.—We have just returned from Dorking, whither I went a fortnight ago to have solitude, while George took his journey to Hofwyl to see **Journal, 1863.**

Journal, 1863.

Bertie. The weather was severely cold for several days of my stay, and I was often ailing. That has been the way with me for a month and more, and in consequence I am backward with my July number of 'Romola'—the last part but one.

> I remember my wife telling me, at Witley, how cruelly she had suffered at Dorking from working under a leaden weight at this time. The writing of 'Romola' ploughed into her more than any of her other books. She told me she could put her finger on it as marking a well-defined transition in her life. In her own words, "I began it a young woman,—I finished it an old woman."

Letter to Madame Bodichon, 12th May 1863.

Yes! we shall be in town in June. Your coming would be reason good enough, but we have others—chiefly, that we are up to the ears in boydom and imperious parental duties. All is as happy and prosperous with us as heart can lawfully desire, except my health. I have been a mere wretch for several months past. You will come to me like the morning sunlight, and make me a little less of a flaccid cabbage-plant.

It is a very pretty life you are leading at Hastings, with your painting all morning, and fair mothers and children to look at the rest of the day.

I am terribly frightened about Mrs ——. She wrote to me telling me that we were sure to suit each other, neither of us holding the opinions of the *Moutons de Panurge.* Nothing could have been more decisive of the opposite prospect to me. If there is one attitude more odious to me than any other of the many attitudes of "knowingness," it is that air of lofty superiority to the vulgar. However, she will soon find out that I am a very commonplace woman. Letter to Madame Bodichon, 12th May 1863.

May 16.—Finished Part XIII. Killed Tito in great excitement. Journal, 1863.

May 18.—Began Part XIV.—the last! Yesterday George saw Count Arrivabene, who wishes to translate 'Romola,' and says the Italians are indebted to me.

Health seems, to those who want it, enough to make daylight a gladness. But the explanation of evils is never consoling except to the explainer. We are just as we were, thinking about the questionable house (The Priory), and wondering what would be the right thing to do; hardly liking to lock up any money in land and bricks, and yet frightened lest we should not get a quiet place just when we want it. But I daresay we shall have it after all. Letter to Mrs Bray, 1st June 1863.

Journal, 1863.

June 6.—We had a little evening party with music, intended to celebrate the completion of 'Romola,' which, however, is not absolutely completed, for I have still to alter the epilogue.

June 9.—Put the last stroke to 'Romola.' *Ebenezer!* Went in the evening to hear "La Gazza Ladra."

The manuscript of 'Romola' bears the following inscription:—

"To the Husband whose perfect love has been the best source of her insight and strength, this manuscript is given by his devoted wife, the writer."

Letter to Miss Sara Hennell, 10th June 1863.

How impossible it is for strong healthy people to understand the way in which bodily *malaise* and suffering eats at the root of one's life! The philosophy that is true—the religion that is strength to the healthy—is constantly emptiness to one when the head is distracted and every sensation is oppressive.

Journal, 1863.

June 16.—George and I set off to-day to the Isle of Wight, where we had a delightful holiday. On Friday, the 19th, we settled for a week at Niton, which, I think, is the prettiest place in all the island. On the following Friday we went on to Freshwater, and failed, from threatening rain, in an attempt to walk to Alum Bay, so that we rather repented of our choice. The consolation was that we shall know better than to go to Freshwater another time. On the Saturday morning we drove to Ryde, and remained there until Monday the 29th. Journal, 1863.

Your letter was a welcome addition to our sunshine this Sabbath morning. For in this particular we seem to have been more fortunate than you, having had almost constant sunshine since we arrived at Sandown, on Tuesday evening. Letter to Miss Sara Hennell, 21st June 1863, from Niton.

This place is perfect, reminding me of Jersey, in its combination of luxuriant greenth with the delights of a sandy beach. At the *end* of our week, if the weather is warmer, we shall go on to Freshwater for our remaining few days. But the wind at present is a little colder than one desires it, when the object is to get rid of a cough, and unless it gets milder, we shall go back to Shanklin. I am enjoying the hedgerow grasses and flowers with something like a released prisoner's feeling—it is so long since I had a bit of real English country.

I am very happy in my holiday, finding quite a fresh charm in the hedgerow grasses and flowers after my long banishment from them. We have a flower-garden just round us, and then a sheltered grassy walk, on which the sun shines through the best part of the day; and then a wide meadow, and Letter to Charles L. Lewes, 21st June 1863, from Niton.

Letter to Charles L. Lewes, 21st June 1863, from Niton.

beyond that trees and the sea. Moreover, our landlady has cows, and we get the quintessence of cream — excellent bread and butter also, and a young lady, with a large crinoline, to wait upon us, —all for 25s. per week; or rather, we get the apartment in which we enjoy those primitive and modern blessings for that moderate sum.

Journal, 1863.

July 4.—Went to see Ristori in "Adrienne Lecouvreur," and did not like it. I have had hemicrania for several days, and have been almost idle since my return home.

Letter to Miss Sara Hennell, 11th July 1863.

Constant languor from the new heat has made me shirk all exertion not imperative. And just now there are not only those excitements of the season, which even we quiet people get our share of, but there is an additional boy to be cared for —Thornie, who is this week passing his momentous examination.

A pretty thing has happened to an acquaintance of mine, which is quite a tonic to one's hope. She has all her life been working hard in various ways, as housekeeper, governess, and several et ceteras that I can't think of at this moment — a dear little dot, about four feet eleven in height; pleasant to look at, and clever; a working woman, without any of those epicene queernesses that belong to the class. Her life has been a history of family troubles, and she has that susceptible nature which makes such troubles hard to bear. More than once she has told me that courage quite forsook her. She felt as if there were no good in living and striving: it was difficult to discern or believe in any results for others, and there seemed none worth having for herself. Well! a man of fortune and accomplishments has just fallen in love with her, now she is thirty-three. It is the prettiest story of a swift decided passion, and made me cry for joy. Mme. Bodichon and I went with her to buy her wedding clothes. The future husband is also thirty-three—old enough to make his selection an honour. Fond of travelling and science and other good things, such as a man deserves to be fond of who chooses a poor woman in the teeth of grand relatives: brought up a Unitarian just turned Catholic. If you will only imagine everything I have not said, you will think this a very charming fairy tale.

Letter to Miss Sara Hennell, 11th July 1863.

We are going this evening to see the French actress in "Juliet" (Stella Colas) who is astonishing the town. Last week we saw Ristori, the other night heard the "Faust," and next week we are going to hear the "Elisir d'Amore" and "Faust" again! So

Letter to Miss Sara Hennell, 11th July 1863.

you see we are trying to get some compensation for the necessity of living among bricks in this sweet summer time. I can bear the opera better than any other evening entertainment, because the house is airy and the stalls are comfortable. The opera is a great, great product—pity we can't always have fine *Weltgeschichtliche* dramatic motives wedded with fine music, instead of trivalities or hideousnesses. Perhaps this last is too strong a word for anything except the "Traviata." Rigoletto is unpleasant, but it is a superlatively fine tragedy in the Nemesis. I think I don't know a finer.

We are really going to buy The Priory after all. You would think it very pretty if you saw it now, with the roses blooming about it.

Journal, 1863.

July 12.—I am now in the middle of G.'s 'Aristotle,' which gives me great delight.

July 23.—Reading Mommsen, and Story's 'Roba di Roma;' also Liddell's 'Rome,' for a narrative to accompany Mommsen's analysis.

July 29.—In the evening we went to Covent Garden to hear "Faust" for the third time. On our return we found a letter from Frederick Maurice—the greatest, most generous tribute ever given to me in my life.[1]

[1] I regret that I have not been able to find this letter.

I have wanted for several days to make some feeble sign in writing that I think of your trouble. But one claim after another has arisen as a hindrance. Conceive us, please, with three boys at home, all bigger than their father! It is a congestion of youthfulness on our mature brains that disturbs the course of our lives a little, and makes us think of most things as good to be deferred till the boys are settled again. I tell you so much to make you understand that "omission" is not with me equivalent to "neglect," and that I *do* care for what happens to you.

Letter to Mrs Peter Taylor, 30th July 1863.

Renan is a favourite with me. I feel more kinship with his mind than with that of any other living French author. But I think I shall not do more than look through the Introduction to his 'Vie de Jésus'—unless I happen to be more fascinated by the constructive part than I expect to be from the specimens I have seen. For minds acquainted with the European culture of this last half-century, Renan's book can furnish no new result; and they are likely to set little store by the too facile construction of a life from materials of which the biographical significance becomes more dubious as they are more closely examined. It seems to me the soul of Christianity lies not at all in the facts of an indi-

Letter to Mrs Peter Taylor, 30th July 1863.

vidual life, but in the ideas of which that life was the meeting-point and the new starting-point. We can never have a satisfactory basis for the history of the man Jesus, but that negation does not affect the Idea of the Christ either in its historical influence or its great symbolic meanings. Still such books as Renan's have their value in helping the popular imagination to feel that the sacred past is of one woof with that human present, which ought to be sacred too.

You mention Renan in your note, and the mention has sent me off into rather gratuitous remarks, you perceive. But such scrappy talk about great subjects may have a better excuse than usual, if it just serves to divert your mind from the sad things that must be importuning you now.

Letter to R. H. Hutton, 8th Aug. 1863.

After reading your article on 'Romola,' with careful reference to the questions you put to me in your letter, I can answer sincerely that I find nothing fanciful in your interpretation. On the contrary, I am confirmed in the satisfaction I felt when I first listened to the article, at finding that certain chief elements of my intention have impressed themselves so strongly on your mind, notwithstanding the imperfect degree in which I have been able to give form to my ideas. Of course if I had been called on to expound my own book, there are other things that I should want to say, or things that I should say somewhat otherwise; but I can point to nothing in your exposition of which my consciousness tells me that it is erroneous, in the sense of saying something which I neither thought nor felt. You have seized with a fulness which I had hardly hoped that my book could suggest, what it was my effort to express in the presentation of Bardo and Baldassarre; and also the relation of the Florentine political life to the development of Tito's nature. Perhaps even a judge so discerning as yourself could not infer from the imperfect result how strict a self-control and selection were exercised in the presentation of details. I believe there is scarcely a phrase, an incident, an allusion, that did not gather its value to me from its supposed subservience to my main artistic objects. But it is likely enough that my mental constitution would always render the issue of my labour something excessive—wanting due proportion. It is the habit of my imagination to strive after as full a vision of the medium in which a character moves as of the character itself. The psychological causes which prompted me to give such details of Florentine life and history as I

Letter to R. H. Hutton 8th Aug. 1863.

Letter to R. H. Hutton, 8th Aug. 1863.

have given, are precisely the same as those which determined me in giving the details of English village life in 'Silas Marner,' or the "Dodson" life, out of which were developed the destinies of poor Tom and Maggie. But you have correctly pointed out the reason why my tendency to excess in this effort after artistic vision makes the impression of a fault in 'Romola' much more perceptibly than in my previous books. And I am not surprised at your dissatisfaction with Romola herself. I can well believe that the many difficulties belonging to the treatment of such a character have not been overcome, and that I have failed to bring out my conception with adequate fulness. I am sorry she has attracted you so little; for the great problem of her life, which essentially coincides with a chief problem in Savonarola's, is one that readers need helping to understand. But with regard to that and to my whole book, my predominant feeling is,—not that I have achieved anything, but—that great, great facts have struggled to find a voice through me, and have only been able to speak brokenly. That consciousness makes me cherish the more any proof that my work has been seen to have some true significance by minds prepared not simply by instruction, but by that religious and moral sympathy with the historical life of man which is the larger half of culture.

Aug. 10.—Went to Worthing. A sweet letter from Mrs Hare, wife of Julius Hare, and Maurice's sister. Journal, 1863.

Aug. 18.—Returned home much invigorated by the week of change; but my spirits seem to droop as usual, now I am in London again.

I was at Worthing when your letter came, spending all my daylight hours out of doors, and trying with all my might to get health and cheerfulness. I will tell you the true reason why I did not go to Hastings. I thought you would be all the better for not having that solicitation of your kindness that the fact of my presence there might have caused. What you needed was precisely to get away from people to whom you would inevitably want to be doing something friendly, instead of giving yourself up to passive enjoyment. Else, of course, I should have liked everything you write about and invite me to. Letter to Madame Bodichon, 19th Aug. 1863.

We only got home last night, and I suppose we shall hardly be able to leave town again till after the two younger boys have left us, and after we have moved into the new house.

Letter to Madame Bodichon, 19th Aug. 1863.

Since I saw you I have had some sweet woman's tenderness shown me by Mrs Hare, the widow of Archdeacon Hare, and the sister of Frederick Maurice.

I *know* how you are enjoying the country. I have just been having the joy myself. The wide sky, the *not* London, makes a new creature of me in half an hour. I wonder, then, why I am ever depressed — why I am so shaken by agitations. I come back to London, and again the air is full of demons.

Letter to Mrs Bray and Miss Sara Hennell, 1st Sept. 1863.

I think I get a little freshness from the breeze that blows on you—a little lifting of heart from your wide sky and Welsh mountains. And the edge of autumn on the morning air makes even London a place in which one can believe in beauty and delight. Delicate scent of dried rose-leaves and the coming on of the autumnal airs are two things that make me feel happy before I know why.

The Priory is all scaffolding and paint; and we are still in a nightmare of uncertainty about our boys. But then I have by my side a dear companion, who is a perpetual fountain of courage and cheerfulness, and of considerate tenderness for my lack of those virtues. And besides that, I have Roman history! Perhaps that sounds like a bitter joke to you, who are looking at the sea and sky, and not thinking of Roman history at all. But this too, read aright, has its gospel and revelation. I read it much as I used to read a chapter in the Acts or Epistles. Mommsen's 'History of Rome' is so fine, that I count all minds graceless who read it without the deepest stirrings.

Letter to Mrs Bray and Miss Sara Hennell, 1st Sept. 1863.

I cannot be quite easy without sending this little sign of love and good wishes on the eve of your journey. I shall think of you with all the more delight, because I shall imagine you winding along the Riviera, and then settling in sight of beautiful things not quite unknown to me. I hope your life will be enriched very much by these coming months; but above all, I hope that Mr Congreve will come back strong. Tell him I have been greatly moved by the 'Discours Préliminaire.'[1]

Letter to Mrs Congreve, Oct. 1863.

If I wait to write until I have anything very profitable to say, you will have time to think that I have forgotten you or else to forget me—and both consequences would be unpleasant to me.

Letter to Miss Sara Hennell, 16th Oct. 1863.

Well, our poor boy Thornie parted from us to-day, and set out on his voyage to Natal. I say "poor,"

[1] Auguste Comte's.

Letter to Miss Sara Hennell, 16th Oct. 1863.

as one does about all beings that are gone away from us for a long while. But he went away in excellent spirits, with a large packet of recommendatory letters to all sorts of people, and with what he cares much more for—a first-rate rifle and revolver,—and already with a smattering of Dutch Zulu, picked up from his grammars and dictionaries.

What are you working at, I wonder? Cara says you are writing; and, though I desire not to ask prying questions, I should feel much joy in your being able to tell me that you are at work on something which gives you a life apart from circumstantial things.

I am taking a deep bath of other peoples' thoughts, and all doings of my own seem a long way off me. But my bath will be sorely interrupted soon by the miserable details of removal from one house to another. Happily Mr Owen Jones has undertaken the ornamentation of the drawing-room, and will prescribe all about chairs, &c. I think, after all, I like a clean kitchen better than any other room.

We are far on in correcting the proofs of the new edition of 'Goethe,' and are about to begin the printing of the 'Aristotle,' which is to appear at Christmas or Easter.

Nov. 5.—We moved into our new house—The Priory, 21 North Bank, Regents' Park. Journal, 1863.

Nov. 14.—We are now nearly in order, only wanting a few details of furniture to finish our equipment for a new stage in our life's journey. I long very much to have done thinking of upholstery, and to get again a consciousness that there are better things than that to reconcile one with life.

At last we are in our new home, with only a few details still left to arrange. Such fringing away of precious life, in thinking of carpets and tables, is an affliction to me, and seems like a nightmare from which I shall find it bliss to awake into my old world of care for things quite apart from upholstery. Letter to Mrs Bray, 14th Nov. 1863.

I have kissed your letter in sign of my joy at getting it. But the cold draughts of your Florentine room came across my joy rather harshly. I know you have good reasons for what you do, yet I cannot help saying, Why do you stay at Florence, the city of draughts rather than of flowers? Letter to Mrs Congreve, 28th Nov. 1863.

Mr Congreve's suffering during the journey, and your suffering in watching him, saddens me as I think of it. For a long while to come I suppose

Letter to Mrs Congreve, 28th Nov. 1863.

human energy will be greatly taken up with resignation rather than action. I wish my feeling for you could travel by some helpful vibrations good for pains.

For ourselves, we have enough ease now to be able to give some of it away. But our removal into our new home on the 5th of November was not so easy as it might have been, seeing that I was only half recovered from a severe attack of influenza, which had caused me more terrible pains in the head and throat than I have known for years. However, the crisis is past now, and we think our little home altogether charming and comfortable. Mr Owen Jones has been unwearied in taking trouble that everything about us may be pretty. He stayed two nights till after twelve o'clock, that he might see every engraving hung in the right place; and as you know I care even more about the fact of kindness than its effects, you will understand that I enjoy being grateful for all this friendliness on our behalf. But so tardy a business is furnishing, that it was not until Monday last that we had got everything in its place in preparation for the next day—Charlie's twenty-first birthday, which made our house-warming a doubly interesting epoch. I wish your sweet presence could have adorned our drawing-room, and made it look still more agreeable in the eyes of all beholders. You would have liked to hear Jansa play on his violin; and you would perhaps have been amused to see an affectionate but dowdy friend of yours, splendid in a grey moire antique—the consequence of a severe lecture from Owen Jones on her general neglect of personal adornment. I am glad to have got over this crisis of maternal and housekeeping duty. My soul never flourishes on attention to details which others can manage quite gracefully without any conscious loss of power for wider thoughts and cares. Before we began to move, I was swimming in Comte and Euripides and Latin Christianity: *now* I am sitting among puddles, and can get sight of no deep water. *Now* I have a mind made up of old carpets fitted in new places, and new carpets suffering from accidents; chairs, tables, and prices; muslin curtains and down-draughts in cold chimneys. I have made a vow never to think of my own furniture again, but only of other people's. Letter to Mrs Congreve, 28th Nov. 1863.

The book[1] is come, with its precious inscription, and I have read a great piece of it already (11 A.M.), besides looking through it to get an idea of its Letter to Mrs Bray, 4th Dec. 1863.

[1] 'Physiology for Schools.' By Mrs Bray.

Letter to Mrs Bray, 4th Dec. 1863.

general plan. See how fascination shifts its quarter as our life goes on! I cannot be induced to lay aside my regular books for half an hour to read 'Mrs Lirriper's Lodgings,' but I pounce on a book like yours, which tries to tell me as much as it can in brief space of the "natural order," and am seduced into making it my after-breakfast reading instead of the work I had prescribed for myself in that pleasant quiet time. I read so slowly and read so few books, that this small fact among my small habits seems a great matter to me. I thank you, dear Cara, not simply for giving me the book, but for having put so much faithful labour in a worthy direction, and created a lasting benefit which I can share with others. Whether the circulation of a book be large or small, there is always this supreme satisfaction about solid honest work, that as far as it goes its effect must be good; and as all effects spread immeasurably, what we have to care for is *kind*, and not quantity. I am a shabby correspondent, being in ardent practice of the piano just now, which makes my days shorter than usual.

Letter to Madame Bodichon, 4th Dec. 1863.

I am rather ashamed to hear of any one trying to be useful just now, for I am doing nothing but indulging myself—enjoying being petted very much, enjoying great books, enjoying our new pretty quiet home, and the study of Beethoven's sonatas for piano and violin, with the mild-faced old Jansa, and not being at all unhappy as you imagine me. I sit taking deep draughts of reading—'Politique Positive,' Euripides, Latin Christianity, and so forth, and remaining in glorous ignorance of "the current literature." Such is our life: and you perceive that instead of being miserable, I am rather following a wicked example, and saying to my soul, "Soul, take thine ease." I am sorry to think of you without any artistic society to help you and feed your faith. It is hard to believe long together that anything is "worth while," unless there is some eye to kindle in common with our own, some brief word uttered now and then to imply that what is infinitely precious to us is precious alike to another mind. I fancy that to do without that guarantee, one must be rather insane—one must be a bad poet, or a spinner of impossible theories, or an inventor of impossible machinery. However, it is but brief space either of time or distance that divides you from those who thoroughly share your cares and joys—always excepting that portion which is the hidden private lot of every human being. In the most entire confidence even of husband and wife

Letter to Madame Bodichon, 4th Dec. 1863.

there is always the unspoken residue—the *undivined* residue—perhaps of what is most sinful, perhaps of what is most exalted and unselfish.

Letter to Miss Sara Hennell, 26th Dec. 1863.

I get less and less inclined to write any but the briefest letters. My books seem to get so far off me when once I have written them, that I should be afraid of looking into 'The Mill;' but it was written faithfully and with intense feeling when it was written, so I will hope that it will do no mortal any harm. I am indulging myself frightfully: reading everything except the "current literature," and getting more and more out of *rapport* with the public taste. I have read Renan's book, however, which has proved to be eminently *in* the public taste. It will have a good influence on the whole, I imagine; but this 'Vie de Jésus,' and still more, Renan's "Letter to Berthelot" in the 'Revue des Deux Mondes,' have compelled me to give up the high estimate I had formed of his mind. Judging from the indications in some other writings of his, I had reckoned him amongst the finest thinkers of the time. Still his 'Life of Jesus' has so much artistic merit, that it will do a great deal towards the culture of ordinary minds, by giving them a sense of unity between that far-off past and our present.

We are enjoying our new house—enjoying its quiet and freedom from perpetual stair-mounting—enjoying also the prettiness of colouring and arrangement, all of which we owe to our dear good friend, Mr Owen Jones. He has determined every detail, so that we can have the pleasure of admiring what is our own without vanity. And another magnificent friend has given me the most splendid reclining chair conceivable, so that I am in danger of being envied by the gods, especially as my health is thoroughly good withal. I should like to be sure that you are just as comfortable externally and internally. I daresay you are, being less of a cormorant in your demands on life than I am; and it is *that* difference which chiefly distinguishes human lots when once the absolute needs are satisfied.

Letter to Mrs Bray, 26th Dec. 1863.

Your affectionate greeting comes as one of the many blessings that are brightening this happy Christmas.

Letter to Mrs Peter Taylor, 28th Dec. 1863.

We have been giving our evenings up to parental duties—*i.e.*, to games and music for the amusement of the youngsters. I am wonderfully well in body, but rather in a self-indulgent state mentally, saying, "Soul, take thine ease," after a dangerous example.

Letter to Mrs Peter Taylor, 28th Dec. 1863.

Of course, I shall be glad to see your fair face whenever it can shine upon me; but I can well imagine, with your multitudinous connections, Christmas and the New Year are times when all *unappointed* visits must be impossible to you.

All good to you and yours through the coming year! and amongst the good, may you continue to feel some love for me; for love is one of the conditions in which it is even better to give than to receive.

Letter to Mrs Congreve, 19th Jan. 1864.

According to your plans, you must be in Rome. I have been in good spirits about you ever since I last heard from you; and the foggy twilight which, for the last week, has followed the severe frost, has made me rejoice the more that you are in a better climate and amongst lovelier scenes than we are groping in. I please myself with thinking that you will all come back with stores of strength and delightful memories. Only, if this were the best of all possible worlds, Mr Lewes and I should be able to meet you in some beautiful place before you turn your backs on Italy. As it is, there is no hope of such a meeting. March is Charlie's holiday month, and when he goes out we like to stay at home for the sake of recovering for that short time our unbroken *tête-à-tête*. We have every reason to be cheerful if the fog would let us. Last night I finished reading the last proofs of the 'Aristotle,' which makes an octavo volume of rather less than 400 pages. I think it is a book which will be interesting and valuable to the few, but perhaps *only* to the few. However, George's happiness in writing his books makes him less dependent than most authors on the audience they find. He felt that a thorough account of Aristotle's science was a bit of work which needed doing, and he has given his utmost pains to do it worthily. These are the two most important conditions of authorship; all the rest belong to the "less modifiable" order of things. I have been playing energetically on the piano lately, and taking lessons in accompanying the violin from Herr Jansa, one of the old Beethoven Quartette players. It has given me a fresh kind of muscular exercise, as well as nervous stimulus, and, I think, has done its part towards making my health better. In fact, I am very well physically. I wish I could be as clever and active as you about our garden, which might be made much prettier this spring if I had judgment and industry enough to do the right thing. But it is a native vice of mine to like all such matters attended to by some one else, and to fold my arms and enjoy the result.

Letter to Mrs Congreve, 19th Jan. 1864.

Some people are born to make life pretty, and others to grumble that it is not pretty enough. But pray make a point of liking me in spite of my deficiencies.

Letter to Mrs Peter Taylor, 21st Jan. 1864.

I comfort myself with the belief that your nature is less rebellious under trouble than mine—less craving and discontented.

Resignation to trial, which can never have a *personal* compensation, is a part of our life task which has been too much obscured for us by unveracious attempts at universal consolation. I think we should be more tender to each other while we live, if that wretched falsity which makes men quite comfortable about their fellows' troubles were thoroughly got rid of.

Letter to Miss Sara Hennell, 22d Jan. 1864.

I often imagine you, not without a little longing, turning out into the fields whenever you list, as we used to do in the old days at Rosehill. That power of turning out into the fields is a great possession in life—worth many luxuries.

Here is a bit of news not, I think, too insignificant for you to tell Cara. The other day Mr Spencer, senior (Herbert Spencer's father) called on us, and knowing that he has been engaged in education all his life, that he is a man of extensive and accurate knowledge, and that, on his son's showing, he is a very able teacher, I showed him Cara's 'British Empire.' Yesterday Herbert Spencer came, and on my inquiring told me that his father was pleased with Cara's book, and thought highly of it. Such testimonies as this, given apart from personal influence and by a practised judge, are, I should think, more gratifying than any other sort of praise to all faithful writers.

Letter to Miss Sara Hennell, 22d Jan. 1864.

Jan. 30.—We had Browning, Dallas, and Burton to dine with us, and in the evening a gentlemen's party.

Journal, 1864.

Feb. 14.—Mr Burton dined with us, and asked me to let him take my portrait.

It was pleasant to have news of you through the fog, which reduces my faith in all good and lovely things to its lowest ebb.

Letter to Mrs Peter Taylor, 3d March 1864.

I hope you are less abjectly under the control of the skiey influences than I am. The soul's calm sunshine in me is half made up of the outer sunshine. However, we are going on Friday to hear the "Judas Maccabæus," and Handel's music always brings me a revival.

I have had a great personal loss lately in the death of a sweet woman,[1] to whom I have sometimes

[1] Mrs Julius Hare, who gave her Maurice's book on the Lord's Prayer.

Letter to Mrs Peter Taylor, 3d March 1864.

gone, and hoped to go again, for a little moral strength. She had long been confined to her room by consumption, which has now taken her quite out of reach except to memory, which makes all dear human beings undying to us as long as we ourselves live.

I am glad to know that you have been interested in "David Gray."[1] It is good for us all that these true stories should be well told. Even those to whom the power of helping rarely comes, have their imaginations instructed so as to be more just and tender in their thoughts about the lot of their fellows.

Letter to Miss Sara Hennell, 7th March 1864.

I felt it long since I had had news from you, but my days go by, each seeming too short for what I must do, and I don't like to molest you with mere questions.

I have been spoiled for correspondence by Mr Lewes's goodness in always writing letters for me where a proxy is admissible. And so it has come to be a great affair with me to write even a note, while people who keep up a large correspondence, and set apart their hour for it, find it easy to cover reams of paper with talk from the end of the pen.

You say nothing of yourself, which is rather un-

[1] A story by Mr Robert Buchanan in the 'Cornhill,' Feb. 1864.

kind. We are enjoying a perfect *tête-à-tête*. On Friday we are going to hear the "Judas Maccabæus," and try if possible to be stirred to something heroic by "Sound an alarm." Letter to Miss Sara Hennell, 7th March 1864.

I was more sorry than it is usually possible to be about the death of a person utterly unknown to me, when I read of Maria Martineau's death. She was a person whose office in life seemed so thoroughly defined and so valuable. For an invalid like Harriet Martineau to be deprived of a beloved nurse and companion, is a sorrow that makes one ashamed of one's small grumblings. But, oh dear, oh dear! when *will* people leave off their foolish talk about all human lots being equal; as if anybody with a sound stomach ever knew misery comparable to the misery of a dyspeptic.

Farewell, dear Sara: be generous, and don't always wait an age in silence because I don't write.

If you were anybody but yourself I should dislike you, because I have to write letters to you. As it is, your qualities triumph even over the vice of being in Italy (too far off for a note of three lines), and expecting to hear from me, though I fear I should be graceless enough to let you expect in vain if I did not care very much to hear from Letter to Mrs Congreve, 8th March 1864.

Letter to Mrs Congreve, 8th March 1864.

you, and did not find myself getting uneasy when many weeks have been passed in ignorance about you. I do hope to hear that you got your fortnight of sight-seeing before leaving Rome—at least, you would surely go well over the great galleries. If not, I shall be vexed with you, and I shall only be consoled for your not going to Venice by the chance of the Austrians being driven or bought out of it—on no slighter grounds. For I suppose you will not go to Italy again for a long, long while, so as to leave any prospect of the omission being made up for by-and-by.

Letter to Miss Sara Hennell, 20th March 1864.

We run off to Scotland for the Easter week, setting out on Sunday evening; so if the spring runs away again, I hope it will run northward. We shall return on Monday the 4th April. Some news of your inwards and outwards would be acceptable; but don't write unless you really *like* to write. You see Strauss has come out with a *popular* 'Life of Jesus.'

Letter to Mrs Peter Taylor, 25th March 1864.

Fog, east wind, and headache: there is my week's history. But this morning, when your letter came to me, I had got up well, and was reading the sorrows of the aged Hecuba with great enjoyment. I wish an immortal drama could be got out of *my* sorrows, that people might be the better for them two thousand years hence. But fog, east wind, and headache are not great dramatic motives.

Letter to Mrs Peter Taylor, 25th March 1864.

Your letter was a reinforcement of the delicious sense of *bien être* that comes with the departure of bodily pain; and I am glad, retrospectively, that beyond our fog lay your moonlight and your view of the glorious sea. It is not difficult to me to believe that you look a new creature already. Mr Lewes tells me the country air has always a magical effect on me, even in the first hour; but it is not the air alone, is it? It is the wide sky and the hills and the wild flowers which are linked with all calming thoughts, just as every object in town has its perturbing associations.

I share your joy in the Federal successes—with that check that attends all joy in a war not absolutely ended. But you have worked and earned more joy than those who have been merely passives.

Journal, 1864.

April 6.—Mr Spencer called for the first time after a long correspondence on the subject of his relation to Comte.

Letter to Miss Sara Hennell, 9th April 1864.

Yes! I am come back from Scotland—came back last Saturday night.

I was much pleased to see Cara so wonderfully well and cheerful. She seems to me ten times

Letter to Miss Sara Hennell, 9th April 1864.

more cheerful than in the old days. I am interested to know more about your work which is filling your life now, but I suppose I shall know nothing until it is in print—and perhaps that is the only form in which one can do any one's work full justice. It is very disappointing to me to hear that Cara has at present so little promise of monetary results from her conscientious labour. I fear the fatal system of half profits is working against her as against others. We are going to the opera to-night to hear the "Favorita." It was the first opera I ever *saw* (with you I saw it!), and I have never seen it since — that is the reason I was anxious to go to-night.

This afternoon we go to see Mulready's pictures —so the day will be a full one.

Journal, 1864.

April 18.—We went to the Crystal Palace to see Garibaldi.

Letter to Miss Sara Hennell, 30th April 1864.

Only think! next Wednesday morning we start for Italy. The move is quite a sudden one. We need a good shake for our bodies and minds, and must take the spring-time before the weather becomes too hot. We shall not be away more than a month or six weeks at the utmost. Our friend Mr Burton, the artist, will be our companion for at least part of the time. He has just painted a divine picture, which is now to be seen at the old Water-Colour Exhibition. The subject is from a Norse legend; but that is no matter—the picture tells its story. A knight in mailed armour and surcoat has met the fair tall woman he (secretly) loves, on a turret stair. By an uncontrollable movement he has seized her arm and is kissing it. She, amazed, has dropped the flowers she held in her other hand. The subject might have been made the most vulgar thing in the world—the artist has raised it to the highest pitch of refined emotion. The kiss is on the fur-lined *sleeve* that covers the arm, and the face of the knight is the face of a man to whom the kiss is a sacrament.

Letter to Miss Sara Hennell, 30th April 1864.

How I should like a good long talk with you! From what you say of your book that is to come, I expect to be very much interested in it. I think I hardly ever read a book of the kind you describe without getting some help from it. It is to this strong influence that is felt in all personal statements of inward experience, that we must perhaps refer the excessive publication of religious journals.

May 4.—We started for Italy with Mr Burton.

Journal, 1864.

June 20.—Arrived at our pretty home again after an absence of seven weeks.

Letter to Miss Sara Hennell, 25th June 1864.

Your letter has affected me deeply. Thank you very much for writing it. It seems as if a close view of almost every human lot would disclose some suffering that makes life a doubtful good—except perhaps at certain epochs of fresh love, fresh creative activity, or unusual power of helping others. One such epoch we are witnessing in a young life that is very near to us. Our "boy," Charles, has just become engaged, and it is very pretty to see the happiness of a pure first love, full at present of nothing but promise. It will interest you to know that the young lady who has won his heart, and seems to have given him her own with equal ardour and entireness, is the grand-daughter of Dr Southwood Smith, whom he adopted when she was three years old, and brought up under his own eye. She is very handsome, and has a splendid contralto voice. Altogether Pater and I rejoice; for though the engagement has taken place earlier than we expected, or should perhaps have chosen, there are counterbalancing advantages. I always hoped Charlie would be able to choose, or rather find, the other half of himself by the time he was twenty-three—the event has only come a year and a half sooner. This is the news that greeted us on our return! We had seen before we went that the acquaintance, which was first made eighteen months or more ago, had become supremely interesting to Charlie. Altogether we rejoice.

Letter to Miss Sara Hennell, 25th June 1864.

Our journey was delightful in spite of Mr Lewes's frequent *malaise;* for his cheerful nature is rarely subdued even by bodily discomfort. We saw only one place that we had not seen before—namely, Brescia; but all the rest seemed more glorious to us than they had seemed four years ago. Our course was to Venice, where we stayed a fortnight, pausing only at Paris, Turin, and Milan on our way thither, and taking Padua, Verona, Brescia, and again Milan, as points of rest on our way back. Our friend Mr Burton's company was very stimulating from his great knowledge, not of pictures only, but of almost all other subjects. He has had the advantage of living in Germany for five or six years, and has gained those large serious views of history which are a special product of German culture, and this was his first visit to Italy, so you may imagine his eager enjoyment in finding it beautiful beyond his hopes. We crossed the Alps by the St Gothard, and stayed a day or two at Lucerne; and this, again, was a first sight of Switzerland to him.

Letter to Mrs Congreve, July 1864.

Looking at my little mats this morning while I was dressing, I felt very grateful for them, and remembered that I had not shown my gratitude when you gave them to me. If I were a "conceited" poet, I should say your presence was the sun and the mats were the tapers; but now you are away I delight in the tapers. How pretty the pattern is—and your brain counted it out! They will never be worn quite away while I live, or my little purse for coppers either.

Journal, 1864.

July 17.—Horrible scepticism about all things paralysing my mind. Shall I ever be good for anything again? Ever do anything again?

July 19.—Reading Gibbon, vol. i., in connection with Mosheim; also Gieseler on the condition of the world at the appearance of Christianity.

Letter to Miss Sara Hennell, 28th Aug. 1864.

I am distressed to find that I have let a week pass without writing in answer to your letter, which made me very glad when I got it. Remembering you just a minute ago, I started up from Max Müller's new volume, with which I was consoling myself under a sore throat, and rushed to the desk that I might not risk any further delay.

It was just what I wanted to hear about you, that you were having some change, and I think the freshness of the companionship must help other good influences, not to speak of the "Apologia," which breathed much life into me when I read it. Pray mark that beautiful passage in which he thanks his friend Ambrose St John. I know hardly anything that delights me more than such evidences of sweet brotherly love being a reality in the world. I envy you your opportunity of seeing and hearing Newman, and should like to make an expedition to Birmingham for that sole end.

Letter to Miss Sara Hennell, 28th Aug. 1864.

My trouble now is George's delicate health. He gets thinner and thinner. He is going to try what horseback will do, and I am looking forward to that with some hope.

Our boy's love-story runs smoothly, and seems to promise nothing but good. His attraction to Hampstead gives George and me more of our dear old *tête-à-tête*, which we can't help being glad to recover.

Dear Cara and Mr Bray! I wish they too had joy instead of sadness from the young life they have been caring for these many years. When you write to Cara, or see her, assure her that she is remembered in my most affectionate thoughts, and that I often bring her present experience before my mind—more or less truly—for we can but blunder about each other, we poor mortals.

Write to me whenever you can, dear Sara. I should have answered immediately but for sickness, visitors, business, &c.

Journal, 1864.

Sept. 6.—*I am reading about Spain, and trying a drama on a subject that has fascinated me—have written the prologue, and am beginning the First Act. But I have little hope of making anything satisfactory.*

Sept. 13 *to* 30.—Went to Harrogate and Scarborough, seeing York Minster and Peterborough.

Letter to Miss Sara Hennell, 15th Sept. 1864, from Harrogate.

We journeyed hither on Tuesday, and found the place quite as pretty as we expected. The great merit of Harrogate is that one is everywhere close to lovely open walks. Your "plan" has been a delightful reference for Mr Lewes, who takes it out of his pocket every time we walk. At present, of course, there is not much improvement in health to be boasted of, but we hope that the delicious bracing air — and also the chalybeate waters, which have not yet been tried—will not be without good effect. The journey was long. How hideous those towns of Holbeach and Wakefield are! It is difficult to keep up one's faith in a millennium within sight of this modern civilisation which consists in "development of industries." Egypt and her big calm gods seems quite as good.

Letter to Miss Sara Hennell, 26th Sept. 1864, from Scarborough.

We migrated on Friday last from delightful Harrogate, pausing at York to see the glorious Cathedral. The weather is perfect, the sea blue as a sapphire, so that we see to utmost advantage the fine line of coast here, and the magnificent breadth of sand. Even the Tenby sands are not so fine as these. Better than all, Mr Lewes, in spite of a sad check of a few days, is strengthened beyond our most hopeful expectations by this brief trial of fresh conditions. He is wonderful for the rapidity with which he "picks up" after looking alarmingly feeble, and even wasted. We paid a visit to Knaresborough the very last day of our stay at Harrogate, and were rejoiced that we had not missed the sight of that pretty characteristic northern town. There is a ruined castle here too, standing just where one's eyes would desire it on a grand line of cliff; but perhaps you know the place. Its only defect is that it is too large, and therefore a little too smoky; but except in Wales or Devonshire, I have seen no sea place on our English coast that has greater natural advantages. I don't know quite why I should write you this note all about ourselves — except that your goodness having helped us to the benefit we have got, I like you to know of the said benefit.

Letter to Mrs Congreve, Sunday, Oct. (?) 1864.

The wished-for opportunity is coming very soon. Next Saturday, Charlie will go to Hastings, and will not return till Sunday evening. Will you—can you—arrange to come to us on Saturday to lunch or dinner, and stay with us till Sunday evening? We shall be very proud and happy if you will consent to put up with such travelling quarters as we can give you. You will be rejoicing our hearts by coming; and I know that for the sake of cheering others, you would endure even large privations as well as small ones.

Letter to Mrs Congreve, Monday-week following.

What a pure delight it was to have you with us! I feel the better for it in spite of a cold which I caught yesterday—perhaps owing to the loss of your sunny presence all of a sudden.

Letter to Miss Sara Hennell, 2d Oct. 1864.

It makes me very, very happy to see George so much better, and to return with that chief satisfaction to the quiet comforts of home. We register Harrogate among the places to be revisited.

I have had a fit of Spanish history lately, and have been learning Spanish grammar—the easiest of all the Romance grammars—since we have been away. Mr Lewes has been rubbing up his Spanish by reading 'Don Quixote' in these weeks of *idlesse;* and I have read aloud and translated to him, like a good child. I find it so much easier to learn anything than to feel that I have anything worth teaching. Letter to Miss Sara Hennell, 2d Oct. 1864.

All is perfectly well with us, now the "little Pater" is stronger, and we are especially thankful for Charlie's prospect of marriage. We could not have desired anything more suited to his character and more likely to make his life a good one. But this blessing which has befallen us, only makes me feel the more acutely the cutting off of a like satisfaction from the friends I chiefly love.

Oct. 5.—Finished the first draught of the First Act of my drama, and read it to George. Journal, 1864.

Oct. 15.—Went to the Maestro (Burton) for a sitting.

Nov. 4.—Read my Second Act to George. It is written in verse—my first serious attempt at blank verse. G. praises, and encourages me.

Nov. 10.—I have been at a very low ebb, body and mind, for the last few days, sticking in the mud continually in the construction of my 3d, 4th, and 5th Acts. Yesterday Browning came to tell us of a bust of Savonarola in terra-cotta, just discovered at Florence.

I believe I have thought of you every day for the last fortnight, and I remembered the birthday —and "everything." But I was a little cross, be- Letter to Miss Sara Hennell, 23d Nov. 1864.

Letter to Miss Sara Hennell, 23d Nov. 1864.

cause I had heard nothing of you since Mr Bray's visit. And I said to myself, "If she wanted to write she *would* write." I confess I was a little ashamed when I saw the outside of your letter ten minutes ago, feeling that I should read within it the proof that you were as thoughtful and mindful as ever.

Yes, I do heartily give my greeting—*had* given it already. And I desire very much that the work which is absorbing you, may give you some happiness besides that which belongs to the activity of production.

It is very kind of you to remember Charlie's date too. He is as happy as the day is long—and very good: one of those creatures to whom goodness comes naturally,—not any exalted goodness, but everyday serviceable goodness, such as wears through life. Whereas exalted goodness comes in brief inspirations, and requires a man to die lest he should spoil his work.

I have been ill, but now am pretty well, with much to occupy and interest me, and with no trouble except those bodily ailments.

I could chat a long while with you—but I restrain myself, because I must not carry on my letter writing into the "solid day."

Your precious letter *did* come last night, and crowned the day's enjoyment. Our family party went off very well, entirely by dint of George's exertions. I wish you had seen him acting charades, and heard him make an after-supper speech. You would have understood all the self-forgetful goodness that lay under the assumption of boyish animal spirits. A horrible German whom I have been obliged to see, has been talking for two hours, with the hardest eyes, blind to all possibilities that he was boring us, and so I have been robbed of all the time I wanted for writing to you. I can only say now that I bore you on my heart—you and all yours known to me—even before I had had your letter yesterday. Indeed, you are not apart from any delight I have in life: I long always that you should share it—if not otherwise, at least by knowing of it, which to you is a sort of sharing. Our double loves and best wishes for all of you—Rough being included, as I trust you include Ben. Are they not idlers with us? Also a title to regard as well as being *collaborateurs*. Letter to Mrs Congreve, Christmas Day, 1864.

Dec. 24.—A family party in the evening. Journal, 1864.

Dec. 25.—I read the Third Act of my drama to George, who praised it highly. We spent a perfectly quiet evening, intending to have our Christmas Day's jollity on Tuesday, when the boys are at home.

Journal, 1865.

Jan. 1.—The last year has been unmarked by any trouble except bad health. The bright spots in the year have been the publication of 'Aristotle,' and our journey to Venice. With me the year has not been fruitful. I have written three Acts of my drama, and am now in a condition of body and mind to make me hope for better things in the coming year. The last quarter has made an epoch for me, by the fact that, for the first time in my serious authorship, I have written verse. In each other we are happier than ever. I am more grateful to my dear husband for his perfect love, which helps me in all good and checks me in all evil—more conscious that in him I have the greatest of blessings.

Letter to Mrs Congreve, 3d Jan. 1865.

I hope the wish that this New Year may be a happy one to you does not seem to be made a mockery by any troubles or anxieties pressing on you.

I enclose a cheque, which I shall be obliged if you will offer to Mr Congreve, as I know he prefers that payments should be made at the beginning of the year.

I shall think of you on the nineteenth. I wonder how many there really were in that "small upper room" 1866 years ago.

Jan. 8.—Mrs Congreve staying with us for a couple of nights. Yesterday we went to Mr Burton's to see my portrait, with which she was much pleased. Since last Monday I have been writing a poem, the matter of which was written in prose three or four years ago—"My Vegetarian Friend." Journal, 1865.

Jan. 15 *to* 25.—Visit to Paris.

Are we not happy to have reached home on Wednesday, before this real winter came? We enjoyed our visit to Paris greatly, in spite of bad weather, going to the theatre or opera nearly every night, and seeing sights all day long. I think the most interesting sight we saw was Comte's dwelling. Such places, that knew the great dead, always move me deeply; and I had an unexpected sight of interest in the photograph taken at the very last. M. Thomas was very friendly, and pleasant to talk to because of his simple manners. We gave your remembrances to him, and promised to assure you of his pleasure in hearing of you. I wish some truer representation of Mr Congreve hung up in the Salon instead of that (to me) exasperating photograph. Letter to Mrs Congreve, Friday (?), 27th Jan. 1865.

We thought the apartment very *freundlich*, and I flattered myself that I could have written better in the little study there than in my own. Such self-flattery is usually the most amiable phase of discontent with one's own inferiority.

I am really stronger for the change.

Journal, 1865.

Jan. 28.—Finished my poem on "Utopias."

Letter to Miss Sara Hennell, 6th Feb. 1865.

I suspect you have come to dislike letters, but until you say so, I must write now and then to gratify myself. I want to send my love, lest all the old messages shall have lost their scent, like old lavender bags.

Since I wrote to you last we have actually been to Paris! A little business was an excuse for getting a great deal of pleasure; and I, for whom change of air and scene is always the best tonic, am much brightened by our wintry expedition, which ended just in time for us to escape the heavy fall of snow.

We are very happy, having almost recovered our old *tête-à-tête*, of which I am so selfishly fond, that I am beginning to feel it an heroic effort when I make up my mind to invite half-a-dozen visitors. But it is necessary to strive against this unsocial disposition, so we are going to have some open evenings.

There is great talk of a new periodical—a fortnightly apparition, partly on the plan of the 'Revue des Deux Mondes.' Mr Lewes has consented to become its editor, if the preliminaries are settled so as to satisfy him. Letter to Miss Sara Hennell, 6th Feb. 1865.

Ecco! I have told you a little of our news, not daring to ask you anything about yourself, since you evidently don't want to tell me anything.

The party was a "mull." The weather was bad. Some of the invited were ill and sent regrets, others were not ardent enough to brave the damp evening—in fine, only twelve came. We had a charade, which, like our neighbours, was no better than it should have been, and some rather languid music, our best musicians half failing us—so ill is merit rewarded in this world! If the severest sense of fulfilling a duty could make one's parties pleasant, who so deserving as I? I turn my inward shudders into outward smiles, and talk fast with a sense of lead on my tongue. However, Mr Pigott made a woman's part in the charade so irresistibly comic, that I tittered at it at intervals in my sleepless hours. I am rather uncomfortable about you, because you seemed so much less well and strong the other day than your average. Let me hear before long how you and Mr Congreve are. Letter to Mrs Congreve, 19th Feb. 1865.

Feb. 21.—Ill and very miserable. George has taken my drama away from me. Journal, 1865.

Letter to Mrs Congreve, 27th Feb. 1865.

The sun shone through my window on your letter as I read it, adding to its cheeriness. It was good of you to write it. I was ill last week, and had mental troubles besides—happily such as are unconnected with any one's experience except my own. I am still ailing, but striving hard "not to mind," and not to diffuse my inward trouble, according to Madame de Vaux's excellent maxim. I shall not, I fear, be able to get to you till near the end of next week—towards the 11th. I think of you very often, and especially when my own *malaise* reminds me how much of your time is spent in the same sort of endurance. Mr Spencer told us yesterday that Dr Ransom said he had cured himself of dyspepsia by leaving off stimulants—the full benefit manifesting itself after two or three months of abstinence. I am going to try. All best regards to Mr Congreve and tenderest sisterly love to yourself.

Journal, 1865.

March 1.—I wrote an article for the 'Pall Mall Gazette'—"A Word for the Germans."

March 12.—Went to Wandsworth, to spend the Sunday and Monday with Mr and Mrs Congreve. Feeling very ailing; in constant dull pain, which makes all effort burthensome.

Letter to Mrs Congreve, 16th March 1865.

I did not promise, like Mr Collins, that you should receive a letter of thanks for your kind entertain-

Letter to Mrs Congreve, 16th March 1865.

ment of me; but I feel the need of writing a word or two to break the change from your presence to my complete absence from you. It was really an enjoyment to be with you, in spite of the bodily uneasiness which robbed me of half my mind. One thing only I regret—that in my talk with you I think I was rather merciless to other people. Whatever vices I have, seem to be exaggerated by my *malaise*—such "chastening" not answering the purpose of purification in my case. Pray set down any unpleasant notions I have suggested about others to my account—*i.e.*, as being *my* unpleasantness, and not theirs. When one is bilious, other people's complexions look yellow, and one of their eyes higher than the other—all the fault of one's own evil interior. I long to hear from you that you are better, and if you are not better, still to hear from you before too long an interval. Mr Congreve's condition is really cheering, and he goes about with me as a pleasant picture—like that Raffaelle the Tuscan duke chose always to carry with him.

I got worse after I left you; but to-day I am better, and begin to think there is nothing serious the matter with me except the "weather," which every one else is alleging as the cause of their symptoms.

Letter to Mrs Bray, 18th March 1865.

I believe you are one of the few who can understand that in certain crises direct expression of sympathy is the least possible to those who most feel sympathy. If I could have been with you in bodily presence, I should have sat silent, thinking silence a sign of feeling that speech, trying to be wise, must always spoil. The truest things one can say about great Death are the oldest, simplest things that everybody knows by rote, but that no one knows really till death has come very close. And when that inward teaching is going on, it seems pitiful presumption for those who are outside to be saying anything. There is no such thing as consolation when we have made the lot of another our own. I don't know whether you strongly share, as I do, the old belief that made men say the gods loved those who died young. It seems to me truer than ever, now life has become more complex, and more and more difficult problems have to be worked out. Life, though a good to men on the whole, is a doubtful good to many, and to some not a good at all. To my thought, it is a source of constant mental distortion to make the denial of this a part of religion—to go on pretending things are better than they are. To me early death takes the aspect of salvation; though I feel, too, that those who live and suffer may sometimes have the greater blessedness of *being* a salvation. But I will not write of judgments and opinions. What I want my letter to tell you is that I love you truly, gratefully, unchangeably. Letter to Mrs Bray, 18th March 1865.

March 25.—I am in deep depression, feeling powerless. I have written nothing but beginnings since I finished a little article for the 'Pall Mall,' on the "Logic of Servants." Dear George is all activity, yet is in very frail health. How I worship his good humour, his good sense, his affectionate care for every one who has claims on him! That worship is my best life. Journal, 1865.

March 29.—Sent a letter on "Futile Lying," from Saccharissa, to the 'Pall Mall.'

I have begun a novel ('Felix Holt').

We are wondering if, by any coincidence or condition of things, you could come to us on Thursday, when we have our last evening party—wondering how you are—wondering everything about you, and knowing nothing. Could you resolve some of our wonderings into cheering knowledge? It is ages since you made any sign to us. Are *we* to be blamed, or you? I hope you are not unfavourably affected by the sudden warmth which comes with the beautiful sunshine. Some word of you, in pity! Letter to Mrs Congreve, 11th April 1865.

Letter to Mrs Congreve, 22d April 1865.

If the sun goes on shining in this glorious way, I shall think of your journey with pleasure. The sight of the country *must* be a good when the trees are bursting into leaf. But I will remember your warning to Emily, and not insist too much on the advantages of paying visits. Let us hear of you sometimes, and think of us as very busy and very happy, but always including you in our world, and getting uneasy when we are left too much to our imaginations about you. Tell Emily that Ben and I are the better for having seen her. He has added to his store of memories, and will recognise her when she comes again.

Journal, 1865.

May 4.—Sent an article on Lecky's 'History of Rationalism' for the 'Fortnightly.' For nearly a fortnight I have been ill, one way or other.

May 10.—Finished a letter of Saccharissa for the 'Pall Mall.' Reading Æschylus, 'Theatre of the Greeks,' Klein's 'History of the Drama,' &c.

Letter to Mrs Congreve, 11th May 1865.

This note will greet you on your return, and tell you that we were glad to hear of you in your absence, even though the news was not of the brightest. Next week we are going away—I don't yet know exactly where; but it is firmly settled that we start on Monday. It will be good for the carpets, and it will be still better for us, who need a wholesome shaking, even more than the carpets do. Letter to Mrs Congreve, 11th May 1865.

The first number of the 'Review' was done with last Monday, and will be out on the 15th. You will be glad to hear that Mr Harrison's article is excellent, but the "mull" which George declares to be the fatality with all first numbers is so far incurred with regard to this very article, that from overwhelming alarm at its length George put it (perhaps too hastily) into the smaller type. I hope the importance of the subject and the excellence of the treatment will overcome that disadvantage.

Nurse all pleasant thoughts in your solitude, and count our affection among them.

We have just returned from a five days' holiday at the coast, and are much invigorated by the tonic breezes. Letter to Miss Sara Hennell, 18th May 1865.

We have nothing to do with the 'Fortnightly' as a money speculation. Mr Lewes has simply accepted the post of editor, and it was seemly that I should write a little in it. But do not suppose that I am going into periodical writing. And your friendship is not required to read one syllable for our sakes. On the contrary, you have my full sympathy in abstaining. Rest in peace, dear Sara, and finish your work, that you may have the sense of having spoken out what was within you. That is really a good — I mean when it is done in all seriousness and sincerity.

Journal, 1865.

May 28.—Finished Bamford's 'Passages from the Life of a Radical.' Have just begun again Mill's 'Political Economy,' and Comte's 'Social Science,' in Miss Martineau's edition.

June 7.—Finished 'Annual Register' for 1832. Reading Blackstone. Mill's second article on "Comte," to appear in the 'Westminster,' lent me by Mr Spencer. My health has been better of late.

June 15.—Read again Aristotle's "Poetics" with fresh admiration.

June 20.—Read the opening of my novel to G. Yesterday we drove to Wandsworth. Walked together on Wimbledon Common, in outer and inner sunshine, as of old; then dined with Mr and Mrs Congreve, and had much pleasant talk.

June 25. — Reading English History, reign of George III.; Shakspeare's "King John." Yesterday G. dined at Greenwich with the multitude of so-called writers for the 'Saturday.' He heard much commendation of the 'Fortnightly,' especially of Bagehot's articles, which last is reassuring after Mr Trollope's strong objections.

July 3.—Went to hear the "Faust" at Covent Garden: Mario, Lucca, and Graziani. I was much thrilled by the great symbolical situations, and by the music—more, I think, than I had ever been before. Journal, 1865.

July 9 (Sunday).—We had Browning, Huxley, Mr Warren, Mr Bagehot, and Mr Crompton, and talk was pleasant.

Letter to Mrs Peter Taylor, Sunday, 10th July 1865.

Success to the canvassing! It is "very meet and right and your bounden duty" to be with Mr Taylor in this time of hard work, and I am glad that your health has made no impediment. I should have liked to be present when you were cheered. The expression of a common feeling by a large mass of men, when the feeling is one of good-will, moves me like music. A public tribute to any man who has done the world a service with brain or hand, has on me the effect of a great religious rite, with pealing organ and full-voiced choir.

I agree with you in your feeling about Mill. Some of his works have been frequently my companions of late, and I have been going through many *actions de grâce* towards him. I am not anxious that he should be in Parliament: thinkers can do more outside than inside the House. But it

Letter to Mrs Peter Taylor, Sunday, 10th July 1865.

would have been a fine precedent, and would have made an epoch, for such a man to have been asked for and elected solely on the ground of his mental eminence. As it is, I suppose it is pretty certain that he will *not* be elected.

I am glad you have been interested in Mr Lewes's article. His great anxiety about the 'Fortnightly' is to make it the vehicle for sincere writing—real contributions of opinion on important topics. But it is more difficult than the inexperienced could imagine to get the sort of writing which will correspond to that desire of his.

Journal, 1865.

July 16.—Madame Bohn, niece of Professor Scherer, called. She said certain things about 'Romola' which showed that she had felt what I meant my readers to feel. She said she knew the book had produced the same effect on many others. I wish I could be encouraged by this.

July 22.—Sat for my portrait—I suppose for the last time.

July 23.—I am going doggedly to work at my novel, seeing what determination can do in the face of despair. Reading Neale's 'History of the Puritans.'

Letter to Mrs Peter Taylor, 1st Aug. 1865.

I received yesterday the circular about the Mazzini Fund. Mr Lewes and I would have liked to subscribe to a tribute to Mazzini, or to a fund for his use, of which the application was defined and guaranteed by his own word. As it is, the application of the desired fund is only intimated in the vaguest manner by the Florentine committee. The reflection is inevitable, that the application may ultimately be the promotion of conspiracy, the precise character of which is necessarily unknown to subscribers. Now, though I believe there are cases in which conspiracy may be a sacred, necessary struggle against organised wrong, there are also cases in which it is hopeless, and can produce nothing but misery; or needless, because it is not the best means attainable of reaching the desired end; or unjustifiable, because it resorts to acts which are more unsocial in their character than the very wrong they are directed to extinguish: and in these three supposable cases it seems to me that it would be a social crime to further conspiracy even by the impulse of a little finger, to which one may well compare a small money subscription.

Letter to Mrs Peter Taylor, 1st Aug. 1865.

I think many persons to whom the circular might be sent would take something like this view, and would grieve, as we do, that a proposition intended to honour Mazzini should come in a form to which they cannot conscientiously subscribe.

Letter to Mrs Peter Taylor, 1st Aug. 1865.

I trouble you and Mr Taylor with this explanation, because both Mr Lewes and I have a real reverence for Mazzini, and could not therefore be content to give a silent negative.

Letter to Mrs Congreve, 1st Aug. 1865.

I fear that my languor on Saturday prevented me from fairly showing you how sweet and precious your presence was to me then, as at all times. We have almost made up our minds to start some time in this month for a run in Normandy and Brittany. We both need the change; though when I receive, as I did yesterday, a letter from some friend telling me of cares and trials from which I am quite free, I am ashamed of wanting anything.

Journal, 1865.

Aug. 2.—Finished the 'Agamemnon' second time.

Letter to Mrs Congreve, 6th Aug. 1865.

When I wrote to you last, I quite hoped that I should see you and Emily before we left home; but now it is settled that we start on Thursday morning, and I have so many little things to remember and to do that I dare not set apart any of the intervening time for the quiet enjoyment of a visit from you. It is not quite so cheerful a picture as I should like to carry with me, that of you and Emily so long alone, with Mr Congreve working at Bradford. But your friends are sure to think of you, and want to see you. I hope you did not suffer so severely as we did from the arctic cold that rushed in after the oppressive heat. Mr T. Trollope came from Italy just when it began. He says it is always the same when he comes to England,—people always say it has just been very hot, and he believes that means they had a few days in which they were not obliged to blow on their fingers.

Letter to Mrs Congreve, 6th Aug. 1865.

When you write to Mr Congreve, pray tell him that we were very grateful for his Itinerary, which is likely to be useful to us—indeed, has already been useful in determining our route.

Sept. 7.—We returned home after an expedition into Brittany. Our course was from Boulogne to St Valéry, Dieppe, Rouen, Caen, Bayeux, St Lô, Vire, Avranches, Dol, St Malo, Rennes, Avray, and Carnac,—back by Nantes, Tours, Le Mans, Chartres, Paris, Rouen, Dieppe, Abbeville, and so again to Boulogne.

Journal, 1865.

We came home again on Thursday night—this day week—after a month's absence in Normandy and Brittany. I have been thinking of you very often since, but believed that you did not care to have the interruption of letters just now, and would rather defer correspondence till your mind was

Letter to Miss Sara Hennell, 14th Sept. 1865.

Letter to Miss Sara Hennell, 14th Sept. 1865.

freer. If I had *suspected* that you would feel any want satisfied by a letter, I should certainly have written. I had not heard of Miss Bonham Carter's death, else I should have conceived something of your state of mind. I think you and I are alike in this, that we can get no good out of pretended comforts, which are the devices of self-love, but would rather, in spite of pain, grow into the endurance of all "naked truths." So I say no word about your great loss, except that I love you, and sorrow with you.

The circumstances of life—the changes that take place in ourselves—hem in the expression of affections and memories that live within us, and enter almost into every day, and long separations often make intercourse difficult when the opportunity comes. But the delight I had in you, and in the hours we spent together, and in all your acts of friendship to me, is really part of my life, and can never die out of me. I see distinctly how much poorer I should have been if I had never known you. If you had seen more of me in late years, you would not have such almost cruel thoughts as that the book into which you have faithfully put your experience and best convictions could make you "repugnant" to me. Whatever else my growth

Letter to Miss Sara Hennell, 14th Sept. 1865.

may have been, it has not been towards irreverence and ready rejection of what other minds can give me. You once unhappily mistook my feeling and point of view in something I wrote *apropos* of an argument in your 'Aids to Faith,' and *that* made me think it better that we should not write on large and difficult subjects in hasty letters. But it has often been painful to me—I should say, it has constantly been painful to me—that you have ever since inferred me to be in a hard and unsympathetic state about your views and your writing. But I am habitually disposed myself to the same unbelief in the sympathy that is given me, and am the last person who should be allowed to complain of such unbelief in another. And it is very likely that I may have been faulty and disagreeable in my expressions.

Excuse all my many mistakes, dear Sara, and never believe otherwise than that I have a glow of joy when you write to me, as if my existence were some good to you. I know that I am, and can be, very little practically; but to have the least value for your thought is what I care much to be assured of.

Perhaps, in the cooler part of the autumn, when your book is out of your hands, you will like to move from home a little and see your London friends?

Letter to Miss Sara Hennell, 14th Sept. 1865.

Our travelling in Brittany was a good deal marred and obstructed by the Emperor's *fête*, which sent all the world on our track towards Cherbourg and Brest. But the Norman churches, the great cathedrals at Le Mans, Tours, and Chartres, with their marvellous painted glass, were worth much scrambling to see.

Letter to Miss Sara Hennell, 28th Oct. 1865.

I have read Mr Masson's book on 'Recent Philosophy.' The earlier part is a useful and creditable survey, and the classification ingenious. The later part I thought poor. If, by what he says of Positivism, you mean what he says at p. 246, I should answer it is simply "stuff"—he might as well have written a dozen lines of jargon. There are a few observations about Comte, scattered here and there, which are true and just enough. But it seems to me much better to read a man's own writing than to read what others say about him, especially when the man is first-rate and the "others" are third-rate. As Goethe said long ago about Spinoza, "Ich zog immer vor von dem Menschen zu erfahren *wie er dachte* als von einem anderen zu hören *wie er hätte denken sollen*."[1] However, I am not fond of expressing criticism or disapproba-

[1] "I always preferred to learn from the man himself what *he* thought, rather than to hear from some one else what *he ought to have thought*."

tion. The difficulty is to digest and live upon any valuable truth one's self.

Nov. 15.—During the last three weeks George has been very poorly, but now he is better. I have been reading Fawcett's 'Economic Condition of the Working Classes,' Mill's 'Liberty,' looking into Strauss's second 'Life of Jesus,' and reading Neale's 'History of the Puritans,' of which I have reached the fourth volume. Yesterday the news came of Mrs Gaskell's death. She died suddenly while reading aloud to her daughter. Journal 1865.

Nov. 16.—Writing Mr Lyon's story, which I have determined to insert as a narrative. Reading the Bible.

Nov. 24.—Finished Neale's 'History of the Puritans.' Began Hallam's 'Middle Ages.'

Dec. 4.—Finished second volume of Hallam. The other day read to the end of chapter ix. of my novel to George, who was much pleased, and found no fault.

We send to-day 'Orley Farm,' 'The Small House at Allington,' and 'The Story of Elizabeth.' 'The Small House' is rather lighter than 'Orley Farm.' 'The Story of Elizabeth' is by Miss Thackeray. It is not so cheerful as Trollope, but is charmingly written. You can taste it and reject it if it is too Letter to Mrs Congreve, 4th Dec. 1865.

melancholy. I think more of you than you are likely to imagine, and I believe we talk of you all more than of any other mortals.

Letter to Miss Sara Hennell, 7th Dec. 1865.

It is worth your while to send for the last 'Fortnightly' to read an article of Professor Tyndall's "On the Constitution of the Universe." It is a splendid piece of writing on the higher physics, which I know will interest you. *Apropos* of the feminine intellect, I had a bit of experience with a superior woman the other day, which reminded me of Sydney Smith's story about his sermon on the Being of a God. He says, that after he had delivered his painstaking argument, an old parishioner said to him, "I don't agree wi' you, Mr Smith; *I think there be a God.*"

Journal, 1865.

Dec. 11.—For the last three days I have been foundering from a miserable state of head. I have written chapter x. This evening read again Macaulay's Introduction.

Dec. 15.—To-day is the first for nearly a week on which I have been able to write anything fresh. I am reading Macaulay and Blackstone. This evening we went to hear the "Messiah" at Exeter Hall.

Letter to Miss Sara Hennell, 21st Dec. 1865.

"A merry Christmas and a Happy New Year" is a sort of hieroglyph for I love you and wish you well all the year round. Christmas to me is like a great many other pleasures, which I am glad to imagine as enjoyed by others, but have no delight in myself. Berried holly, and smiling faces, and snapdragon, grandmamma and the children, turkey and plum-pudding,—they are all precious things, and I would not have the world without them; but they tire me a little. I enjoy the common days of the year more. But for the sake of those who are stronger, I rejoice in Christmas.

Letter to Miss Sara Hennell, 21st Dec. 1865.

Dec. 24.—For two days I have been sticking in the mud from doubt about my construction. I have just consulted G., and he confirms my choice of incidents.

Journal, 1865.

Dec. 31.—The last day of 1865. I will say nothing but that I trust—I will strive—to add more ardent effort towards a good result from all the outward good that is given to me. My health is at a lower ebb than usual, and so is George's. Bertie is spending his holidays with us, and shows hopeful characteristics. Charles is happy.

SUMMARY.

JANUARY 1862 TO DECEMBER 1865.

Begins 'Romola' again—Letter to Miss Hennell—Max Müller's book—'Orley Farm'—Anthony Trollope—T. A. Trollope's 'Beata'—Acquaintance with Mr Burton and Mr W. G. Clark—George Smith, publisher, suggests a "magnificent offer"—Depression about 'Romola'—Letter to Mrs Bray asking for loan of music—Pantomime—First visit to Dorking—Letter to Madame Bodichon—Impatience of concealment—Anxiety about war with America—Sympathy with Queen—Mr Lewes begins 'History of Science'—Mrs Browning's "Casa Guidi Windows"—Depression—George Smith offers £10,000 for 'Romola' for the 'Cornhill'—Idea given up—Visit to Englefield Green—Working under a weight—Second visit to Dorking for three weeks—Delight in spring—Accepts £7000 for 'Romola' in 'Cornhill'—Regret at leaving Blackwood—Palsy in writing—Visit to Littlehampton and to Dorking third time—Letter to Mrs Congreve—Mr Lewes at Spa—George Eliot in better spirits—Letter to Miss Hennell—Joachim's playing—New Literary Club—Reading Poliziano—Suggestion of Tennyson's "Palace of Art"—Visit from Browning—Depression—Letter to Madame Bodichon—No negative propaganda—Letter to Mrs Peter Taylor—The "Messiah" on Christmas Day—Letter to Miss Hennell—St Paul's "Charity"—The Poetry of Christianity—The Bible—Adieu to year 1862—Letter to Miss Hennell—Encouragement about 'Romola'—Literary Club dissolves—Miss Cobbe—Letter to Mrs Congreve—Depression—Fourth visit to Dorking for fortnight—Letter to Charles Lewes on Thackeray's Lectures—The effect of writing 'Romola'—Letter to Madame Bodichon — Odiousness of intellectual superciliousness —

Letter to Mrs Bray—Thinking of the Priory—'Romola' finished—Inscription—Visit to Isle of Wight—Ristori—Letter to Miss Hennell—Thornton Lewes—London amusements—Opera—Reading Mommsen, Liddell's 'Rome,' and 'Roba di Roma'—Letter from Frederick Maurice referred to as most generous tribute ever given—Letter to Mrs Peter Taylor—Renan's 'Vie de Jésus'—Visit to Worthing—Mrs Hare—Return to London—Depression—Letter to R. H. Hutton on 'Romola'—The importance of the medium in which characters move—Letter to Madame Bodichon—Effect of London on health—Letter to Mrs Bray—Delight in autumn—Mommsen's History—Letter to Mrs Congreve—'The Discours Préliminaire'—Removal to the Priory—Mr Owen Jones decorates the house—Jansa the violinist—Letter to Mrs Bray—'Physiology for Schools'—Letter to Madame Bodichon—Enjoying rest, and music with Jansa—Letter to Miss Hennell—Renan—Letter to Mrs Bray—Enjoyment of Priory—Letter to Mrs Congreve—Mr Lewes's 'Aristotle' finished—Letter to Mrs Peter Taylor—Compensation—Letter to Mrs P. A. Taylor—Effect of sunshine—Death of Mrs Hare—"David Gray"—Letter to Miss Hennell—Dislike of note writing—Visit to Scotland—Letter to Mrs Peter Taylor—Joy in Federal successes—Crystal Palace to see Garibaldi—Mr Burton's picture of a Legendary Knight in Armour—Third Visit to Italy with Mr Burton for seven weeks—Return to London—Charles Lewes's engagement to Miss Gertrude Hill—Pleasure in Mr Burton's companionship in travel—Letter to Mrs Congreve — Present of mats — Depression — Reading Gibbon—Gieseler—Letter to Miss Hennell—Reading Max Müller—Reference to the 'Apologia'—Newman—Reading about Spain—Trying a drama—Letter to Miss Hennell—Harrogate — Development of Industries — Scarborough — Letters to Mrs Congreve—Pleasure in her visit—Letter to Miss Hennell — Learning Spanish — Two Acts of drama written—Sticking in construction of remainder—Letter to Mrs Congreve — Christmas greeting — Retrospect of year 1864—Letter to Mrs Congreve—First payment to Positivist Fund—Comparison with "small upper room" 1866 years ago—Mrs Congreve staying at The Priory — Poem "My Vegetarian Friend" written—Visit to Paris—Letter to Mrs Congreve—Visit to Comte's apartment in Paris—Finished Poem on "Utopias"—Letter to Miss Sara Hennell—Delight in dual solitude—'Fortnightly Review'—Letter to Mrs Congreve—Charades—Depression—Mr Lewes takes away drama —Article for the 'Pall Mall,' "A Word for the Germans"—Letter to Mrs Congreve—Visit to Wandsworth—Depression —Letter to Mrs Congreve after visit—Letter to Mrs Bray on a young friend's death—Deep depression—Admiration of Mr Lewes's good spirits—'Felix Holt' begun—Article on Lecky's 'History of Rationalism' in 'Fortnightly'—Reading Æschylus, 'Theatre of the Greeks'—Klein's 'History of the Drama'—Letter to Mrs Congreve — First number of the 'Fortnightly'—Frederic Harrison's article—Reading Mill, Comte, and Blackstone—Aristotle's "Poetics"—Dine with Congreves at Wandsworth—Faust at Covent Garden—Sunday reception—Browning—Huxley and Bagehot—Mr Burton's portrait finished—Letter to Mrs Peter Taylor on J. S. Mill—The 'Fortnightly Review'—Mazzini subscription—Letter of adieu to Mrs Congreve—Expedition to Brittany for month—Letter to Miss Hennell—"Pretended comforts"—Recollection of early feelings—Delight in her friendship—Masson's 'Recent Philosophy'—Comte—Goethe on Spinoza—Reading Fawcett's 'Economic Condition of Working Classes'—Mill's 'Liberty'—Strauss's second 'Life of Jesus'—Neale's 'History of the Puritans' — Hallam's 'Middle Ages' — Letter to Miss Hennell on Tyndall's article on "The Constitution of the Universe"—View of Christmas Day —Retrospect of 1865.

CHAPTER XIII.

I HAVE had it in my mind to write to you for many days, wanting to tell you, yet feeling there might be some impertinence in doing so, of the delight and gratitude I felt in reading your article on Industrial Co-operation. Certain points admirably brought out in that article would, I think, be worth the labour of a life if one could help in winning them thorough recognition. I don't mean that my thinking so is of any consequence, but simply that it is of consequence to me when I find your energetic writing confirm my own faith. Letter Frederic Harrison, 5th Jan. 1866.

It would be fortunate for us if you had nothing better to do than look in on us on Tuesday evening. Professor Huxley will be with us, and one or two others whom you know, and your presence would make us all the brighter.

Jan. 9.—Professors Huxley and Beesley, Mr Journal, 1866.

Burton and Mr Spencer, dined with us. Mr Harrison in the evening.

Letter to Frederic Harrison, 12th Jan. 1866.

The ample and clear statement you have sent me with kind promptness has put me in high spirits—as high spirits as can belong to an unhopeful author. Your hypothetical case of a settlement suits my needs surprisingly well. I shall be thankful to let Sugden alone, and throw myself entirely on your goodness, especially as what I want is simply a basis of legal possibilities, and not any command of details. I want to be sure that my chords will not offend a critic accomplished in thorough-bass—not at all to present an exercise in thorough-bass.

I was going to write you a long story, but on consideration it seems to me that I should tax your time less, and arrive more readily at a resolution of my doubts on various points not yet mentioned to you, if you could let me speak instead of writing to you.

On Wednesday afternoons I am always at home but on any day when I could be sure of your coming, I would set everything aside for the sake of a consultation so valuable to me.

Journal, 1866.

Jan. 20.—For the last fortnight I have been unusually disabled by ill health. I have been consulting Mr Harrison about the law in my book with satisfactory result.

I had not any opportunity, or not enough presence of mind, to tell you yesterday how much I felt your kindness in writing me that last little note of sympathy.

Letter to Frederic Harrison, 22d Jan. 1866.

In proportion as compliments (always beside the mark) are discouraging and nauseating, at least to a writer who has any serious aims, genuine words from one capable of understanding one's conceptions are precious and strengthening.

Yet I have no confidence that the book will ever be worthily written. And now I have something else to ask. It is, that if anything strikes you as untrue in cases where my drama has a bearing on momentous questions, especially of a public nature, you will do me the great kindness to tell me of your doubts.

On a few moral points, which have been made clear to me by my experience, I feel sufficiently confident,—without such confidence I could not write at all. But in every other direction I am so much in need of fuller instruction, as to be constantly under the sense that I am more likely to be wrong than right.

Hitherto I have read my MS. (I mean of my

Letter to Frederic Harrison, 22d Jan. 1866.

previous books) to Mr Lewes, by forty or fifty pages at a time, and he has told me if he felt an objection to anything. No one else has had any knowledge of my writings before their publication. (I except, of course, the publishers.)

But now that you are good enough to incur the trouble of reading my MS., I am anxious to get the full benefit of your participation.

Letter to Mrs Congreve, 28th Jan. 1866.

We arrived here on Tuesday, and have been walking about four hours each day, and the walks are so various that each time we have turned out we have found a new one. George is already much the better for the perfect rest, quiet, and fresh air. Will you give my thanks to Mr Congreve for the 'Synthèse,' which I have brought with me and am reading? I expect to understand three chapters well enough to get some edification.

George had talked of our taking the train to Dover to pay you a "morning call." He observes that it would have been a "dreadful sell" if we had done so. Your letter, therefore, was providential—and without doubt it came from a dear little Providence of mine that sits in your heart.

Letter to Frederic Harrison, 31st Jan. 1866.

I have received both your precious letters—the second edition of the case, and the subsequent note. The story is sufficiently in the track of ordinary probability; and the careful trouble you have so generously given to it, has enabled me to feel a satisfaction in my plot which beforehand I had sighed for as unattainable.

Letter to Frederic Harrison, 31st Jan. 1866.

There is still a question or two which I shall want to ask you, but I am afraid of taxing your time and patience in an unconscionable manner. So, since we expect to return to town at the end of next week, I think I will reserve my questions until I have the pleasure and advantage of an interview with you, in which *pros* and *cons* can be more rapidly determined than by letter. It seems to me that you have fitted my phenomena with a *rationale* quite beautifully. If there is any one who could have done it better, I am sure I know of no man who *would.* Please to put your help of me among your good deeds for this year of 1866.

To-day we have resolute rain, for the first time since we came down. You don't yet know what it is to be a sickly wretch, dependent on these skiey influences. But Heine says illness "spiritualises the members." It had need do some good in return for one's misery.

Letter to Miss Sara Hennell, 12th Feb. 1866.

Thanks for your kind letter. Alas! we had chiefly bad weather in the country. George was a

Letter to Miss Sara Hennell, 12th Feb. 1866.

little benefited, but only a little. He is too far "run down" to be wound up in a very short time. We enjoyed our return to our comfortable house, and perhaps that freshness of home was the chief gain from our absence.

You see, to counterbalance all the great and good things that life has given us beyond what our fellows have, we hardly know now what it is to be free from bodily *malaise.*

After the notion I have given you of my health, you will not wonder if I say that I don't know when anything of mine will appear. I can never reckon on myself.

Journal, 1866.

March 7.—I am reading Mill's 'Logic' again. Theocritus still, and English History and Law.

March 17.—To St James's Hall hearing Joachim, Piatti, and Hallé in glorious Beethoven music.

Letter to Miss Sara Hennell, 9th April 1866.

Don't think any evil of me for not writing. Just now the days are short, and art is long to artists with feeble bodies. If people don't say expressly that they want anything from me, I easily conclude that they will do better without me, and have a good weight of idleness, or rather bodily fatigue, which puts itself into the scale of modesty. I torment myself less with fruitless regrets that my particular life has not been more perfect. The young things are growing, and to me it is not melancholy but joyous that the world will be brighter after I am gone than it has been in the brief time of my existence. You see my pen runs into very old reflections. The fact is, I have no details to tell that would much interest you. It is true that I am going to bring out another book, but just *when* is not certain.

Letter to Miss Sara Hennell, 9th April 1866.

The happiness in your letter was delightful to me, as you guessed it would be. See how much better things may turn out for all mankind, since they mend for single mortals even in this confused state of the bodies social and politic.

Letter to Madame Bodichon, 10th April 1866.

As soon as we can leave we shall go away, probably to Germany, for six weeks or so. But that will not be till June. I am finishing a book which has been growing slowly like a sickly child, because of my own ailments; but now I am in the later acts of it, I can't move till it is done.

You know all the news, public and private—all about the sad cattle plague, and the Reform Bill, and who is going to be married and who is dead. So I need tell you nothing. You will find the English world extremely like what it was when you left it—conversation more or less trivial and insincere, literature just now not much better, and poli-

Letter to Madame Bodichon, 10th April 1866.

tics worse than either. Bring some sincerity and energy to make a little draught of pure air in your particular world. I shall expect you to be a heroine in the best sense, now you are happier after a time of suffering. See what a talent I have for telling other people to be good!

We are getting patriarchal, and think of old age and death as journeys not far off. All knowledge, all thought, all achievement seems more precious and enjoyable to me than it ever was before in life. But as soon as one has found the key of life, "it opes the gates of death." Youth has not learned the *art* of living, and we go on bungling till our experience can only serve us for a very brief space. That is the "external order" we must submit to.

I am too busy to write except when I am tired, and don't know very well what to say, so you must not be surprised if I write in a dreamy way.

Journal, 1866.

April 21.—Sent MS. of two volumes to Blackwood.

April 25.—Blackwood has written to offer me £5000 for 'Felix Holt.' I have been ailing, and uncertain in my strokes, and yesterday got no further than p. 52 of vol. iii.

Letter to John Blackwood, 25th April 1866.

It is a great pleasure to me to be writing to you again, as in the old days. After your kind letters,

I am chiefly anxious that the publication of 'Felix Holt' may be a satisfaction to you from beginning to end.

Letter to John Blackwood, 25th April 1866.

Mr Lewes writes about other business matters, so I will only say that I am desirous to have the proofs as soon and as rapidly as will be practicable.

They will require correcting with great care, and there are large spaces in the day when I am unable to write, in which I could be attending to my proofs.

I think I ought to tell you that I have consulted a legal friend about my law, to guard against errors. The friend is a Chancery barrister, who "ought to know."

After I had written the first volume, I applied to him, and he has since read through my MS.

How very good it was of you to write me a letter which is a guarantee to me of the pleasantest kind that I have made myself understood.

Letter to John Blackwood, 27th April 1866.

The tone of the prevalent literature just now is not encouraging to a writer who at least wishes to be serious and sincere; and, owing to my want of health, a great deal of this book has been written under so much depression as to its practical effectiveness, that I have sometimes been ready to give it up.

Letter to John Blackwood, 27th April 1866.

Your letter has made me feel, more strongly than any other testimony, that it would have been a pity if I had listened to the tempter Despondency. I took a great deal of pains to get a true idea of the period. My own recollections of it are childish, and of course disjointed, but they help to illuminate my reading. I went through the 'Times' of 1832-33 at the British Museum, to be sure of as many details as I could. It is amazing what strong language was used in those days, especially about the Church. "Bloated pluralists," "Stall-fed dignitaries," &c., are the sort of phrases conspicuous. There is one passage of prophecy which I longed to quote, but I thought it wiser to abstain: "Now, the beauty of the Reform Bill is, that under its mature operation the people must and will become free agents"—a prophecy which I hope is true, only the maturity of the operation has not arrived yet.

Mr Lewes is well satisfied with the portion of the third volume already written; and as I am better in health just now, I hope to go on with spirit, especially with the help of your cordial sympathy. I trust you will see, when it comes, that the third volume is the natural issue prepared for by the first and second.

A thousand thanks for your note. Do not worry yourself so much about those two questions that you will be forced to hate me. On Tuesday next we are to go to Dorking for probably a fortnight. I wished you to read the first 100 pages of my third volume; but I fear now that I must be content to wait and send you a duplicate proof of a chapter or two that are likely to make a lawyer shudder by their poetic licence. Please to be in great distress some time for want of my advice, and tease me considerably to get it, that I may prove my grateful memory of these days.

Letter to Frederic Harrison, 27th April 1866.

To-morrow we go—Mr Lewes's bad health driving us—to Dorking, where everything will reach me as quickly as in London.

Letter to John Blackwood, 30th April 1866.

I am in a horrible fidget about certain points which I want to be sure of in correcting my proofs. They are chiefly two questions. I wish to know—

1. Whether in Napoleon's war with England, after the breaking up of the Treaty of Amiens, the seizure and imprisonment of civilians was exceptional, or whether it was continued throughout the war?

2. Whether in 1833, in the case of transportation to one of the colonies, when the sentence did not involve hard labour, the sentenced person might be at large on his arrival in the colony?

Letter to John Blackwood, 30th April 1866.

It is possible you may have some one near at hand who will answer these questions. I am sure you will help me if you can, and will sympathise in my anxiety not to have even an allusion that involves practical impossibilities.

One can never be perfectly accurate, even with one's best effort, but the effort must be made.

Journal, 1866.

May 31.—Finished 'Felix Holt.'

The manuscript bears the following inscription:—

"From George Eliot to her dear Husband, this thirteenth year of their united life, in which the deepening sense of her own imperfectness has the consolation of their deepening love."

Letter to Mrs Congreve, 5th June 1866.

My last hope of seeing you before we start has vanished. I find that the things urged upon me to be done, in addition to my own small matters of preparation, will leave me no time to enjoy anything that I should have chosen if I had been at leisure. Last Thursday only I finished writing, in a state of nervous excitement that had been making my head throb and my heart palpitate all the week before. As soon as I had finished I felt well. You know how we had counted on a parting sight of you; and I should have particularly liked to see Emily, and witness the good effect of Derbyshire.

But send us a word or two if you can, just to say how you *all three* are. We start on Thursday evening for Brussels. Then to Antwerp, The Hague, and Amsterdam. Out of Holland we are to find our way to Schwalbach. Let your love go with us, as mine will hover about you and all yours—that group of three which the word "Wandsworth" always means for us. Letter to Mrs Congreve, 5th June 1866.

I finished writing ['Felix Holt'] on the last day of May, after days and nights of throbbing and palpitation—chiefly, I suppose, from a nervous excitement which I was not strong enough to support well. As soon as I had done I felt better, and have been a new creature ever since, though a little overdone with visits from friends, and attention (*miserabile dictu!*) to petticoats, &c. Letter to Mrs Bray, 5th June 1866.

I can't help being a little vexed that the course of things hinders my having the great delight of seeing you again—during this visit to town. Now that my mind is quite free, I don't know anything I should have chosen sooner than to have a long, long, quiet day with you.

June 7.—Set off on our journey to Holland. Journal, 1866.

I wish you could know how idle I feel—how utterly disinclined to anything but mere self-indulgence—because that knowledge would enable Letter to Mrs Congreve, 25th June 1866.

Letter to Mrs Congreve, 25th June 1866.

you to estimate the affection and anxiety which prompt me to write in spite of disinclination. June is so far gone, that by the time you get this letter you will surely have some result of the examination to tell me of; and I can't bear to deprive myself of that news by not letting you know where we are. "In Paradise," George says; but the Paradise is in the fields and woods of beech and fir, where we walk in uninterrupted solitude in spite of the excellent roads and delightful resting-places, which seem to have been prepared for visitors in general. The promenade, where the ladies—chiefly Russian and German, with only a small sprinkling of English and Americans—display their ornamental petticoats and various hats, is only the outskirt of Paradise; but we amuse ourselves there for an hour or so in the early morning and evening, listening to the music and learning the faces of our neighbours. There is a deficiency of men, children, and dogs: otherwise the winding walks, the luxuriant trees and grass, and the abundant seats of the promenade, have every charm one can expect at a German bath. We arrived here last Thursday, after a fortnight spent in Belgium and Holland; and we still fall to interjections of delight whenever we walk out—first at the beauty of the place, and next at our own happiness in not having been frightened away from it by the predictions of travellers and hotel-keepers, that we should find no one here — that the Prussians would break up the railways, &c., &c.—Nassau being one of the majority of small States who are against Prussia. I fear we are a little in danger of becoming like the Bürger in "Faust," and making it too much the entertainment of our holiday to have a

Letter to Mrs Congreve, 25th June 1866.

> "Gespräch von Krieg und Kriegsgeschrei
> Wenn hinten, weit, in der Türkei,
> Die Völker auf einander schlagen."

Idle people are so eager for newspapers that tell them of other people's energetic enthusiasm! A few soldiers are quartered here, and we see them wisely using their leisure to drink at the Brunnen. They are the only suggestion of war that meets our eyes among these woody hills. Already we feel great benefit from our quiet journeying and repose. George is looking remarkably well, and seems to have nothing the matter with him. You know how magically quick his recoveries seem. I am too refined to say anything about our excellent quarters and good meals; but one detail, I know, will touch your sympathy. We dine in our own

Letter to Mrs Congreve, 25th June 1866, from Schwalbach.

room! It would have marred the *Kur* for me if I had had every day to undergo a *table d'hôte* where almost all the guests are English, presided over by the British chaplain. Please don't suspect me of being scornful towards my fellow country men or women: the fault is all mine that I am miserably *gênée* by the glances of strange eyes.

We want news from you to complete our satisfaction, and no one can give it but yourself. Send us as many matter-of-fact details as you have the patience to write. We shall not be here after the 4th, but at Schlangenbad.

Letter to Mrs Congreve, 3d Aug. 1866.

We got home last night, after a rough passage from Ostend. You have been so continually a recurrent thought to me ever since I had your letter at Schwalbach, that it is only natural I should write to you as soon as I am at my old desk again. The news of Mr Congreve's examination being over made me feel for several days that something had happened, which caused me unusual lightness of heart. I would not dwell on the possibility of your having to leave Wandsworth, which, I know, would cause you many sacrifices. I clung solely to the great cheering fact that a load of anxiety had been lifted from Mr Congreve's mind. May we not put in a petition for some of his time now? And will he not come with you and Emily to dine with us next week, on any day except Wednesday and Friday? The dinner-hour seems more propitious for talk and enjoyment than lunch-time; but in all respects choose what will best suit your health and habits —only let us see you.

Letter to Mrs Congreve, 3d Aug. 1866.

We returned from our health-seeking journey on Thursday evening, and your letter was the most delightful thing that awaited me at home. Be sure it will be much read and meditated; and may I not take it as an earnest that your help, which has already done so much for me, will be continued? I mean, that you will help me by your thoughts and your sympathy—not that you will be teased with my proofs.

Letter to Frederic Harrison, 4th Aug. 1866.

I meant to write you a long letter about the æsthetic problem: but Mr Lewes, who is still tormented with headachy effects from our rough passage, comes and asks me to walk to Hampstead with him, so I send these hasty lines. Come and see us soon.

We got home on Thursday evening, and are still feeling some unpleasant effects from our very rough passage—an inconvenience which we had waited some days at Ostend to avoid. But the wind took no notice of us, and went on blowing.

Letter to John Blackwood, 4th Aug. 1866.

Letter to John Blackwood, 4th Aug. 1866.

I was much pleased with the handsome appearance of the three volumes, which were lying ready for me. My hatred of bad paper and bad print, and my love of their opposites, naturally get stronger as my eyes get weaker; and certainly that taste could hardly be better gratified than it is by Messrs Blackwood & Sons.

Colonel Hamley's volume is another example of that fact. It lies now on my revolving desk as one of the books I mean first to read. I am really grateful to have such a medium of knowledge, and I expect it to make some pages of history much less dim to me.

My impression of Colonel Hamley, when we had that pleasant dinner at Greenwich, and afterwards when he called in Blandford Square, was quite in keeping with the high opinion you express. Mr Lewes liked the article on 'Felix' in the Magazine very much. He read it the first thing yesterday morning, and told me it was written in a nice spirit, and the extracts judiciously made.

Letter to Miss Sara Hennell, 10th Aug. 1866.

I have had a delightful holiday, and find my double self very much the better for it. We made a great round in our journeying. From Antwerp to Rotterdam, The Hague, Leyden, Amsterdam, Cologne; then up the Rhine to Coblentz, and thence to Schwalbach, where we stayed a fortnight. From Schwalbach to Schlangenbad, where we stayed till we feared the boats would cease to go to and fro; and in fact, only left just in time to get down the Rhine to Bonn by the Dutch steamer. From Bonn, after two days, we went to Aix; then to dear old Liège, where we had been together thirteen years before: and, to avoid the King of the Belgians, ten minutes backwards to the baths of pretty Chaudfontaine, where we remained three days. Then to Louvain, Ghent, and Bruges; and, last of all, to Ostend, where we waited for a fine day and calm sea, until we secured—a very rough passage indeed.

Letter to Miss Sara Hennell, 10th Aug. 1866.

Ought we not to be a great deal wiser, and more efficient personages, or else to be ashamed of ourselves? Unhappily, this last alternative is not a compensation for wisdom.

I thought of you — to mention one occasion amongst many — when we had the good fortune, at Antwerp, to see a placard announcing that the company from the Ober-Ammergau, Bavaria, would represent, that Sunday evening, the *Lebensgeschichte* of our Saviour Christ, at the Théatre des Variétés. I remembered that you had seen the representation with deep interest—and these actors are doubtless

Letter to Miss Sara Hennell, 10th Aug. 1866.

the successors of those you saw. Of course we went to the theatre. And the Christ was, without exaggeration, beautiful. All the rest was inferior, and might even have had a painful approach to the ludicrous; but both the person and the action of the Jesus were fine enough to overpower all meaner impressions. Mr Lewes, who, you know, is keenly alive to everything "stagey" in physiognomy and gesture, felt what I am saying quite as much as I did, and was much moved.

Rotterdam, with the grand approach to it by the broad river; the rich, red brick of the houses; the canals, uniformly planted with trees, and crowded with the bright brown masts of the Dutch boats,—is far finer than Amsterdam. The colour of Amsterdam is ugly: the houses are of a chocolate colour, almost black (an artificial tinge given to the bricks), and the woodwork on them screams out in ugly patches of cream-colour; the canals have no trees along their sides, and the boats are infrequent. We looked about for the very Portuguese synagogue, where Spinoza was nearly assassinated as he came from worship. But it no longer exists. There are no less than three Portuguese synagogues now—very large and handsome. And in the evening we went to see the worship there. Not a woman was present, but of devout men not a few,—a curious reversal of what one sees in other temples. The chanting and the swaying about of the bodies—almost a wriggling—are not beautiful to the sense; but I fairly cried at witnessing this faint symbolism of a religion of sublime, far-off memories. The skulls of St Ursula's eleven thousand virgins seem a modern suggestion compared with the Jewish Synagogue. At Schwalbach and Schlangenbad our life was led chiefly in the beech woods, which we had all to ourselves, the guests usually confining themselves to the nearer promenades. The guests, of course, were few in that serious time,—and between war and cholera we felt our position as health—and pleasure—seekers somewhat contemptible.

Letter to Miss Sara Hennell, 10th Aug. 1866.

There is no end to what one could say, if one did not feel that long letters cut pieces not to be spared out of the solid day.

I think I have earned that you should write me one of those perfect letters in which you make me see everything you like about yourself and others.

Aug. 30.—I have taken up the idea of my drama, 'The Spanish Gypsy,' again, and am reading on Spanish subjects—Bouterwek, Sismondi, Depping, Llorente, &c.

Journal, 1866.

Letter to Frederic Harrison, 15th Aug. 1866.

I have read several times your letter of the 19th, which I found awaiting me on my return, and I shall read it many times again. Pray do not even say, or inwardly suspect, that anything you take the trouble to write to me will not be valued. On the contrary, please to imagine as well as you can the experience of a mind morbidly desponding, of a consciousness tending more and more to consist in memories of error and imperfection rather than in a strengthening sense of achievement—and then consider how such a mind must need the support of sympathy and approval from those who are capable of understanding its aims. I assure you your letter is an evidence of a fuller understanding than I have ever had expressed to me before. And if I needed to give emphasis to this simple statement, I should suggest to you all the miseries one's obstinate egoism endures from the fact of being a writer of novels—books which the dullest and silliest reader thinks himself competent to deliver an opinion on. But I despise myself for feeling any annoyance at these trivial things.

That is a tremendously difficult problem which you have laid before me; and I think you see its difficulties, though they can hardly press upon you as they do on me, who have gone through again and again the severe effort of trying to make certain ideas thoroughly incarnate, as if they had revealed themselves to me first in the flesh and not in the spirit. I think æsthetic teaching is the highest of all teaching, because it deals with life in its highest complexity. But if it ceases to be purely æsthetic —if it lapses anywhere from the picture to the diagram—it becomes the most offensive of all teaching. Avowed Utopias are not offensive, because they are understood to have a scientific and expository character: they do not pretend to work on the emotions, or couldn't do it if they did pretend. I am sure, from your own statement, that you see this quite clearly. Well, then, consider the sort of agonising labour to an English-fed imagination to make out a sufficiently real background for the desired picture,—to get breathing individual forms, and group them in the needful relations, so that the presentation will lay hold on the emotions as human experience—will, as you say, "flash" conviction on the world by means of aroused sympathy.

Letter to Frederic Harrison, 15th Aug. 1866.

I took unspeakable pains in preparing to write 'Romola'—neglecting nothing I could find that would help me to what I may call the "idiom" of Florence, in the largest sense one could stretch the word to: and then I was only trying to give *some*

Letter to Frederic Harrison, 15th Aug. 1866.

out of the normal relations. I felt that the necessary idealisation could only be attained by adopting the clothing of the past. And again, it is my way (rather too much so perhaps) to urge the human sanctities through tragedy—through pity and terror, as well as admiration and delight. I only say all this to show the tenfold arduousness of such a work as the one your problem demands. On the other hand, my whole soul goes with your desire that it should be done; and I shall at least keep the great possibility (or impossibility) perpetually in my mind, as something towards which I must strive, though it may be that I can do so only in a fragmentary way.

At present I am going to take up again a work which I laid down before writing 'Felix.' It is—*but please, let this be a secret between ourselves*—an attempt at a drama, which I put aside at Mr Lewes's request, after writing four acts, precisely because it was in that stage of creation—or *Werden*—in which the idea of the characters predominates over the incarnation. Now I read it again, I find it impossible to abandon it: the conceptions move me deeply, and they have never been wrought out before. There is not a thought or symbol that I do not long to use: but the whole requires recasting; and, as I never recast anything before, I think of the issue very doubtfully. When one has to work out the dramatic action for one's self, under the inspiration of an idea, instead of having a grand myth or an Italian novel ready to one's hand, one feels anything but omnipotent. Not that I should have done any better if I had had the myth or the novel, for I am not a good user of opportunities. I think I have the right *locus* and historic conditions, but much else is wanting. Letter to Frederic Harrison, 15th Aug. 1866.

I have not, of course, said half what I meant to say; but I hope opportunities of exchanging thoughts will not be wanting between us.

It is so long since we exchanged letters, that I feel inclined to break the silence by telling you that I have been reading with much interest the 'Operations of War,' which you enriched me with. Also that I have had a pretty note, in aged handwriting, from Dean Ramsay, with a present of his 'Reminiscences of Scottish Life.' I suppose you know him quite well, but I never heard you mention him. Also—what will amuse you—that my readers take quite a tender care of my text, writing to me to tell me of a misprint, or of "one phrase" which they entreat to have altered, that no blemish may disfigure 'Felix.' Dr Althaus has sent me word of a misprint which I am glad to know of—or rather of Letter to John Blackwood, 6th Sept. 1866.

Letter to John Blackwood, 6th Sept. 1866.

a word slipped out in the third volume. 'She *saw* streaks of light, &c. . . . *and* sounds. It must be corrected when the opportunity comes.

We are very well, and I am swimming in Spanish history and literature. I feel as if I were molesting you with a letter without any good excuse, but you are not bound to write again until a wet day makes golf impossible, and creates a dreariness in which even letter-writing seems like a recreation.

Letter to John Blackwood, 11th Sept. 1866.

I am glad to know that Dean Ramsay is a friend of yours. His sympathy was worth having, and I at once wrote to thank him. Another wonderfully lively old man—Sir Henry Holland—came to see me about two Sundays ago, to bid me good-bye before going on an excursion to—North America!—and to tell me that he had just been re-reading 'Adam Bede' for the fourth time. "I often read in it, you know, besides. But this is the fourth time quite through." I, of course, with the mother's egoism on behalf of the youngest born, was jealous for 'Felix.' Is there any possibility of satisfying an author? But one or two things that George read out to me from an article in 'Macmillan's Magazine' by Mr Mozley did satisfy me. And yet I sicken again with despondency under the sense that the most carefully written books lie, both outside and inside people's minds, deep undermost in a heap of trash.

Sept. 15.—Finished Depping's 'Juifs au Moyen Âge.' Reading Chaucer, to study English. Also reading on Acoustics, Musical instruments, &c. Journal, 1866.

Oct. 15.—Recommenced 'The Spanish Gypsy,' intending to give it a new form.

For a wonder, I remembered the day of the month, and felt a delightful confidence that I should have a letter from her who always remembers such things at the right moment. You will hardly believe in my imbecility. I can never be quite sure whether your birthday is the 21st or the 23d. I know every one must think the worse of me for this want of retentiveness that seems a part of affection; and it is only justice that they should. Nevertheless I am not quite destitute of lovingness and gratitude, and perhaps the consciousness of my own defect makes me feel your goodness the more keenly. I shall reckon it part of the next year's happiness for me if it brings a great deal of happiness to you. That will depend somewhat—perhaps chiefly—on the satisfaction you have in giving shape to your ideas. But you say nothing on that subject. Letter to Miss Sara Hennell, 22d Nov. 1866.

We knew about Faraday's preaching, but not of

Letter to Miss Sara Hennell, 22d Nov. 1866.

his loss of faculty. I begin to think of such things as very near to me—I mean decay of power and health. But I find age has its fresh elements of cheerfulness.

Bless you, dear Sara, for all the kindness of many years, and for the newest kindness that comes to me this morning. I am very well now, and able to enjoy my happiness. One has happiness sometimes without being able to enjoy it.

Journal, 1866.

Nov. 22.—Reading Renan's 'Histoire des Langues Sémitiques'—Ticknor's 'Spanish Literature.'

Dec. 6.—We returned from Tunbridge Wells, where we have been for a week. I have been reading Cornewall Lewis's 'Astronomy of the Ancients,' Ockley's 'History of the Saracens,' 'Astronomical Geography,' and Spanish ballads on Bernardo del Carpio.

Letter to Miss Sara Hennell, 7th Dec. 1866.

We have been to Tunbridge Wells for a week, hoping to get plenty of fresh air, and walking in that sandy undulating country. But for three days it rained incessantly!

No; I don't feel as if my faculties were failing me. On the contrary, I enjoy all subjects — all study — more than I ever did in my life before. But that very fact makes me more in need of resignation to the certain approach of age and death. Science, history, poetry — I don't know which draws me most, and there is little time left me for any one of them. I learned Spanish last year but one, and see new vistas everywhere. That makes me think of time thrown away when I was young—time that I should be so glad of now. I could enjoy everything, from arithmetic to antiquarianism, if I had large spaces of life before me. But instead of that I have a very small space. Unfeigned, unselfish, cheerful resignation is difficult. But I strive to get it.

Letter to Miss Sara Hennell, 7th Dec. 1866.

Dec. 11.—Ill ever since I came home, so that the days seem to have made a muddy flood, sweeping away all labour and all growth.

Journal, 1866.

Just before we received Dr Congreve's letter, we had changed our plans. George's increasing weakness, and the more and more frequent intervals in which he became unable to work, made me at last urge him to give up the idea of "finishing," which often besets us vainly. It will really be better for the work as well as for himself that he should let it wait. However, I care about nothing just now except that he should be doing all he can to get better. So we start next Thursday for Bordeaux, staying two days in Paris on our way. Madame Mohl writes us word that she hears from friends of the

Letter to Mrs Congreve, 22d Dec. 1866.

Letter to Mrs Congreve, 22d Dec. 1866.

delicious weather—mild, sunny weather—to be had now on the French south-western and south-eastern coast. You will all wish us well on our journey, I know. But *I* wish I could carry a happier thought about you than that of your being an invalid. I shall write to you when we are at Biarritz or some other place that suits us, and when I have something good to tell. No; in any case I shall write, because I shall want to hear all about you. Tell Dr Congreve we carry the 'Politique' with us. Mr Lewes gets more and more impressed by it, and also by what he is able to understand of the 'Synthèse.' I am writing in the dark. Farewell. With best love to Emily, and dutiful regards to Dr Congreve.

Journal, 1866.

Dec. 27.—Set off in the evening on our journey to the south.

SUMMARY.

JANUARY 1866 TO DECEMBER 1866.

Letters to Frederic Harrison on Industrial Co-operation—Consults him about law in 'Felix Holt'—Asks his opinion on other questions—Letter to Mrs Congreve—Visit to Tunbridge Wells—Reading Comte's 'Synthèse'—Letter to F. Harrison on "case" for 'Felix Holt'—Letter to Miss Hennell

—Joy in the world getting better—Letter to Madame Bodichon—'Felix Holt' growing like a sickly child—Want of sincerity in England—Desire for knowledge increases—Blackwood offers £5000 for 'Felix Holt'—Letters to John Blackwood renewing correspondence—Thanks for encouragement—Painstaking with 'Felix Holt'—Letter to F. Harrison on legal points—The book finished—Inscription—Letter of adieu to Mrs Congreve—Letter to Mrs Bray—Excitement of finishing 'Felix Holt'—Journey to Holland and Germany—Letter to Mrs Congreve from Schwalbach—Return to The Priory—Letter to F. Harrison asking for sympathy—Letter to John Blackwood—Colonel Hamley—Letter to Miss Hennell describing German trip—Miracle play at Antwerp—Amsterdam synagogue—Takes up drama 'The Spanish Gypsy' again—Reading on Spanish subjects—Letter to F. Harrison—Need of sympathy—Æsthetic teaching—Tells him of the proposed drama—Letters to John Blackwood—Dean Ramsay—Sir Henry Holland—Article on 'Felix Holt' in 'Macmillan's Magazine'—'The Spanish Gypsy' recommenced—Reading Renan's 'Histoire des Langues Sémitiques' and Ticknor's Spanish Literature—Visit to Tunbridge Wells for a week—Reading Cornewall Lewis's 'Astronomy of the Ancients'—Ockley's 'History of the Saracens' and Spanish Ballads—Letter to Miss Hennell—Enjoyment of study—Depression—Letter of adieu to Mrs Congreve—Set off on journey to Spain.

END OF THE SECOND VOLUME.

PRINTED BY WILLIAM BLACKWOOD AND SONS

Facsimile of a portion of GEORGE ELIOT'S M.S. from Notes on "THE SPANISH GYPSY."

The subject of the Spanish Gypsy was originally suggested to me by a picture which hangs in the Scuola di San Rocco at Venice, over the door of the large Sala containing Tintoretto's frescoes. It is an Annunciation said to be by Titian. Of course I had seen numerous pictures of this subject before; & the subject had always attracted me. But on this my second visit to the Scuola di San Rocco, this small picture of Titian's pointed out to me for the first time, brought a new train of thought. It occurred to me that here was a great dramatic motive of the same class as those used by the Greek dramatists, yet specifically differing from them. A young maiden believing herself to be on the eve of the chief event of her life - marriage - about to share in the ordinary lot of womanhood, full of young hope, has suddenly announced to her that

She is chosen to fulfil a great destiny entailing a terribly different experience from that of ordinary womanhood. She is chosen, not by any momentary arbitrariness, but as a result of foregoing hereditary conditions: she obeys. "Behold the handmaid of the Lord." Here I thought is a subject grander than that of Iphigenia, & it has never been used. I came home with this in my mind, meaning to give the motive a clothing in some suitable set of historical & local conditions. — My reflections brought me nothing that would serve me except that moment in Spanish history when the struggle with the Moors was attaining its climax, & when there was the gypsy race present under such conditions as would enable me to get my heroine & the hereditary claim on her among the gypsies. I required the opposition of race to give the need for renouncing the expectation of marriage: I could not use the Jews or the Moors